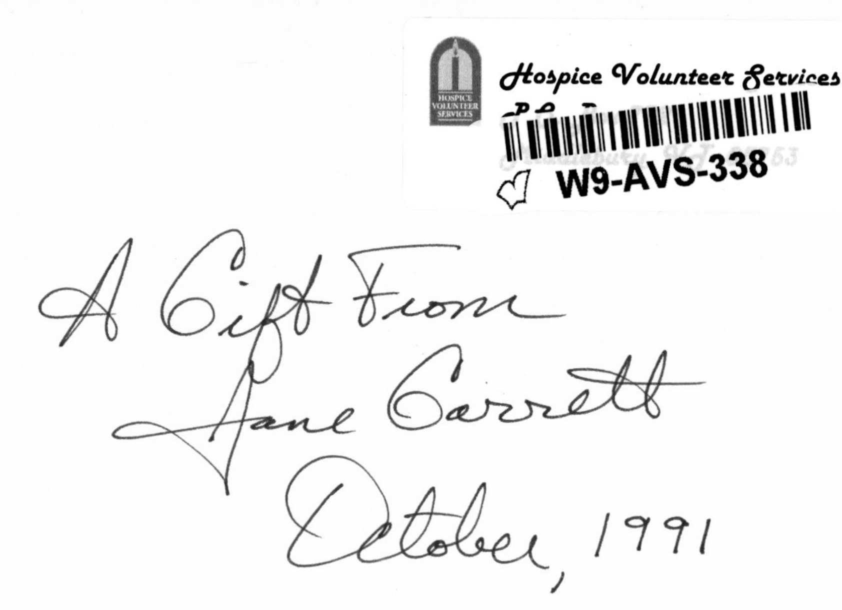
Hospice Volunteer Services
W9-AVS-338
A Gift From
Jane Garrett
October, 1991

THE BETRAYAL OF HEALTH

THE BETRAYAL OF HEALTH

The Impact of Nutrition, Environment, and Lifestyle on Illness in America

Joseph D. Beasley, M.D.

TIMES BOOKS
RANDOM HOUSE

Published in the United States by Times Books, a division of
Random House, Inc., New York, and simultaneously in Canada by
Random House of Canada Limited, Toronto. Portions of this work
were originally published in *The Kellogg Report.*

Library of Congress Cataloging-in-Publication Data
Beasley, Joseph D.
The betrayal of health : the impact of nutrition, environment, and
lifestyle on illness in America / Joseph D. Beasley. — 1st ed.
p. cm.
ISBN 0-812-91897-5
1. Social medicine—United States. 2. Medical care—United
States. 3. United States—Social conditions—1980– I. Title.
RA418.3.U6B43 1991
362.1'0973—dc20 90-71448

Permissions acknowledgments appear on p. v.

Manufactured in the United States of America

9 8 7 6 5 4 3 2

First Edition

PERMISSIONS ACKNOWLEDGEMENTS

Grateful acknowledgment is made to the following for permission to reprint previously published material:

American Association for the Advancement of Science: Excerpts from "Toward a National Nutritional Policy" by Dr. Jean Mayer from the April 21, 1972, issue of *Science* magazine (Volume 176, pages 237–241). Copyright © 1972 by the AAAS. Reprinted by permission of the American Association for the Advancement of Science.

American Medical Association: Excerpts from "Vitamin Preparations as Dietary Supplements and as Therapeutic Agents" by The American Medical Association Council on Scientific Affairs from the April 10, 1987, issue of the *Journal of the American Medical Association* (Volume 257, #14, page 1931). Copyright © 1987 by the American Medical Association. Reprinted by permission.

American Pharmaceutical Association: Excerpts from "The Chemical Age" by the Special Commission on Internal Pollution. Copyright © 1977 by the American Pharmaceutical Association. Originally published in the *Journal of the American Pharmaceutical Association* NS 17: 369–373, June 1977. Reprinted by permission of the American Pharmaceutical Association.

Association of American Medical Colleges: Excerpt from "Final Report of the Commission on Medical Education," AAMC, 1932. Reprinted by permission from the Association on American Medical Colleges (AAMC).

Helen Caldicott, M.D.: Excerpts from "Radiation, Unsafe at Any Level" by Helen Caldicott, M.D. from the December 1978 issue of *The Progressive*. Reprinted by permission.

The New York Times: Excerpt from "U.S. Social Tolerance of Drugs Found on the Rise" by Glenn Collins, from the March 21, 1983, issue of *The New York Times*. Copyright © 1983 by the New York Times Company, Reprinted by permission.

To the W. K. Kellogg Foundation for
its support and leadership in
promoting health and preventing
disease; and to the late Jerry Swift,
who worked with me from 1980 until
1987 on the report on which this
book is based

Acknowledgments

The Betrayal of Health is a distillation and condensation of *The Impact of Nutrition, Environment, and Lifestyle on the Health of Americans: A Report to the Kellogg Foundation.* That report, which I wrote with the late Jerry Swift, M.A., was released in 1989 under the auspices of the Institute of Health Policy and Practice of the Bard College Center in Annandale-on-Hudson, New York.

I WISH to thank Catherine Heusel, whose research and editing skills added greatly to the substance of the original report and without whom this book simply would not have been possible. I am also grateful to Steve Wasserman, editorial director of Times Books, for convincing me that the original 300,000-word report could afford to shed a few pounds, and that the result would be a better, more readable work. His prescribed diet was rigorous and, I confess, difficult to stay on. With the encouragement and help of his gifted colleagues and associate editors, Ruth Fecych and Paul Golob, I nevertheless managed it.

Others, too, were enormously helpful and important during the seven years that went into the making of this book. The research was originally funded by grants from the W. K. Kellogg Foundation and the Ford Foundation. The staff of the W. K. Kellogg Foundation provided invaluable criticism and support over this period. The views and ideas expressed in the book are, of course, entirely my own and are not intended to reflect the views of these foundations. Many friends and colleagues were of critical help. A mere listing of their names in no way reflects the profound debt I owe to their manifold contributions. Still, I should be remiss if I didn't take this opportunity to thank David Bell, formerly of the Ford Foundation; Helen Bernstein; Alvin Bicker, Ph.D.; Virginia Bontje; President Leon Botstein and Dimitri Papadimitriou of Bard College; Dr. Thomas A. Bruce; Robert Burger; the late Mrs. Cynthia Calhoun of the Calhoun Foundation; Peter Dolgenos; the late Dr. Grace Goldsmith of Tulane University; Professor Roger Grimson; Dr. David Harris; Jerome Joffe; Jim Kelly; Miriam Kent; Frank King; Dr. Philip R. Lee; Kimley MacDonald; Gene Mason; Michael J-S McNally; Lorraine Miller; Christopher Norwood; Dr. William Rea; the late Dr. Arthur Sackler; Dr. Robert Sparks; Loretta Shum; Dr. William Steibel; Paul Swift; Roberta Thumin; Robert Timmerman; Susan Van Kleeck; the late Dr. Roger Williams.

Finally, I should like to thank my wife, Kim, and my son, Malcolm, for their cheerful and unwavering support throughout the long and arduous process of development that produced first a report, and then this book.

THIS BOOK is not intended for use in diagnosing or treating any individual. Persons who feel they may have a health problem should consult a physician or other qualified health professional.

Contents

THE BETRAYAL OF HEALTH

Introduction

HUMANITY is in the midst of a world crisis. We are rendering ourselves toxic and malnourished while simultaneously destroying the ecological balance that supports life on earth. The rate of population growth has far outstripped the rate of ecologically sound production, geometrically complicating an already perilous world state.

The many problems that now face the United States are symptoms of this basic planetary condition—manifestations of a global bioecological catastrophe that is finally coming home to roost. The symptoms of this crisis are seen in the headlines nearly every day—toxic spills, polluted beaches, the drug and alcohol epidemic, the spread of AIDS, high infant mortality rates and low birth weights, and a national health-care bill that exceeds $600 billion a year. It is reflected in calls to "Just say no," eat oat bran, avoid fats, and not use aerosols.

On an individual level, it is felt most acutely in the doctor's office, where patients are asking for explanations that physicians simply cannot provide. Modern medicine, for all its wondrous technology, has only succeeded in describing and treating the various symptoms of the crisis. It is currently almost completely unprepared to diagnose and treat the underlying causes.

The chronic conditions that challenge us today—from hypertension to learning disabilities—do not respond to the simple formula of "identify the cause and eliminate it" that worked so well for infectious diseases. Until relatively recently, the great threats to our health were fairly specific—viruses such as influenza and smallpox, bacteria such as salmonella and shigella, and traumatic injuries. Today, however, health is compromised on many levels at once. The interaction of many factors dictates our health, not just an individual event or agent. Health, or the lack of it, is determined by the interrelationship of the human organism with its food supply, its environment, and other humans.

Research has uncovered a tremendous amount of valuable information on the effect of the complex and delicate balance that exists between the environment, nutrition, and lifestyle and our health. Yet this research has not found its way to the physicians who are entrusted with caring for us or to the policymakers who make decisions that radically affect our futures. As a result, many physicians are still looking for the magic bullet that will cure hypertension, and many policymakers are seeking "the" solution to teen pregnancy, drunk/drugged driving, and high drop-out rates.

The chronic diseases—both social and medical—are really symptoms of a much more vast underlying problem. They are the culmination of years of inadequate nutrition, a toxic environment, sedentary lifestyles, familial and social disruptions, and dependence on artificial agents (from cigarettes to cocaine) for happiness. Every cell in our bodies—from the brain to the immune system—is affected by these abuses. The effects are particularly devastating in developing children—both in and out of the womb. The massive and irreversible loss of human potential in the children of this world is the most disturbing aspect of this planetary destruction. With each underweight, malnourished child born to a malnourished, poorly educated, drug- or alcohol-addicted mother another bit of the future is lost.

Reversing this trend requires a much more comprehensive approach than that currently offered by most physicians, politicians, and public-policy makers. It requires an approach that looks at the full spectrum of ills that are afflicting our planet, from the destruction of the seas and rain forests to the compromising of the human immune system.

This book is an attempt to present such an approach. It is the product of ten years of research on the interaction of the environment, nutrition, and lifestyle and the effect this interaction has on our health. It is based on the assumption that there is a profound connection between sickness and society. I know this from personal experience. Between 1964 and 1974 I worked on the related problems of family planning, health-delivery systems, and nutrition among the poor of the South and of underdeveloped countries. This experience exposed me to thousands of cases of illness in the developing countries and to the more overt clinical effects of malnutrition. I was profoundly influenced by the cases of protein malnutrition or kwashiorkor (in Ghanese, literally, "red boy") that I saw in the tropics. Here I observed children removed from the breast at around two years of age in an environment that did not supply the protein and essential nutrients of the breast milk, much less meet the increased nutrient demands of childhood growth. These children first became apathetic, depressed, irritable, and withdrawn; then they developed edema, hypertension, and skin and hair changes. If untreated they eventually died of an acute infection or chronic diarrhea.

It was remarkable to see both these profound symptoms resulting from malnutrition and in turn the rapid "cure" that could be evoked in a child with adequate protein and essential nutrients. The swelling went down, the mental symptoms disappeared, and in a matter of days the child's outlook changed from severely abnormal to that of an alert, friendly youngster with sparkling energy and bright eyes.

During this period I also began to understand that perhaps a majority of children in the Third World have lost a significant portion of their mental capacity, and hence potential, through the devastating cycle in which they are caught: malnourished and sick women becoming pregnant repeatedly, without planning or preparation; the unborn afflicted with intrauterine malnutrition; infants and children constantly hungry, increasing their susceptibility to the ravages of a host of infectious diseases; the young girls who survive soon becoming pregnant themselves in a state of damage and debility, beginning the cycle again. This irreversible loss of the cutting edge of brain potential in a large segment of the world's children seemed to me, more than any other factor, to limit both the future and the quality of human life around the world.

Since 1975 I have practiced clinical medicine in America and I focused intensively on patients with a wide range of chronic noninfectious conditions. Many of these bloated, poorly nourished, hypertensive, mentally troubled patients—seen so often in doctors' offices here—reminded me hauntingly of the early stages of kwashiorkor I had observed in children overseas. These patients, of course, were not afflicted by the rampant infectious diseases and diarrhea of the Third World. But their poor condition and low resistance left them vulnerable to our own society's scourges, notably the toxifying effects of our rapidly changing lifestyle and environment. Alcohol, smoking, high stress, lack of exercise, overuse of medications and other drugs, thousands of man-made chemicals polluting the outdoors or woven into our clothing, cosmetics, and furniture—not to mention the food supply: I found all of these facts of life implicated in the various chronic conditions I encountered.

In treating these patients, I wanted to understand each individual in the context of his or her unique past and daily life at present. I not only carried out the usual medical history, physical exam, and routine laboratory work, but I carefully evaluated their nutritional status and diet; food and chemical allergies or sensitivities; home and work environments; activity levels and handling of stress; use of medications, alcohol, nicotine, caffeine, and street drugs; and other dimensions of their lifestyle and personal habits.

Only then was the patient's presenting complaint diagnosed—within this comprehensive picture of his or her health status. Moreover, the presumptive diagnosis and treatment plan did not stop at the original complaint but addressed the patient's entire state of health. My objective was both to do a more effective job of treating the complaint (by getting at the underlying systems of health and illness in the patient) and also—given the chronic disease epidemic threatening us all—to practice preventive medicine in a concrete, specific, and effective manner.

I would begin treatment by detoxifying the patient so far as feasible from drugs of all kinds, suspect chemical exposures, highly processed additive-laden food products, excessive sugar and refined carbohydrates, and simultaneously restoring him or her metabolically with a highly nutritious diet, nutrient supplementation as indicated, and an appropriate stress-management and exercise program. Within this rehabilitative context I pursued strictly classical medical treatment of specific complaints, including a conservative approach to the prescribing of drugs.

The results of this procedure were gratifying. Many cases of essential hypertension, arthritis, diabetes mellitus, obesity, alcoholism, mental illness, anxiety, depression, and other chronic conditions became manageable without drugs, and frequently the symptoms simply disappeared. I do not understand all of the exact mechanisms by which these changes occurred, but clinical records indicate they did so in too high a proportion of cases to be by chance alone. In addition, it proved possible to remove and then reinduce symptoms in a patient simply by adjusting these variables in relation to the individual's metabolism.

In 1978, to better understand the clinical results I was able to obtain with this broader approach, I began a review of the relevant medical literature. My appointment in 1980 as the Bard Fellow in Medicine and Science and the awards of research grants from the Ford Foundation and the W. K. Kellogg Foundation allowed me to devote a major portion of my time to this pursuit. To my surprise, the literature often either corroborated or strongly suggested the direction I was taking. Amid the voluminous research findings being published each year, I found substantial and significant, although often unpublicized, work being done by first-rate researchers in biochemistry, nutritional science, endocrinology, neuropathology, immunology, toxicology, and related disciplines. Many of these findings shed light on individuals' pathological responses to dietary, environmental, or lifestyle factors endemic in our society today. Though simple cause-effect links were rare, chronic diseases were the conditions most frequently involved.

The data were in the literature but, as I knew from my own experience, they were not being applied in the day-to-day practice of medicine. One reason for this state of affairs was that nobody had pulled the superspecialists' findings together into practical form for physicians to use. And workable syntheses are equally important for lawmakers, health officials, and the millions of individuals who are concerned about their health. The present book is such a synthesis. Its focus is the biological basis of contemporary health problems. It seeks to demonstrate the prime importance of basic biological factors in the rise, etiology, prevention and treatment of chronic conditions and reproductive problems. We all recognize that the human body is composed of various *organic* systems: respiratory, circulatory, gastrointestinal, genitourinary, nervous, immune. But, more basically, the human organism is the product of a network of great *biological* systems. How we don't know, but *genetics* emerged in the primordial chemical "soup" of the oceans as the starting point of life itself and of every individual's life. Why we don't know, but all genetic creatures require *nutrition* to survive and function. In ways we are only beginning to appreciate, the *environment* or the living being's ecology is an essential factor in its health and viability. Even living beings' own *behavior*—most of all human beings'—becomes a complex system affecting their well-being. Finally, there is always the uncontrollable world of randomness, chance *events* that help us or cut into our lives and health. Together these systems and all their interactions form a vital network in which each of us came to life and finds health (and illness) and our length of days.

Yet, even though we can maintain our health only in and through these systems, most of the research on them—in molecular biology, biochemistry, nutrition science, environmental medicine, and so on—is not yet applied in medical practice or appreciated by the public. Moreover, their interacting roles in the various chronic conditions are only beginning to be explored. Indeed, most disease today is the result of individuals' lifestyle, their nutrition or lack of it, their chemical environment and personal behavior—smoking, drinking too much, working under stress, chronic depression, drug use of one kind or another, failure to exercise, overeating.

In conducting my research, I have worked from the following premises:

1. Biology is profoundly important to all questions of human performance. This fact is only now being recognized.
2. The biology of human performance is very little understood even by the scientists involved—far less than the public realizes.
3. Perhaps least understood of all are the longer-term risks inherent in rapid biological changes—whether in genetics or nutrition or the environment or our behavior and lifestyle.
4. Where these risks have come to be recognized and assessed, they have usually turned out to be worse than had been assumed.
5. Thus, the enthusiastic pursuit of technological change by industry, Madison Avenue, the military, medicine, and researchers poses known and unknown biological risks for all of us.
6. As a society, our best protection against technological damage is a conservative attitude and careful policies that control the direction and pace of technological change. With biology, so far as possible, we should take only known risks, and only for proportionately larger benefits.

More than anything, we must return to our biological base. Since the broader dimensions of long-term health or illness are routinely ignored by mainstream medical institutions, this book attempts to fill a critically important role in health promotion and disease prevention. A survey of the literature suggests that a variety of basic biological processes are involved in the chronic conditions that plague us—from learning disabilities to cancer. At the same time, there do not appear to be straightforward, generalizable cause-effect links between any one factor and any one disturbance. A better framework for viewing these relationships appears to be a systems approach to health that facilitates a multifaceted methodology.

It is not enough to remove or irradiate tumors, transplant hearts, institutionalize "difficult" children, or jail drug addicts. We must stop these tragedies from occurring in the first place. It makes no sense to insist on treating a dysfunctional child only psychosocially or with medications, when that child may have started life in a uterine existence of maternal alcoholism, stress, or prescription drugs, been raised in a house coated with lead-based paint, played near roadways flowing with exhaust fumes, and be living now on Coca-Cola and candy bars.

The better we understand these biological implications, the sooner we will shape a more nutritious food system, a cleaner environment, and a healthier lifestyle. In and of themselves, these steps will go far toward reducing youths' developmental difficulties. They may also help turn back the tide of degenerative diseases among older (and not so much older) adults.

1

The Genetic Foundation of Health

PEOPLE HAVE recognized for millennia that children inherit not merely property and political opinions from their parents but, in some unknown way, many characteristics of their very being. Prehistoric Hebrew customs, later codified in the Talmud, omitted circumcision for boys born into the families of bleeders. And a 6,000-year-old Babylonian tablet shows the pedigrees of horses and diagrams for crossbreeding traits.

At the same time, ***heredity*** was always one of the most baffling and mysterious phenomena of nature. Resemblances were partial at best and they were completely unpredictable. ***Variation*** was common and obvious. If Suzie looked just like her lovely mother, Sylvia, little brother Sammy, with his jug ears and freckles, didn't look like anybody at all. Still—and this was the mystery—despite abundant and continuous variation, heredity persevered, if not apparent in one generation or the next, then cropping up in the one after that.

Even the outburst of scientific knowledge in the seventeenth, eighteenth, and nineteenth centuries couldn't make heads or tails of the hodgepodge of heredity and variation among all biological species. Darwin himself subscribed to the old "blood" theory (blue blood, pure-blooded, mixed blood, new blood, and so on), which held that the mother's and father's contributions blended, like blood, in the offspring and flowed on to the third generation as an average of the two. The problem with the blended-blood theory was that it always broke down when, in the next generation or two, an ancestor's pure trait (blue eyes, red hair, or a rare albino complexion, for example) resurfaced in all its purity. "Yes, that's Uncle Henry's nose all right. Poor kid."

Ironically, the genius that broke the riddle was a monk who never had children. And the science of the day gave him so much trouble that he couldn't pass the qualifying exam even for a high school teaching license. Some of his lowest marks, in fact, were in biology. Of course, this was Gregor Mendel, the obscure priest in the small town of Brun, Austria, who crossbred peas in the monastery garden and kept track of the results. When in 1866 he published his findings, plus a theory to explain them, in two articles in the local science society's journal, they were passed over without interest.

When his articles were rediscovered in 1900, Mendel's insights took the scientific world by storm. They were soon extended to form the groundwork of the new field of genetics. Mendel's theory laid the foundation for stunning progress in plant breeding, including the bonanza of American agriculture in this century and the Green Revolution of high-yield grains in the Third World. Indeed, virtually all advances in biology since 1900 and many breakthroughs in medicine and related disciplines reflect his approach. Of the various systems that, together, determine our health, none is so fundamental as the inborn genetics we inherit from our parents.

Scientists now know that each of us is genetically unique and that our personal gene system—built into every cell in our bodies—plays a basic role in all aspects of our functioning. At the same time, our genes rarely have the final say. Nutrition, the environment, and our personal behavior all have a tremendous impact on our lives and health. Correspondingly, none of these affect us apart from our inborn genetics. The gene's blueprinting inspires and governs the responses of all our cells, organs, and systems to the encompassing web of life.

The genetic system has often been called the blueprint of life, and there is a good deal of truth to the metaphor. Of biological life's two root functions—the individual's growth and activity, and the species' continuation through reproduction—the genetic system encodes both. Like a game of blackjack played with hundreds of thousands of cards, earlier rounds (inherited genetics) determine which cards are in the deck at this point. Then the chance of the deal governs which cards actually show up in the present hand (our genotype), and the strength of the cards (genetic dominance) determines the outcome—the particular person. Thus, genes are really a double set of blueprints, both for life as lived and life as passed on.

Yet the metaphor tells only half the story. If genes are the blueprints, they are also the construction company that transforms the blueprints into flesh and blood. In this age of communications and analysis, the gene is revered as the code, the information carrier, the explanation of life. But the larger truth is that genes *are* life.

There are millions of genes activating the human being, intricately organized, governing and carrying out the body/mind's conception, growth, and development; reproduction; and all our life's activity. They do this both directly and indirectly through their primary agents: the proteins. These proteins, in their astounding variety (there are more than a million different kinds throughout the body), are complex molecules, each built of looped chains of amino acids. By assembling the twenty-two acids into thousands of different proteins the genes construct and regulate all living beings.

Genes build proteins very much the way they reproduce themselves, by the *genetic code.* Genes are made of DNA (deoxyribonucleic acid)—a twisting ladder of four repeating "base" molecules. Each human cell contains about six feet of this genetic silk, packed into forty-six chromosomes.

The ever-changing order in which the four DNA base molecules (adenine, cytosine, guanine, and thymine) occur is the *genetic code.* Each DNA sequence of three bases—called a codon—dictates which of the twenty-two amino acids is to be added next to the protein that is being built, until the codon for STOP is reached and that protein is complete. Then another is started. Proteins, from hundreds to tens of thousands of amino acids long, are continually being assembled like this in each cell.

Proteins then, are the very substance of the body, the chief constituent of our flesh, hair, and nails, all external and internal organs, blood and lymph, indeed *all* the body's cells. They are also central to most of its operating systems: the nervous system, the enzymes that regulate our vital processes, the antibodies that destroy invaders, even some of the hormones and amino acids that become neurotransmitters and communicate from organ to organ and cell to cell.

Besides dictating proteins, the genes of each cell also manage the overall process of development by regulating which cells reproduce when and at what rate, and which proteins each cell produces at any given time. In this way, from fertilization on, genes begin allocating particular roles to particular cells. As it proceeds, this differentiating of cells develops into the formation of the various organs and shape of the body as we know it.

Among the proteins genes produce, the most powerful and important are the enzymes. Each gene encodes a particular enzyme and no other, while the enzyme in turn catalyzes a specific bodily reaction.

Since the body is primarily a catalytic enterprise, it requires tens of thousands of these special agents to carry out its operations efficiently. One of the first clues to the complexity and individuality of this system was discovered around 1900, when Karl Landsteiner deduced why some people died from blood transfusions that saved others' lives. The ABO blood types he discovered were the first known genetically determined biochemical marker between apparently similar people. Sir Archibald Garrod—a British physician and biochemist—later followed Landsteiner's lead to investigate diseases that involve bizarre biochemical abnormalities. Garrod theorized that individuals with disorders such as alkaptonuria (a condition characterized by a range of symptoms including the early onset of arthritis) have inherited a missing or defective enzyme, a block at some specific point in one or more metabolic pathways. He called these abnormalities "inborn errors of metabolism."

Since Garrod presented his hypothesis to the Royal College of Physicians in 1908, thousands of inborn errors of metabolism have been identified, and more are being discovered all the time. Two of the best known of these disorders are lactose intolerance, in which the individual is missing the enzyme necessary to digest the natural sugar in milk, and phenylketonuria (PKU), in which the enzyme needed to break down phenylalanine is disturbed.

Inborn errors of this type have a metabolic domino effect. A block at any point in the system of metabolic conversion causes disorders throughout the system. In infants with PKU, for example, phenylalanine accumulates in the brain, blocking normal development and causing irritability, hyperactivity, vomiting, seizures, and other neurological damage.

Fortunately, it is possible to detect disorders such as PKU and lactose intolerance within the first few days after birth, and dietary restrictions can prevent future problems. But these are only two of the more dramatic examples of possible inborn errors. Garrod himself realized that these phenomena might not be "errors" at all. In a letter to *The Lancet* in December of 1902 he wrote:

> The thought naturally presents itself that these are merely extreme variations of chemical behavior which are probably everywhere present in minor degrees and that just as no two individuals in a species are absolutely identical in bodily structure neither are their chemical processes carried out along exactly the same lines.[1]

When Garrod referred to difference in bodily structure he had little idea how prophetic his statement was. In 1926, Wade Brown and his co-workers at the Rockefeller Institute reported startling differences in organ weights within standard strains of rabbits. Ranges of fivefold to tenfold (per kilo of net body weight) were common, and spleens, to cite the extreme example, varied as much as eighty times in these healthy, "normal," presumably identical animals.[2]

These revelations about biological individuality were extended to human beings by Dr. Barry Anson of Northwestern University in 1951 with the publication of his comprehensive *Atlas of Human Anatomy.*[3] While preparing this manuscript, Anson and his researchers found medical texts containing "facts" that applied to only 15 percent of the population, and discovered wide variations in organ size and shape among individual humans.

These findings, and later research that further illustrated the tremendous differences that exist between supposedly "identical" individuals—from human twins to carefully bred lab rats—have tremendous medical implications. If we are all, in fact, unique, it follows that our "milieu interieur"—the natural balance that the body instinctively maintains—will be unique as well. What is "normal" for one individual (from body temperature to weight distribution) may be quite abnormal for another. Every step in the complicated process of genetics ensures that the resulting individual will be different from all other human beings. Moreover, once the genetic system begins interacting with the other subsystems of health, no two individuals, not even identical twins, are ever the same physically, mentally, or biochemically.

The importance of this truth can scarcely be overemphasized. Despite the popular notion that "genetic" also means fixed and impervious ("He can't help it, he was just born that way"), the reality is far more complex. Heredity and experience are mutually dependent and interacting—inseparable partners in our development. Each new experience, from the foods we eat to the toxins, viruses, and chemicals to which we are exposed, has an impact. As Rene Dubos has written:

> Only a small percentage of the genes are in an active state in any particular organism at any given time. Environmental forces can set in motion within the organism certain physiological processes that determine which parts of the genetic code are activated. The ancient controversy that had for so long put nature in opposition arose from incomplete knowledge of the intimate mechanisms of life.[4]

The uniqueness of the individual affects not only the diseases to which he or she is susceptible but also how that disease will manifest itself and what approach to treatment will prove most effective. Medicine learned this lesson the hard way when it was discovered that penicillin—which worked so miraculously for most patients—could precipitate fatal anaphylaxis in others. Since then we have learned that most drugs, chemicals, and even foods will prompt unusual responses in "some" patients. But we have not made the great cognitive leap of accepting that such "unusual" responses are not really unusual at all.

The many generalizations that medical science—and government agencies—have made about nutritional requirements, chemical exposures, and even many lifestyle factors repeatedly ignored the critical difference made by each individual's own biology. None of these factors has any meaning for health independent of the individual's response to it. When dealing with biologically unique individuals, in the real world, it is (in the words of Sir William Osler) "more important to know what sort of patient has a disease than to know what sort of disease a patient has."

The roots of one's biological individuality, then, are multiple and interlocking. The first, of course, is the unique new genotype in the pinpoint cell from which the individual grew.

The second is the rest of the original cell—the *cytoplasm* in which the genetic nucleus floats. Scientists once believed that genes carried out their assorted tasks immune to life's influences. But then the role of DNA was discovered, and soon after the genetic code was cracked, and it became clear that everything genes do involves the surrounding cytoplasm. From it they draw the amino acids to build their proteins, even the chemicals with which to replicate themselves.

The cytoplasm comes from the mother's body (the original egg cell that was fertilized) plus a contribution from the father (the nongene fraction of the spermatozoon). Hence, the nutritional states of the parents, their lifestyle, the environmental contaminants of their tissues and fluids, all condition the matter and chemistry of the new cell.

Third, as the cell divides and subdivides, the mother's body plays the vital role of supplying nutrients and oxygen-rich blood to the growing embryo. Any lack of *sustenance* in her—whether poor nutrition or anemic (low-oxygen) blood—can hinder or block expression of one or more genes during the development of the embryo and fetus.

A fourth factor is the reverse of sustenance, namely, protection or prophylaxis, freedom from toxicity. Rather than providing what is needed, prophylaxis keeps away what is harmful, safeguarding the fetus from infections, trauma, and toxifying chemicals. Any of these may scarcely bother the mother, yet impair or even kill the vulnerable fetus.

A final factor is timing. Chance events in the mother, from a fall to an alcoholic drink to a medication or an infection, *if they occur at the wrong time*, can block the delicate developmental process. Laboratory evidence has shown that the timing of this "developmental noise" is critical—sometimes just a matter of hours can spell the difference, and the effects, from a mole on the body to mental retardation, can be lifelong. As Richard Lewontin has observed: "Small accidental alterations in the growth pattern of nerve connections in the fetal brain may produce considerable differences in mental functioning."[5]

A number of implications follow from these interactions between the genes, surrounding cytoplasm, nutrients, assaults, and timing—the most fundamental of which is that each individual is unique to the roots of his or her biological being as it developed from the moment of conception.

We all know that human beings vary enormously in how, when, and what they perceive, learn, imagine, and so on, but parents, teachers, and scientists have been slow to recognize that such variations are rooted in idiosyncrasies of each individual's nervous system. One reason is the difficulty in tracing these roots and separating them from the pervasive effects of experience. As a result, it is difficult today to generalize about the genetic basis of learning and behavior. But in 1959 three different breakthroughs pointed to the same genetic source of mind and personality.

- In France, Lejeune, Gautier, and Turpin discovered the cause of Down's syndrome (mongolism): The cells of such individuals simply contain an extra chromosome (no. 21), for a total of forty-seven instead of the usual forty-six in normal humans. An irregularity in gene coding—a surplus rather than a deficiency—produces mental and personality changes.
- Patricia Jacobs and John Strong in England found an extra sex chromosome (the female or X chromosome) to be the cause of Klinefelter's syndrome in males. This disorder results in feminine-type breasts, small testicles, infertility, long slender limbs, little body hair, low sex drive, social and personality disturbances, and often mental retardation.
- Charles Ford and colleagues discovered a *missing* X chromosome in females with Turner's syndrome, another developmental disorder with profound physical and personality abnormalities.

Because, as Garrod noted in 1902, extreme variations "are probably everywhere present in minor degrees," there is reason to expect that the familiar human differences in intellectual ability, style of learning, intuitive power, personality, athletic interests, sexuality, and many behavior patterns may be partly rooted in the gene coding differences that make each of us unique. American society today is increasingly standardized and "medicalized," with the danger that the uniqueness of a child will be quickly branded a "disability" (as in "learning disability") or as "unacceptable behavior" or even "mental illness."

The classical scientist may reply, But if we are all unique, how can there be a general science of biology—or a scientific basis of medicine—at all?

The late Roger Williams, groundbreaking biochemist and champion of biological individuality (and discoverer of two B vitamins), distinguished applied biology from pure biology, noting that pure biology always seeks the illuminating *general patterns* in biological processes and ignores the irrelevant minor variations. In applied biology, on the other hand, when applying these patterns to a unique individual, biochemical individuality is a *crucial* consideration. It is foolish to apply scientific principles "without regard for the biochemical and physiological individuality of the person to be helped." In pure biology's search for operating principles, variation is considered an enemy and must be ignored. But the moment applied biology seeks to help individuals, recognizing the variations among them becomes a powerful ally.

What Williams and others have tried to point out is how little we know so far of the intricate ways of biology and, second, how central biological individuality is to all life's beings and processes. No intelligent approach to the learning and behavioral problems of youth—or the rise of chronic conditions—will ignore our genetic singularity or the widely differing effects on individuals of this century's great changes in environment, nourishment, and behavior.

Genes cannot exist apart from these other subsystems of life. Without nutrients to constitute cells, a fostering environment, and the life-supporting behavior of the organism, genes are lifeless threads of chemicals. Just as there can be no nutrition in and of itself, or an ecology or behavior apart from living beings, genes do not live and cannot function on their own but only in mutual interaction with these other subsystems. It is this codetermining interaction—past and present—of genes, nutrition, ecology, lifestyle, and events that produces at any point in time that priceless, elusive human quality: health.

These interacting systems, not being independent entities, are never absolutes with fixed values. In and of themselves, there is no such thing as excellent nutrition or a clean environment or ideal behavior or perfect genes. Each of these factors, in a living individual, brings a range of *potential* responses and requirements but acquires its *actual* value only when intersecting with the responses and requirement of the others.

Over time, genes can adapt to changing conditions in these systems, eventually transforming the very nature of the species. The source of this adaptability is *mutation*—any change in the coding of a set of genes. Mutation gives genes a repertoire, and *adaptation* is the genes' selection from this repertoire at any given time—tailored to the other varying systems of life. Genetic mutants with survival advantages—that work better in the interaction of available nutrients, ecological conditions, and the organism's behavior—go on to become mainstream genes in the evolving species.

But survival advantages are relative things. The same gene that contributed to survival in one situation may be far less advantageous in another. The great geneticist Theodosius Dobzhansky has called these "adaptively ambivalent genes."[6] Prime examples are the genes that regulate the diseases of sickle-cell anemia and diabetes.

The sickle-cell gene exists today almost exclusively among blacks living in or deriving from a region of central Africa where malaria is endemic. As it happens, *carriers* of the sickle-cell gene (that is, individuals with the "defective" recessive gene and a "normal" dominant) are peculiarly resistant to malaria. Thus, the defective gene is actually an alternative gene that is both advantageous and disadvantageous, depending on one's environment. In central Africa's malaria zone, the genetic advantage of increased resistance to malaria has far outweighed the disadvantage of mild anemia, and the trait has survived accordingly. In contemporary America, it is of no advantage and may even result in crippling anemia in the offspring of two carriers.

Similarly, it is thought that the genetic variation that results in diabetes was once a "thrifty" trait that enabled the body to store and metabolize food more efficiently in times of want. In the classic diabetic state, cells take in far less sugar from the blood than normal, so that, when the diet is rich and abundant, blood glucose levels are quite high. In primitive hunter-gatherer societies, the body may have used blood glucose at a much slower rate. High blood glucose levels coupled with slow glucose absorption rates allowed the body to use this "fuel" for a longer period of time, including during periods of want. Today, our continuous and abundant food supply has virtually eliminated such "dry" periods, and the continuously high blood sugar levels can lead to diabetes.

The diabetic trait is common in desert animals who have irregular access to food and water. Experimental studies on mice with the diabetic gene found that these mice, when placed on a starvation diet, lived considerably longer than their normal counterparts on the same diet. Mice with only one diabetic gene lived 25 to 40 percent longer than controls, while mice with two diabetic genes lived eight times longer than controls.[7]

This survival advantage disappeared when the food supply was increased to one half the usual laboratory diet. On the increased food supply, the mice with two diabetic genes soon developed obesity and all the symptoms of diabetes.

This pattern holds true in various human groups, as well. Aboriginal people such as the Polynesians and Native Americans have dramatically higher rates of diabetes than their Western counterparts. Indeed, among the Pima Indians living on reservations in Arizona, approximately half of the adult population now has diabetes.[8] This condition may be due to the relatively recent and abrupt change from a hunter-gatherer lifestyle.

In time, the sickle-cell and diabetic traits will probably die out of their own accord in Western nations, having outlived their usefulness to the species. But such natural selection takes millions of years. In the meantime we must deal with these and other problematic legacies from our hunter-gatherer ancestors, even as we complicate matters by inducing mutations of our own.

The mutations that led to our development as a species took thousands of years to develop and gain a genetic "foothold." The swift environmental changes that we are causing—in the physical environment, the food supply, our very lifestyles—may be exceeding our species's ability to adapt.

Because of technology's ventures into ionizing radiation and synthetic chemistry, the human beings of our age, as well as the food chain on which we live, may be undergoing a far higher mutation rate than biology has been accustomed to. By a conservative estimate, in the last few decades we have roughly doubled nature's spontaneous mutation rate. All along the genetic pipeline—from the body's building of proteins and dividing of cells to the construction by sex cells of new genotypes and the dividing of chromosomes preparatory to reproduction—man-made mutations are damaging the intricate chemistry of our being. These *induced mutations* play a major role in the high twentieth-century cancer rate and undoubtedly in a number of the other chronic conditions prevalent in advanced societies today.

As for the species's longer-term prospects, can there be any hope that today's higher mutation rate will mean greater possibilities of adaptation in the ages to come? Or are there qualitative differences between the spontaneous mutations of gene chemistry and the gene damage wrought by outside agents? These are grave questions about which we know very little. Too little is known about genes to equate chemico/radiation gene damage with the spontaneous mutations of evolutionary history. The consensus among experts is that induced mutations must be strictly minimized, not only for our own health but for the future of the race. There is no justification great enough to take the risk. In the gloomy conclusion of Macfarlane Burnet, "If the standard social pattern of today in Western communities continues indefinitely, there can be no escape from serious genetic deterioration."[9]

As *programmed* organisms, then, we have many built-in limits that, as *intelligent* organisms, we have to take into account if we want to stay healthy. We have excellent adaptive mechanisms for coping with short-term challenges. But if the challenges endure and become chronic, our constant adapting—which exacts its own toll—can become exhausted and dysfunctional. Gradually we are weighted with one or more maladaptive conditions that in time may worsen into chronic disorders.

In reviewing the evidence, however, we should keep in mind the surpassing complexity of the human biological being, including its individuality and its particular environmental history, nutrition, and the cumulative effects of its own behavior. In light of the way genetics interacts with each of these, it is likely that no particular factor is the sole cause of the chronic disorders—physical or behavioral—but that the pace of change in all these systems is proving to be faster than our genetic endowment can readily adapt.

THE TWENTIETH-CENTURY discovery of the genetic system is one of humankind's greatest breakthroughs. Already this momentous discovery is proving abundantly beneficial. We are gaining great insights into life processes. Specifically, an increasing portion of human disease is being recognized as genetically caused, predisposed, or influenced.

The dawning of the Age of Genetics has meant that tremendous advances are being made in a wholly new genetic attack on human disease. Genetic engineering, meanwhile, has transformed plant and animal breeding programs for improved stocks, resistance, and yield. The promise here is also enormous: food quantities sufficient to provide for any human future; much greater nutrient content and nutrient availability in foodstuffs; fewer food-borne hazards, whether natural or introduced by man; and fewer plant and animal diseases to be fought with pesticides. Indeed, the genetic engineering revolution, only now dawning, may be one of humanity's greatest voyages of discovery.

Whether genetic research and engineering will make significant advances against chronic disease remains to be seen. But no prudent society afflicted with chronic conditions ought to count on genetic technology to pull its chestnuts from the fire.

The inherently ponderous pace of human evolution has put us at significant biological risk in our rapidly changing world. Since it is highly unlikely that we will be able to speed up our "biological clocks" to accommodate the advances of technology, it is imperative that we bring technology into dynamic equilibrium with our genetic heritage. To do so, we must understand not only how our genetic system works but how it interacts with the other biological subsystems of our health—most notably our nutrition, environment, and lifestyle.

2

The Web of Nutrition

EVERY SCHOOLCHILD in the Western world is taught about Vasco da Gama's voyage around the Cape of Good Hope in 1497. What is not so widely taught is that by its end da Gama had lost—from "scurvy"—a hundred of his original crew of 160 men. The cause: unknown. They just started bleeding at the gums and ended up dead. In 1593 this dreaded disease (the result of not eating fruits and vegetables containing vitamin C) accounted for the deaths of 10,000 British seamen.

The remarkable story of nutrition, however, does not begin until 1734, on an English brig running from London to Greenland. Again scurvy broke out. One sailor had a fearful case, and the captain, assuming the disease was infectious and thinking the sacrifice of a lone sailor might save the rest of the crew, put him ashore in the Shetland Islands. No one—including the sailor—expected him to survive more than a few days. Out of sheer hunger, he began to chew the grass growing on the island. Soon he could stand, and then walk. A ship bound for London sighted him and carried him home ahead of his shipmates—who were astounded when he greeted them on the dock.

The "miracle" came to the attention of Dr. James Lind, a surgeon in the British fleet who was concerned about the decimation of crews on long voyages. Hearing of the sailor who ate grass he asked himself a question no one had ever asked before—at least, not in a scientific way. Could the grass have contained some specific substance that was missing from the sailors' usual diet? Could there be a connection between what a man ate and the disease that killed him—or never touched him?

To see if he could answer the question, Lind launched medical science's first controlled clinical study—in 1747 aboard a frigate called the *Salisbury*. The trial was a classic: simple, impeccable, and historic in its outcome. Lind took twelve stricken sailors who were eating standard shipboard fare and altered their diet. He put two men on a quart of cider a day, two on twenty-five drops of elixir vitriol three times a day, two on two teaspoons of vinegar three times a day on an empty stomach, two of the worst cases on nothing but seawater, two others on two oranges and one lemon daily, and the final two on nutmeg. The results? Only two sailors—the ones given two oranges and a lemon a day—returned to duty . . . and in a "miraculous" six days.

Instantly, Lind knew the significance of his findings. By 1753 he had published them in his classic *A Treatise of the Scurvy*. As has happened often in medicine, his work was ridiculed or ignored. Not until 1795, forty-eight years and thousands of deaths later (and a year after Lind himself died), did the British Admiralty order that "lime juice"—citrus fruits—be included in shipboard diets. British sailors, no longer dying by the thousands, soon became known as Limeys.

Great physicians of the past, like the Greek Hippocrates or the Roman Empire's Galen or the Arab Avicenta or the Swiss Paracelsus, had prescribed certain foods (from garlic to cloves to vinegar to fruit) for particular illnesses. But Lind was the first to demonstrate a link between diet and disease, the first to prove the momentous distinction between food, of whatever kind, and true nourishment. In effect, he discovered what we now call *nutrition*.

People had always related *food* to hunger and satiety and survival. Lind was the first to show that "getting enough to eat" wasn't enough. He proved that it can make a life-and-death difference which foods you eat, that foods contain *essential* differences between them that can make the difference between sickness and health.

Lind's work crossed a Rubicon in history, launching the quest to discover how the foods we eat throughout our lives (and exactly which foods, when) give us health, mental health, disease resistance, healing, performance, calmness, energy. Without fully realizing it, he conducted the first demonstration of the link between nutrition and human potential.

NEARLY EVERYTHING known about nutrition has been discovered in the last 75 years. Dr. Lind made his watershed discovery of the difference between food and nourishment about 1750. But the quest to *understand* the difference took another 150 years. First had to come the birth and growth of chemistry (oxygen wasn't discovered until 1772) and then of organic or biochemistry. So it was only in the twentieth century that progress got under way on the mystery of nutrition, which lies at the heart of the chemistry of life. The breakthrough was made in London, by a most unlikely man, in the year 1912.

Beriberi had long been an Oriental disease, involving cracked skin, swollen legs, "pins and needles" in the flesh, and great weakness, leading to insanity. By the late nineteenth century both Dutch East Indies and Japanese medical officers—following in Lind's tracks—had linked beriberi to diets high in polished white rice, and the chemists' search was on for what they called the "missing factor" in the discarded rice polishings. After a frustrating search by top scientists from Wisconsin to Japan to Java to Holland, the "missing factor" was finally isolated by a restless young Pole, Casimir Funk, working at the Lister Institute in London in 1912. Reducing 836 pounds of brown rice down to a precious six ounces, Funk thought he had isolated the long-sought "beriberi factor." He invented the name "vitamine" for the new compound and then, strangely, gave up research.

What Funk had actually discovered was the "missing factor" (now called niacin or vitamin B_3) in another nutrient-deficiency disease, pellagra. The actual "beriberi factor" (vitamin B_1 or thiamine) was finally isolated in Java in 1926 and synthesized in the Merck laboratories in Rahway, New Jersey, in 1936.

Since those decades of discovery about the great deficiency diseases, we've learned a tremendous amount about nutrients, but the larger part of nutrition remains shrouded in mystery. In fact, we have still to discover all the essential nutrients. As recently as the 1970s, silicon, vanadium, nickel, and arsenic were shown to be essential to human life. Yet much of what science knows about nutrition is not being applied in our eating habits, or in medicine or the running of institutions, or in the media or education.

Americans are surprisingly ignorant about nutrition. Studies have long shown that a high proportion of individuals do not know the most elementary facts about health and the human body, including the location of such major organs as the heart, stomach, liver, and kidneys. Regarding more sophisticated concepts such as carbohydrates, fats, proteins, vitamins, minerals, trace elements, and human metabolism, there appears to be both great ignorance and confusion among the American people.

The U.S. Food & Drug Administration's Nutrition Knowledge Survey, conducted in 1974 and 1975, found a majority of consumers holding beliefs about nutrition that were influenced by custom and food fashion rather than fact. The figures revealed wide ignorance about the very basics of nutrition. In the 1974 study, over half of those interviewed could not understand all or part of a typical nutrition label. [1] The follow-up in 1975 confirmed that almost 25 percent of respondents believed that proper nutrition meant being of the right weight. About 40 percent agreed that "if you just eat a variety of foods from the supermarket, you will get enough nutrition." [2]

A study sponsored by the U.S. Department of Agriculture found that on three different nutrition quizzes participants were guessing about as often as they gave correct answers. [3] Nor were these the "ignorant poor." The survey focused on shoppers (94 percent women) in middle-class communities (93 percent white, 65 percent with household incomes above $15,000) with above-average educational background (78 percent or better high school graduates).

In jarring contrast to these facts, consumers believe they are well informed about nutrition. In the USDA study, only 7 percent felt their knowledge of nutrition was inadequate. Other surveys have confirmed the public's confusion about nutrition. Common fallacies include the following, turned up in a 1975 USDA Home Economics Research Report [4] and in an FDA study: [5]

- Some foods by themselves contain all the common nutrients in recommended amounts.
- There are sources of body energy other than food.
- Food eaten between meals is less nutritious than that eaten at meals.
- Synthetic vitamins added to foods are of less benefit than the same vitamins occurring naturally in foods.

In nearly every study this glaring contradiction emerges between consumers' professed understanding of good nutrition and the ignorant beliefs they actually hold on the subject. Worse, the majority of consumers' beliefs about nutrition (right or wrong) bear no particular relationship to how they act in buying food or eating meals.

Hundreds of books written on nutrition were reviewed in the preparation of this book. Nowhere is there a clearer orientation to the subject than in the work of Roger Williams. A summary of his basic theses is as follows:

1. Each individual inherits a distinctive set of nutritional requirements. The "average person"—for whom the National Research Council and the FDA specify Recommended Daily Dietary Allowances (RDAs)—is a myth. The range of individual requirements has been obtained for only a handful of the essential nutrients known to us. These differences range from twofold to fortyfold. This biochemical individuality is of profound importance in the diagnosis, treatment, and prevention of disease; yet it still goes largely unrecognized in medical practice and research.
2. Every basic nutrient is as necessary a part of the body's internal environment as water and oxygen. The proper functioning of body cells depends on all of these nutrients' being present.
3. Nutrients work as a team. Cells do not depend on single nutrients performing single roles of proper body functioning—they depend on total nutritional teamwork. Scarcity of a single nutrient reduces the efficiency of all the nutrients with which it is teamed.
4. In the real world, living species are rarely supplied with optimum nutrition. For humans in industrial societies, such less-than-perfect conditions are exacerbated by the destruction of nutrients in food processing.
5. Common noninfectious diseases sometimes develop because susceptible persons have far greater than "average" requirements for a particular vitamin, mineral, amino acid, or fatty acid—requirements that the ordinary diet does not adequately meet.
6. Greater attention must be paid to the known role of nutrition in strengthening the body's own defenses against invading microorganisms and toxic substances.
7. The discovery of deficiency diseases and the identification of vitamins in the early decades of this century should have led to a

> reorientation of medicine along nutritional lines. Scurvy, beriberi, pellagra, and other disorders caused by a missing food factor were more than a handful of oddity diseases. The fact that their symptoms occurred throughout the body and that the missing nutrients were essential for health pointed to a broad biological relationship between disease and faulty nutrition. But it was a lead that medicine, suddenly taken up with the new "wonder" drugs and emerging technologies, did not follow up.
>
> The result is that medical science today still needs to find out to what extent individuals who are peculiarly susceptible to heart disease, cancer, obesity, arthritis, mental illness, alcoholism, multiple sclerosis, Parkinson's disease, and a host of other chronic illnesses can benefit from nutritional science.

Williams's work suggests that the incorporation of these basic principles of nutrition into medicine on an equal footing with the germ theory of infectious disease will mean a new era in the prevention and management of illness. As we shall see, subsequent findings in biochemistry, immunology, neurophysiology, and related fields support this view.

NUTRIENTS AND the body's process of nutrition are not difficult to understand. Only a few obvious concepts are involved.

- *What is a nutrient?*

A nutrient is any substance that the body has to get *from outside* to stay alive, and that is processed through digestion.

Every species is biochemically different and therefore has a different set of nutrients. Dogs and cats don't eat oranges—and don't need vitamin C because their bodies manufacture ample amounts. Somehow in the course of evolution humans lost the genes and therefore the enzymes to make vitamin C, which is now an essential nutrient for *human* life. Unless we get ascorbic acid (vitamin C) from the outside we end up like those British sailors Dr. Lind wanted to save.

Nutrients, then, are just chemicals, from earth elements like iron to extremely complex organic molecules like vitamin B_{12}. The only thing these particular chemicals have in common is that the human organism happens to need them from outside to conduct its life processes.

• *How many essential nutrients do humans need to keep alive and healthy?*

Given the basic materials (the nutrients) they need, the gene/enzyme complexes of human cells can assemble all the chemical compounds that make up the human body and keep it operating efficiently. There are over fifty thousand of these compounds—or millions if one counts all the different antibodies the body tailors to attack invaders. To build all these compounds, the human body needs only fifty essential nutrients from the outside (table 1). (Essential nutrients are still being discovered—and some experts debate a few items included—so this list is not final.)

—The *major nutrients* form the vast bulk of all the food we eat: over 99.99 percent. We need from ounces up to pounds of them every day, and there are *five* in all (see below).

—The *micronutrients* are those we need just grams or less of each day. In the harmony of nature, they also occur in foods in only minute amounts. (Any more and such essential nutrients as florine or selenium would kill us.) There are *three* types of micronutrients (see below).

• *How much do we need of these fifty essential nutrients?*

Nutrients vary extremely widely in the amount needed—from millionths of a gram to pounds per day. In fact, nutrients are commonly divided into two categories according to the level needed: the major nutrients and the micronutrients.

"Major" and "micro" refer only to quantities needed, not to importance: In time, the body (and mind) become just as sick for lack of an infinitesimal nutrient like folic acid as from a major nutrient like water. Only millionths of a gram of B_{12} are needed to prevent pernicious anemia, a blood disorder that can lead to acute paranoia—"megaloblastic madness"—and death.

The five major (or macro) nutrients are: protein, carbohydrates, fat, water, and fiber. Virtually 100 percent of all food is made up of these five substances in varying concentrations.

The three types of micronutrients are: vitamins, minerals, and trace minerals (or trace elements).

Let's look at each of these eight groups of nutrients.

TABLE 1

The Fifty Essential Nutrients for Human Beings

(Discovered to date)

1. Water	
2. Calories (from fat, carbohydrates, and proteins)	
3. Fiber	
4. Arginine (for children)	Essential Amino Acids
5. Histidine (for children)	Essential Amino Acids
6. Leucine	Essential Amino Acids
7. Isoleucine	Essential Amino Acids
8. Lysine	Essential Amino Acids
9. Methionine	Essential Amino Acids
10. Phenylalanine	Essential Amino Acids
11. Thereonine	Essential Amino Acids
12. Tryptophan	Essential Amino Acids
13. Valine	Essential Amino Acids
14. Linoleic acid	Essential Fatty Acids
15. Linolenic acid	Essential Fatty Acids
16. Arachidonic acid	Essential Fatty Acids
17. Sodium (Na)	Major Minerals
18. Magnesium (Mg)	Major Minerals
19. Phosphorus (P)	Major Minerals
20. Chlorine (Cl)	Major Minerals
21. Potassium (K)	Major Minerals
22. Calcium (Ca)	Major Minerals

Protein

We are animals and we need the "stuff" of animals to live. Protein is *the* key constituent of all animal bodies, accounting for 10 to 20 percent, depending on age and body weight. (Most of the rest is water, fat, and the calcium of bones and teeth.)

Thousands of different proteins are assembled and utilized in the human body. These proteins are key not only to the structure of the

TABLE 1 *(Continued)*

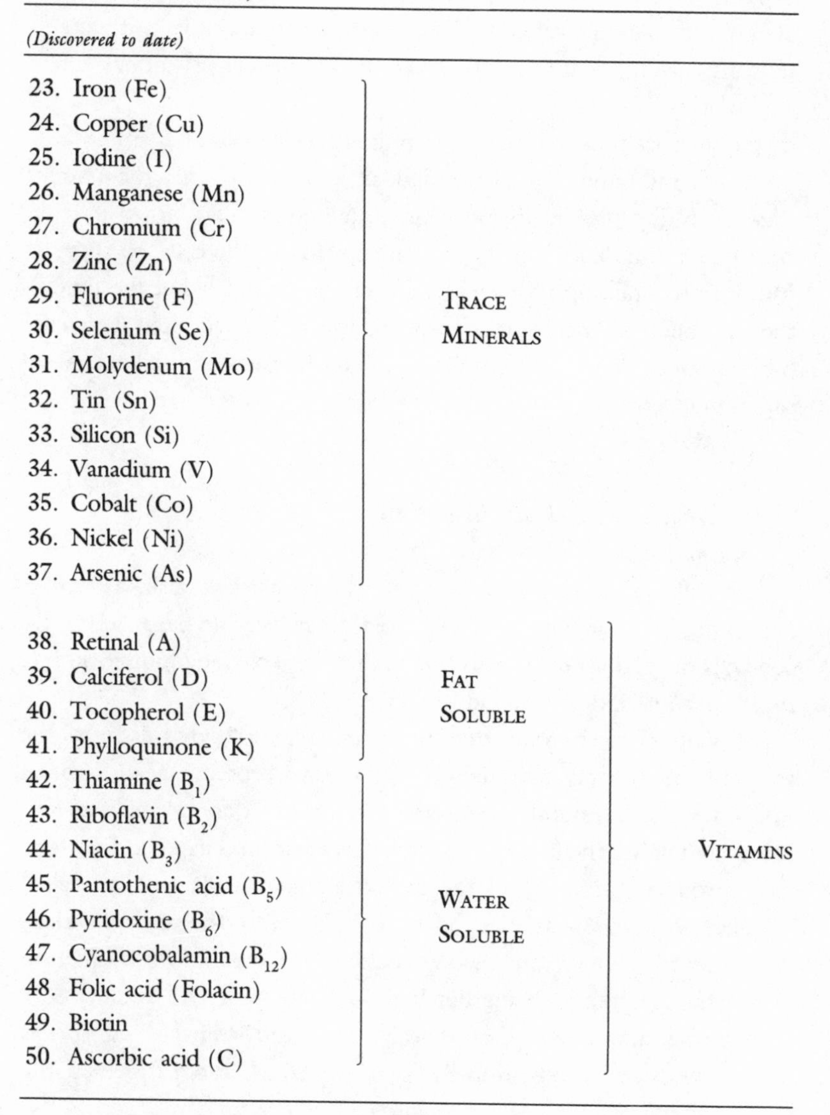

(Discovered to date)		
23. Iron (Fe)	Trace Minerals	
24. Copper (Cu)	Trace Minerals	
25. Iodine (I)	Trace Minerals	
26. Manganese (Mn)	Trace Minerals	
27. Chromium (Cr)	Trace Minerals	
28. Zinc (Zn)	Trace Minerals	
29. Fluorine (F)	Trace Minerals	
30. Selenium (Se)	Trace Minerals	
31. Molydenum (Mo)	Trace Minerals	
32. Tin (Sn)	Trace Minerals	
33. Silicon (Si)	Trace Minerals	
34. Vanadium (V)	Trace Minerals	
35. Cobalt (Co)	Trace Minerals	
36. Nickel (Ni)	Trace Minerals	
37. Arsenic (As)	Trace Minerals	
38. Retinal (A)	Fat Soluble	Vitamins
39. Calciferol (D)	Fat Soluble	Vitamins
40. Tocopherol (E)	Fat Soluble	Vitamins
41. Phylloquinone (K)	Fat Soluble	Vitamins
42. Thiamine (B_1)	Water Soluble	Vitamins
43. Riboflavin (B_2)	Water Soluble	Vitamins
44. Niacin (B_3)	Water Soluble	Vitamins
45. Pantothenic acid (B_5)	Water Soluble	Vitamins
46. Pyridoxine (B_6)	Water Soluble	Vitamins
47. Cyanocobalamin (B_{12})	Water Soluble	Vitamins
48. Folic acid (Folacin)	Water Soluble	Vitamins
49. Biotin	Water Soluble	Vitamins
50. Ascorbic acid (C)	Water Soluble	Vitamins

body (the billions of cells comprising its organs, nerves, muscles, and flesh) but also to its functioning—mainly through enzymes, the tiny managers of body processes. The human body can build all the proteins it needs, but to do so it must have the building blocks of protein—the amino acids. Just as genes are almost endless combinations of four "bases," so proteins are countless combinations of twenty-two amino acids. About half of these amino acids are essential nutrients for humans; given them, the body can build the other "nonessential" amino acids.

To build its proteins, the body must have the essential amino acids present at the same time in the right proportion. We get these amino acids by eating protein foods, which our bodies break down into the constituent amino acids that are then supplied to the cells, so they can use them to build up whatever new proteins are needed at the time. If the diet becomes deficient in protein, the cells encounter difficulties meeting various needs—for example, in building new antibodies to ward off an infection.

- *Where does the body get its protein supply of amino acids?*

Primarily from the animal kingdom: meat, chicken, fish, as well as animal products such as milk, eggs, and other dairy items. A secondary source is the grain/nuts/beans side of the vegetable kingdom, including bread, peanut butter, tofu, and pasta.

Just eating protein foods does not guarantee the body will get all the essential amino acids it needs to build its own proteins. Many protein foods lack certain essential amino acids and must be complemented with foods containing them. The primary sources of protein—the meat and dairy products—contain all the essential amino acids and are called *complete proteins.* But the secondary sources—from the vegetable kingdom—usually contain only *incomplete proteins.* Cereals, for example, are low in the amino acid lysine but high in methionine and cystine. Soybeans, lima beans, and kidney beans have mirror-image amino acid profiles. So when foods from the two groups are eaten together, the body gets the complete set of amino acids it needs.

Many cultures have instinctively developed basic meals that resolve this problem of "protein complementarity." In the Middle East bread and cheese are traditionally eaten together. In Mexico, rice and beans. And in America, breakfast cereals with milk. Protein complementarity is a nutritional problem that vegetarians have to address in order to maintain full health and functioning.

Carbohydrates

Just as protein is the key component of the animal kingdom, so carbohydrates are found almost exclusively in the vegetable kingdom—in fruits, vegetables, and grains. Carbohydrates (organic compounds of carbon, oxygen, and hydrogen) function as *fuel* for the body's cells, which burn them to produce energy and heat. Virtually nonexistent in the structure of our bodies (0.05 to 0.1 percent), carbohydrates nonetheless are the largest portion of most people's diet. (Carbohydrates not needed at the time of digestion are stored in the body as fat.)

Carbohydrate foods range from the complex—called *starches*—to the simple—called *sugars.* We're all familiar with both. Starches are potatoes, rice, corn and other vegetables, bread, cereal, and pasta. Sugars include table sugar, fruit, syrups, honey. Actually the two are connected on a continuous spectrum, with the complex breaking down into the simple. We see this process when we leave a green banana or peach out to ripen: The complex starches of the young fruit gradually break down into the sweet sugars of ripeness.

In the same way, before the individual cell can burn them as fuel, carbohydrates must first be broken down into their simplest form, which is glucose. Starches break down into a number of complex sugars, which then break down into a number of simple sugars, which are then absorbed into the blood, chiefly as glucose. The bloodstream carries the glucose (along with oxygen from the lungs), to all the body's cells, where it is burned—oxidized—into energy. The body's most constant need is for energy—maintaining the level of glucose in the blood.

The level of glucose in the bloodstream is monitored by the pancreas. When blood glucose levels rise, the pancreas secretes insulin, which triggers the cells to absorb the glucose, either for immediate use as energy or for storage. Without insulin, the cells cannot absorb the glucose and will literally starve for lack of fuel.

The importance of insulin's regulatory role cannot be overestimated. Very slight alterations in blood glucose levels can have dramatic physical and mental effects. The brain, which burns one fourth of all the body's fuel, is most sensitive to these changes and is affected every time we eat. A typical example is the drowsiness felt after lunch or a big meal: The digesting food drives up the blood sugar quickly, which triggers a strong insulin response and a sharp drop in blood sugar, experienced as tiredness. In general, it is insulin's steadying influence that keeps blood glucose levels within a "normal" range (80–100 mg/dl), so that the body's cells can function efficiently.

Fat

After water, fat is the most familiar macronutrient. Everybody knows what fat is. But what most don't realize is that fat is basically a good thing for the body, providing nutrients, warmth, and energy. Importantly, several specific forms of fat—the essential fatty acids—are necessary for life. In fact, some of the most promising nutrition research today is focusing on fats—or *lipids,* as they are called technically—which scientists believe may turn out to be as complex as vitamins, once we understand their many roles in the body.

The lipids contain the same elements as carbohydrates, but they contain more carbon and hydrogen, and less oxygen—an important difference when it comes to burning them for energy. With more carbon and hydrogen to burn, lipids liberate almost twice as much energy (and therefore calories) as carbohydrates or protein. An ounce of butter or olive oil means about 255 calories; an ounce of sugar or pure protein 113 calories.

There are many different kinds of lipids, but five in particular have been the subject of debate. The *essential fatty acids*—linoleic, linolenic, and archidonic—which are not synthesized by the body, and the *fat-soluble vitamins* (A, D, E, and K) are vital sets of lipids that occur across all chemical classes.

The third kind, *triglycerides,* makes up over 90 percent of our body fat and as much of 98 percent of the fat in our foods. They are generally differentiated on the basis of "saturation"—a term that refers to the balance of carbon and hydrogen in a given fat molecule. In saturated fats, every carbon bond is occupied by a hydrogen atom. The most obvious consequence of this saturation is that saturated fats tend to be solid at room temperature. The most common sources of saturated fats are animal products such as meat fat, lard, and butter.

In unsaturated fats the carbon atoms bond to each other, and therefore lack two hydrogen atoms. Oleic acid, found in olive oil, is an unsaturated fat.

Polyunsaturated fats have two or more such carbon bonds, and at least four missing hydrogen atoms. Linoleic acid, found in corn oil, is polyunsaturated.

Saturation is a major point of contention nowadays, but the complexity of the issue is rarely realized. Early research on arterial disease implicated saturated fats as the culprit and led to the near canonization of polyunsaturated and hydrogenated oils. More recent research has found that the role fats play in arterial disease is not as clear-cut as was once thought and that polyunsaturated and hydrogenated fats have risks of their own. The unsaturated points in these fats are "weak links" that allow oxygen to attack and turn the oil rancid. Worse yet, processing alters the chemical structure of polyunsaturated fats, making them potentially harmful to the body.

Number four, *cholesterol*, is another problem lipid, the focus of a great deal of attention from the medical establishment and the food industry. When looked at objectively, it is truly remarkable—the central structure of the steroid hormones, a part of the bile acids that digest fat, and a major component of brain and nerve tissue. In the words of nutrition researcher Henry Schroeder, "Without it the skin would dry up, the brain would not function, and there would be no vital hormones of sex and adrenal."[6]

"So," you may ask, "if cholesterol is so important, why are we told to avoid it?" Good question. Basically, research has found a statistical correlation between blood cholesterol levels and heart disease. On the surface, this may seem like reason enough to ban cholesterol, but the fact remains that proving a correlation between two factors in a process as complex as nutrition does not necessarily prove a cause. Years of research have yet to prove that—among normal healthy people eating a good diet—there is a direct link between dietary cholesterol, blood cholesterol, and the likelihood of heart attack or stroke. The complexity of the argument is illustrated in groups such as the Eskimos living above the Arctic Circle. When these individuals maintain their natural lifestyle (in which the bulk of calories come from protein and natural fats) they have no atherosclerosis.

On the other hand, there's significant evidence that processed polyunsaturated oils produce potentially cancer-causing "free radicals." So while we shouldn't eat a pound of lard a day, neither should we assume that margarine, processed oils, or other "no-cholesterol" foods are particularly healthy alternatives.

The *lipoproteins* are not strictly fats, but they play a crucial role in distributing fats to the body's tissues via the blood and lymphatic systems. Since lipids are not water soluble, they must be "packaged" in protein-encased globules—the lipoproteins. These cases come in varying densities and serve different purposes. The low-density lipoproteins (LDLs) are packaged in the liver to carry cholesterol to the body's cells. The LDLs are frequently referred to as "bad" lipoproteins, because they have been associated with the buildup of arterial plaque. High-density lipoproteins (HDLs), on the other hand, are smaller particles thought to play a role in the prevention of heart disease, perhaps by transporting unused cholesterol back to the liver for metabolism and removal, or by inhibiting the uptake of LDLs by arterial walls. The most recent research indicates that the *ratio* between cholesterol, triglycerides, and the various lipoproteins may be the deciding factor in disease development, rather than the concentration of any one of these factors.

Fiber

Roughly speaking, "fiber" includes those substances in our food that are *not* food, that is, which our systems cannot digest and metabolize. These substances occur mainly in the plant kingdom, which needs stationary forms of defense. Fiber substances are found in the protective walls of cells and, on a larger scale, in the outer surfaces of seeds and their mature fruits, including nuts and vegetables. (The most familiar fiber food, bran, is the shell of the wheat grain.) Simply put, fiber is tough and resistant to outside destroyers such as the enzymes of our digestive system.

It may seem strange to call a nonfood—which the body can't digest or get nourishment from—a nutrient. But it is precisely fiber's indigestibility, the fact that it passes through unchanged, that makes it so important in our diet. By not being broken down and utilized by the body, fiber exerts a variety of beneficial effects both on the walls and muscular action of the intestines and on the digesting contents as they make their way through us. Only in the past ten years have researchers begun to study fiber intensively. As a result, we now understand some of its roles in human health, but many suspected benefits remain to be explored or confirmed.

- Fiber is thought to have three important effects on the digestive contents. First, it keeps them moving smoothly, firming up diarrhea or loosening constipation. Second, it is believed to bind many potentially harmful substances and prevent them from toxifying the body. Third, it appears to modify a number of compounds before absorption, such as bile salts (preventing gallstones) and cholesterol and triglycerides (reducing atherosclerosis). Unrefined carbohydrates are also thought by some to be helpful in the prevention and management of diabetes.

- Fiber maintains the normal volume and softness of the contents of the intestinal tract, thereby reducing internal pressure associated with diverticular diseases (splits and pouches in the tract), appendicitis, hiatus hernias, and varicose veins. In addition, fiber may prevent cancers of the bowel by inhibiting carcinogenic activity along its surfaces.

Thus, we need dietary fiber among the essential nutrients, not as a chemical component, like the others, but as a physiological agent: It establishes and maintains the health of the digestive system.

Water

Water is the only substance that is a nutrient for all living creatures. Water is also the most abundant constituent of our bodies, although less as we grow older. The embryo is 98 percent water, babies about 75 percent, and adults from 65 percent down to 50 percent (the more fat, the less water).

Of the fifty or so essential nutrients, water is the "most essential," that is, we have to have more of it, more often, than any other nutrient and we will die sooner for lack of it (within three to five days). Only oxygen is more crucial.

Not only is water a nutrient but it typically contains many other nutrients, notably minerals. As a nutrient, water plays a key role in countless interactions in every organ, system, and function of the body. About 45 percent of an adult's weight is the water within the cells—20 percent is extracellular water surrounding cells.

Through thirst and excretion, the body carefully maintains its total body water level. A rise or drop of just a few percent will make us sick; a drop of about 20 percent is fatal. With moderate activity and no visible sweating, we need about two to three quarts of water a day, which we get in food and beverages, the balance being met by drinking water.

THESE FIVE GROUPS—protein, carbohydrate, fat, fiber, and water—are humans' major nutrients, ranging from ounces to pounds a day and accounting for almost all our food. We will now take a look at the three groups of micronutrients—vitamins, minerals, and trace minerals—substances we need only tiny amounts of, from grams to millionths of a gram.

Minerals

Plants send their roots down into the mineral-laden earth to obtain the basic elements out of which organic life is built; similarly, animals need many of the same minerals, such as iron and phosphorus and copper, to carry out life processes and be healthy. Minerals are divided into two categories, again according to the amounts needed.

- The *trace minerals* or trace elements are those we need only the faintest presence of in our diet, measured down to millionths of a gram.
- The *macrominerals* are those we need in grams down to tenths of a gram per day. There are seven (in order here of descending amount needed): potassium, chlorine, sodium, calcium, phosphorus, magnesium, and sulfur.

One of the more important characteristics of these macrominerals is their ability to form acids or bases, enabling cells to maintain the acidity or alkalinity at which various enzymes work best.

Sodium, in particular, performs a delicate balancing act with potassium in the body's cells. Sodium is concentrated in the fluid surrounding cells, while potassium concentrates within them. The two must stay in balance to maintain the osmotic pressure of the cells and regulate the flow of nutrients and wastes in and out of the cells.

The major acid-forming minerals (calcium, potassium, sodium, and magnesium) are contained mostly in cereals and grains. Meat, poultry, and fish also include them in significant amounts. The major base-forming minerals (chlorine, phosphorus, and sulfur) are primarily found in fruits and vegetables. Milk and milk products contain them both.

Trace Elements

The remaining nutrient minerals are called *trace minerals* (or *trace elements*) because the human organism requires only the smallest amount of them in order to survive. Indeed, higher concentrations of some of these elements (such as arsenic) would be toxic. A few of the trace elements are well known, such as iodine (which is added to salt to prevent goiter) and fluoride (which is added to toothpaste and water supplies). Others, such as selenium, are only recently gaining attention. Selenium has been of interest because some researchers believe it plays a role in preventing cancer, atherosclerosis, and other diseases.

Vitamins

When Casimir Funk coined the dubious term *vitamine* for his "missing factor," he meant the factor was "vital" and an "amine," an organic compound that contains nitrogen. He was right about the "vital" but wrong about the "amine," since vitamin A, ascorbic acid, vitamin D, and others do not contain nitrogen.

However, the word caught on—and a new term *was* needed—so scientists dropped the final *e* and *vitamin* it became. A new term was needed because it had become apparent there were many "missing factors." We now know of at least fourteen of these complex chemicals, and though many have little in common chemically, they are dubbed collectively "the vitamins." In this sense, *vitamin* is a catchall label for the remaining nutrients that are neither protein, carbohydrate, fat, or mineral.

Vitamins have one or two other qualities in common; they are all organic substances needed in only minute quantities—and most of them act as *co-enzymes.* Like keys, they fit into tiny chemical locks that free the body's thousands of enzymes to carry out their tasks. So vitamins are neither building blocks nor sources of energy nor basic elements. But in the gene-enzymes' regulatory networks, each vitamin is a complex organic molecule that fills in specific missing links throughout the body's chemistry. For this reason, no vitamin can substitute for any other, nor does any one carry out a basic function all by itself. Nutrients work as a team, and all are necessary for optimal function. The complete absence of only one nutrient will result in death, and any degree of deficiency will cause systemic malfunctions and illness.

If the human body can't synthesize vitamins, who or what can? Where do we obtain them? The plant kingdom is the chief source of vitamins. For all their structural simplicity, plants perform a number of functions essential to life that animals can't. Fundamentally, they supply our world with oxygen and they synthesize vitamins. Some vitamins, such as C, are found only in fruits and vegetables. Others, like the B complex, are found in animal tissues as well. Among animal tissue, the liver—as the body's chemical plant—is particularly high not only in protein but also in many vitamins. Uniquely, vitamin D is released when sunlight strikes the skin, and the terrible bone disorder rickets (from vitamin D deficiency) occurred commonly among children in fog- and smoke-bound locales of the north.

The vitamins are divided into two distinct groups—ten of them (vitamin C and the nine B complex vitamins) dissolve in water; the other four (A, D, E, and K) dissolve in fat. This difference has several important implications.

- Because the body is a water-based operation, the water-soluble vitamins are readily absorbed but are not stored in high amounts. For this reason, they need to be supplied fairly steadily in the diet, and there is little danger of them building up in the body to toxic levels.
- In contrast, the fat-soluble vitamins should be consumed in the presence of fat in the diet in order to be absorbed. Moreover, the body can build up large stores of them, as it can of fat, so that they don't have to be supplied continuously. Yet, if the stores build too high, vitamins like A and D can reach toxic levels and actually harm the organism or its functioning.

This difference also affects how foods should be stored and cooked if different vitamins are not to be lost.

WE CAN OBTAIN essential nutrients via only two routes: by eating, digesting, and metabolizing food; or by direct nutrient supplementation, either orally or intravenously.

Scientists have kept adult volunteers in good health for weeks by feeding them a chemically defined formula that includes all the known nutrients. However, this "supplementary" route to nutrition has two tremendous disadvantages.

- The first is the incalculable human difference between three good meals a day and a "chemically defined formula." Food means far more to us than "just" essential nutrients.
- The second is scientific: In all likelihood, some essential nutrients have not yet been identified, so that supplementation with known nutrients is almost surely incomplete. Further, it is already known that individuals have nutrient needs quite different from the statistical average of the population.

The concept of fortifying or enriching foods began in the 1800s, when the French chemist Boussingault suggested adding a trace of iodine to table salt to eliminate goiter. The idea worked extremely well (and continues to this day), but other types of "enrichment" have not been so successful. Enrichment and fortification measures today are generally a case of too little, too late.

In the early 1970s, Roger Williams graphically illustrated the limitation of enrichment when he placed one group of rats on a diet of standard supermarket enriched bread and another group on bread that had been supplemented on the basis of current nutritional knowledge.[7] After ninety days, two thirds of the animals on the commercial bread diet were dead, and the survivors were severely stunted. Practically all of the other group were alive and growing. Neither man nor rat can live by today's enriched bread alone.

To obtain essential nutrients, then, eating a variety of foods is the one and only king's highway. And by understanding the relationship of nutrients to food, we can see the proper roles of direct nutrient supplementation.

FOOD IS habitually consumed substances, most of which are (or were) living beings, but some of which—like water or salt—are nonliving. Since nutrients are essential for life, all living things contain nutrients, and many nonliving things contain the mineral nutrients.

No one food contains all the nutrients. Some foods, like sugar and distilled water, contain only one nutrient. Most foods contain several. The term *nutrient density* has recently come into use to suggest the level or concentration of nutrients in any given food compared to the amount of calories (energy) it supplies.

- Eggs are often called the most nearly perfect food, for they contain very high caliber protein (all the essential amino acids in the right balance for us) plus the other nutrients *except* vitamin C and fiber. Other very high nutrient-density foods include wheat germ and liver of all kinds. High nutrient-density foods include fish, fowl, meat, and dairy products; many vegetables, such as broccoli, greens, and sweet potatoes; and some fruits, like watermelon and cantaloupe.
- Iceburg lettuce or peeled cucumbers are examples of foods with very few nutrients at very low levels. They can be described as low nutrient-density foods (except they don't have many calories either). Very low nutrient-density foods are unenriched white rice or white bread, sugared breakfast cereals (nonfortified), chocolate, and most pastries.
- Sugar and hard liquor are the lowest nutrient-density foods, containing no nutrients except calories (energy). These are sometimes called "naked calories." And some researchers claim that since sugar and liquor utilize nutrients in the process of their metabolism, they are actually "anti-nutrients." Other extremely low nutrient-density foods are quite common, such as coffee, tea, candy, and cola and other sugared sodas.

Like ourselves, the plants and animals we depend on for our nutrients depend on the surrounding ecosystem for their nutrients. They are as subject to "poor diet" and malnutrition as we are. As a result there are no eternal, unchanging nutrient values for specific foods. Like us, plants and animals are basically what they eat, and their nutrient content and nutrient density change radically in response to many factors.

Factors Affecting the Nutrient Content of Foods

1. *Genetics.* Broadly speaking, apples are as varied as human beings, not just in size and shape but in genetic makeup. This is true among the

different varietals—Delicious, McIntosh, Granny Smith, and so on—but also within each varietal. One major result of these genetic differences is a wide variation in nutrient content—from variety to variety, and from apple to apple.

What is true of apples is equally true of apricots and avocados—and all other fruits, vegetables, and grains. Because of the genetic diversity of their individual seeds, they all vary widely in nutrient content (although researchers work from standard expectations for standard varieties).

Nutrient variety due to genetics is also found in the animal kingdom, although much less broadly. Animal tissues and products (including fish, fowl, and dairy items) are predominantly water, protein, and fat, and these tend to vary just in their relative proportions. Animal foods also contain vitamins and minerals that vary genetically, although not as widely as in fruits, vegetables, and grains.

2. *Growing Conditions.* These variables have enormous influence on the ultimate nutrient content of our foods. Time of planting, the soil, the weather, fertilizing, all condition the chemical composition of grains, vegetables, and fruits, as well as the animals fed these plant sources and the humans that dine on both.

The condition of the soil is most important: Many essential trace elements, for example, can only reach us by traveling from the soil up the food chain. Yet that same process depletes the soil of these elements, and soil in many regions is already naturally low in some of our essential trace

TABLE 2
Vitamin C in Varieties of Apples
Average C in mg/100 mg

Wegener	19	Jonathan	7
Northern Spy	16	Red Delicious	6
Rome Beauty	11	Stayman	6
Jubilee	10	Spartan	3
Golden Delicious	10	McIntosh	2
Winesap	9		

SOURCE: M. A. Stevens, "Varietal influence on nutritional value," in *Nutritional Qualities of Fresh Fruits and Vegetables*, eds. P. L. White and N. Selvey (Mount Kisco, N.Y.: Futura Publishing, 1974), p. 101. Used by permission.

TABLE 3
*Nutrient Density Varies Widely: Vitamin C**

Food Source	*Mg. of C per Calories in Normal Serving*	*Approximate Nutrient Density*
Peppers, red (raw)	151/23	6
Peppers, green (raw)	94/16	5
Broccoli (cooked)	162/474	4
Brussels sprouts	35/56	3
Cauliflower (cooked)	69/28	2
Spinach (raw)	28/14	2
Cabbage (cooked)	48/29	2
Asparagus (cooked)	16/12	1
Strawberries	88/55	1
Cantaloupe	90/82	1
Tomatoes (raw)	28/27	1
Oranges (Valencia)	48/50	1
Grapefruit	52/56	1
Zucchini squash (cooked)	19/25	1
Potatoes (boiled)	22/88	¼

SOURCE: *Nutritive Value of American Food in Common Units*, Agricultural Handbook #465 (Washington, D.C.: U.S. Dept. of Agriculture, 1975).
* *Nutrient density* is relative to calories. A green pepper supplies about twice as much C as an orange, but calorie for calorie the pepper is five times richer a source.

elements. Crops grown in soil that is deficient in minerals such as phosphorus and cobalt (which are essential to animal nutrition) are nutritionally inferior. Animals raised on such forage are likely to be thin and poorly fleshed. Crops and livestock can be just as iron-deficient as so many American women are today, with obvious links up the food chain.

Farmers fertilize, of course, but largely with commercial nitrogen fertilizers to increase crop yield rather than trace elements to improve nutrient content. Not only do these common commercial fertilizers fail to restore essential trace elements, they deplete such nutrients as iron, vitamin C, and the essential amino acid lysine, which limits protein value.

The same problem does not occur directly in the raising of animal foods—indeed, livestock in the United States receive far more nutrient supplementation per capita than humans. Among livestock the chief problem is the other, nonnutritive chemicals, such feed additives as antibiotics, synthetic hormones, and hormonelike substances, which are supplied in abundance, with long-term risks for human health.

3. *Harvesting.* This process also frequently takes a toll in nutrients. The main loss stems from the practice of picking vegetables and fruits before they ripen in order to meet marketing and transportation dictates.

The loss in taste and nutrition from harvesting "mature green" tomatoes and ripening them in storage has been calculated by the University of California at Davis. For example, vitamin C increases steadily in the ten-day period required for full color development in a vine-ripened tomato; it *declines* from the original "green" level in an early-picked tomato. The difference is about 80 percent of the original value. The result? A tomato that was ripened on the vine has one fourth to one third more ascorbic acid (vitamin C) than one that was machine picked while it was still green.

4. *Handling, Transportation, and Storage.* These also reduce the nutrient content of foodstuffs. A few examples:

- Fifty-three percent of ascorbic acid in coleslaw is lost in two hours when vinegar is used.
- Cucumbers lose 22 percent of their ascorbic acid during slicing, 33 to 35 percent during standing for one hour, and 41 to 49 percent during standing for three hours.
- Cantaloupe slices lose 35 percent of their ascorbic acid during twenty-four hours of refrigeration.
- Orange juice held at 48°F loses 17 percent of its thiamine in twenty-four hours.
- Canned vegetables and fruits lose nutrients just sitting on the shelf: Stored for one year at 65°F losses of thiamine are common; at 80°F the losses go as high as 25 percent.
- Light degrades vitamin B_2 in milk (in plastic bottles in supermarkets, for example). Light also rapidly destroys vitamin A in milk.
- Niacin (B_3) is degraded by the enzymes that age meats.

- Oils do not store well at all, unless refrigerated or tightly sealed. Exposed to air, they become rancid, with direct losses of nutrients, especially essential fatty acids and vitamin A.

5. *Food Processing.* Anything done to modify foodstuffs before they're eaten will change nutrient amounts. A moderate level of processing is both necessary and good. But processing—today usually extensive—is also the single greatest destroyer of nutrient values in the United States. In a land of such abundant food, processing is the chief factor in the serious nutrient deficiencies that are common among Americans.

Processing includes everything done to foodstuffs from killing the chicken to peeling the apple, from cooking potatoes to homogenizing milk to stir-frying vegetables, from slicing onions to toasting bread to canning peaches. It also includes more ambitious schemes of industrial processing that concoct fabricated "food analogs," "imitation foods," or "convenience food products" such as cholesterol-free "eggs"; margarine (and now "imitation margarine"); nondairy creamer; turkey burger; "meat-like products made with extruded soy protein concentrate"; processed cheese products and whipped cream substitutes; sugared snack/breakfast foods; "textured vegetable protein" that can be produced in cubes, chunks, chips, granules, and rolls; imitation mayonnaise; meatless hot dogs; and milk shakes without any ice cream.

There are three genuine nutritional benefits in the moderate processing of many foods. First, certain kinds of processing improve the appearance, taste, and texture—the palatability—of foods, from peeling and slicing cucumbers to steaming rice to cooking meat. Second, washing and cooking eliminate many pathogenic microorganisms and toxic pesticides. Third, most raw foods are more digestible or their nutrients more available when moderately cooked or baked, including grains, eggs, dried beans, brussels sprouts, cabbage, and so on.

The bad news is that every step in processing foods—from the kitchen drainboard to giant factory vats—takes its toll of nutrients. This loss of nutrients occurs during necessary, beneficial processing, but is much greater in the overprocessing our diet is currently subjected to. Needed processing is moderate, with only limited nutrient losses, whereas overprocessing knows no bounds and destroys high percentages of nutrients that Americans are deficient in.

In processing, as in harvesting, transportation, and storage, proteins fare the best and vitamins the worst, especially less stable ones such as C, B_1, or B_5. Since nutrients are not a priority of industry or government, the research on nutrient losses is limited.

Some losses during home preparation are staggering—such as 80 percent of vitamin C in mashed potatoes. Not all nutrients suffer the same losses, but vitamin C is used as a common reference because, being easily destroyed, it is indicative of other nutrient losses. Additional studies of the effects of home preparation have found that:

- Bananas lose half their vitamin C when sliced and exposed to air at room temperature for five hours.
- Fruits cooked in water lose up to 68 percent of their vitamin C and leafy vegetables up to 87 percent.
- In home cooking of roots and tubers (carrots, potatoes, etc.) losses range as high as 33 percent for B_1, 45 percent for B_2, 61 percent for B_3, and 76 percent for vitamin C.
- Well over half the B_3 and B_1 are lost from simply washing raw-milled rice.
- In numerous studies of baking and toasting, B_1 is lost in direct proportion to heating time: After one minute of toasting white bread loses more than 25 percent and whole wheat about 17 percent. In contrast, half a minute of toasting costs 9 percent and 4 percent respectively.
- Meat in the oven? High settings mean B_1 losses of 49 percent from beef and pork, versus "only" 38 percent at low temperatures. Cooking meat also causes losses of up to 55 percent of vitamin B_6, while cooking vegetables destroys up to 30 percent.
- Boiling milk for five seconds decreases free folic acid activity 40 to 90 percent.

The most devastating loss of nutrients, however, occurs in industrial food processing, during the milling of wheat down to "refined" white flour. Some 70 to 80 percent of the thiamine, riboflavin, niacin, and vitamin B_6, and 80 to 90 percent of several trace elements (not to mention most of the fiber) are lost during this extremely common process. Comparable, if not such thorough, losses occur throughout the commercial food-production system. Examples are legion; a scattered sample includes the following:

- In the cafeteria: While potatoes are a good source of vitamin C, dehydrated potato flakes that are reconstituted and held on a steam table for an hour have no vitamin C remaining.
- In the supermarket: The pasteurized orange juice that comes in milk cartons is an unreliable and often a poor source of vitamin C. (In fact, most processed fruit juices—canned or frozen and reconstituted—are notably less nutritious than the original fruit.)
- In the bakery: Vitamin B_1 is completely degraded in chocolate cake.
- At the carryout: Thin hamburgers held warm for several hours have little folic acid left.
- Processed meats? Vitamin B_1 losses range from 15 percent for mild-cured products to 60 percent for irradiated ones.

Food plays many marvelous roles in human life. But its main function is to supply the fifty or so essential nutrients our bodies need to live and thrive.

At the same time, there is no stable, clear-cut relationship between foods and nutrients. The nutrient content of any food portion can vary widely due to unknown complexities of genetics; soil or feeding; growing conditions; the timing and manner of harvesting or slaughter; its transportation, handling, and storage; and finally the amount of refining and processing it is subject to up to the moment it is eaten.

While many of today's growing and food-processing technologies degrade the nutrient value of foods, research on these nutrient losses and how to protect nutrient values is still in its infancy, only marginally funded, and lacking a unified program. Government has shown little interest and industry still less.

In this unsatisfactory situation, the consumer's best defense is a working knowledge of foods and nutrition—and a diet built around fresh whole foods, avoiding highly refined, processed products to the extent possible.

AS WE SAW in the example of sailors dying of scurvy, you can get plenty to eat and still starve to death if just one of the essential nutrients happens to be missing. Strangely enough, it is also quite possible to get plenty of food containing all the essential nutrients and yet still end up malnourished for lack of nutrients *when and where you need them.*

The reason is that nutrition doesn't take place in your mouth, or your stomach, or your intestinal tract. Nutrition—the fitting of those missing keys into their tiny slots in your biochemistry—takes place within the trillions of cells of your body. For nutrition actually to occur, not only do the nutrients have to be in the food you eat but the body has to extract them from the food *(digestion)*, they have to be carried from the digestive tract into the bloodstream *(absorption)* to be transported to all the body's cells, and each cell must be able to employ them *(utilization)* in its many chemical reactions. When it does, that's nutrition.

Unfortunately, the body processes are sometimes happenstance affairs.

- Digestion doesn't always proceed properly, as we all know.
- Absorption into the bloodstream may not take place adequately, or at all.
- Utilization may not occur for a variety of reasons.

To the degree any of these processes is disrupted, nutrients do not make it to their slots and malnutrition occurs, ranging from the indetectable to system-wide.

There are many reasons why the digestion, absorption, or utilization of nutrients may falter. The most important is what might be regarded as the first principle of nutrition—that nutrients work as a team.

During the great decades of vitamin discovery—the 1920s through the 1940s—medicine responded positively, attempting to make use of individual nutrients as remedies for individual maladies. The failure of this approach—just at the time antibiotics and other early "wonder" drugs burst on the scene—led to medicine's disillusionment with and virtual abandonment of nutrition and nutrient therapy, a neglect of nutrition that continues today.

A handful of pioneers in nutrition science, however, stuck with these essential chemicals, striving to decipher how they do in fact work. The very complexity of nutrient research revealed the obvious: *No nutrient plays a solo part*—all nutrients play in ensembles, taking a surprising variety of cooperative roles throughout the organism. This insight had many implications.

- The human organism is not a machinelike collection of parts, fifty nutrients among them, but a vastly complex biochemical system, maintaining its own miracle of life through endlessly interacting processes.

- Human disease in general is not caused by a missing or broken part and cannot be reversed simply by replacing a part (such as one nutrient or another). Rather, illness is the result of progressive breakdowns in cellular or systemic processes involving highly complex biochemical relationships.
- Any missing or insufficient nutrient will be implicated in a variety of dysfunctions throughout the organism.
- Since nutrients are interlocking factors in various foods, it is highly unlikely—probably impossible—to lack just one nutrient, with all the others being in adequate supply.

The first principle of nutrition (and nutrient therapy for illness)—that nutrients do not work singly but only in concert—has been elaborated by many investigators over the last thirty years. The unlikelihood of a single nutrient deficiency was described by the pioneering Westport, Connecticut, physician Morton S. Biskind as long ago as 1953. He pointed out that:

1. Until all the nutrients are identified, there is no possibility of proving a case of a single nutrient deficiency.
2. In the living human being (as opposed to laboratory experiments), the factors that produce the deficiency of a single nutrient (stress, heat, poor diet) necessarily cause multiple deficiencies.
3. All the nutrients studied so far affect at least one other nutrient negatively by their absence.

The case has also been made by Drs. Herman Baker and Oscar Frank of the New Jersey Medical School: "Vitamins by themselves cannot prevent or correct a deficiency."[8] Not only are minerals also needed but protein and in many cases whole foods that contain nutrients whose activity is as yet poorly understood. The interactions of nutrients are so complex that only a few "pairs" are conspicuous for their complementary activity: protein and vitamin A, zinc and A, C and the B complex.

The case of zinc and A is an interesting example. Vitamin A from the diet is first stored in the liver, from which zinc transports it into the bloodstream according to need. A classic sign of vitamin A deficiency is night blindness, yet it was long reported that vitamin A therapy that raised the liver concentration often did not cure the night blindness. Recent studies, however, propose that such patients are often also deficient in zinc, preventing transport of A to the cells, and it has now been shown that supplementation with zinc can rapidly raise bloodstream levels of A.

The fact that nutrients interact and that a single nutrient deficiency is a practical impossibility does not mean that severe nutrient deficiencies do not have specific, repeatable effects. The *limiting nutrient* typically determines the predominant symptoms and is usually easy to identify in a given deficiency disease. For example, serious zinc deficiency reduces or kills the sense of taste, which can often be restored by zinc alone.[9]

To sum up, the concept of a nutrient-deficiency disease (scurvy as a deficiency of vitamin C, for example) is superficial. Any obvious deficiency state has secondary symptoms and subclinical effects. Such a state is really a mixed deficiency syndrome with one nutrient as the most limiting factor among several deficiencies. The web of nutrition cannot be torn at any point without disturbing the whole.

Digestion

Digestion is the process of breaking food down into its constituents so that the nutrients can be absorbed. Digestion is largely the work of enzymes (along with hydrochloric acid and bile), and at each stage many different enzymes are needed. From the moment foods are chewed, specialized enzymes begin their job of chemical dismantling. In the mouth enzymes reduce starch to complex sugars. In the stomach enzymes and hydrochloric acid break proteins down into amino acids. In the small intestine enzymes reduce the complex sugars to simple sugars. Enzymes and bile break down fat into the fatty acids and other components.

Vitamins and minerals are also required in the metabolism of many foodstuffs. To metabolize carbohydrate, for example, the body needs vitamins B_1, B_2, B_3, B_5, B_6, and the minerals phosphorus and magnesium. Ironically, the latter four nutrients are removed from white flour and not added back in "enriched" bread. So the liver has to find these nutrients in other foods in order to properly break down white flour products. If the nutrients are not available, the products are poorly metabolized, reducing the availability of the nutrients they do contain.

The human digestive tract is a remarkable chemical processing system that can free up to 90 percent of all the nutrients in whatever food passes through it, converting them to forms far more readily absorbed. On the other hand, stress, fear, worry, anger, and many drugs, toxins, and pathogens (those causing diarrhea, for example) can greatly disturb digestion, reducing its efficiency even to starvation levels.

Absorption and Transport

The digestive tract is a hollow tube passing through the body from mouth to anus. Its contents, even when fully digested, are not yet part of the body; and unless they are "absorbed" into the body itself, they simply pass out the other end. Specifically, once digestion frees the nutrients from food, they must pass or be "transported" across the intestinal wall into the bloodstream. The bloodstream then carries them to every cell in the body, where they must be carried across the cell wall into the biochemical innards of the cell itself. Without cells there is no life, and without nutrients delivered into cells there is no nutrition.

Not surprisingly, there's no guarantee that—once food is ingested and digested—the nutrients released will be absorbed by the body. This failure to absorb nutrients is called "malabsorption." Malabsorption, and the resulting malnutrition, is one of the leading health problems in the Third World and a significant problem in the United States. Fortunately, this is now being recognized, and absorption studies, though still in their infancy, are becoming one of the most fertile areas of nutrition research.

The first block is the absence of other nutrients necessary for proper absorption. The literature here is relatively recent but extensive. Soluble proteins and sodium ions are important transport mechanisms and must be present in the gut at the time of digestion in order for absorption of many nutrients to take place. And folate and vitamin B_{12} are especially needed for full vitamin absorption. Vitamin D is needed for calcium to be absorbed, and vitamins C and E for iron. Several minerals are also essential for the absorption of many vitamins. This is particularly true among alcoholics, who often do not respond to supplementation with vitamins in which they are deficient (especially the B complex) because the rest of their diet is insufficient.

The vicious cycle of nutrient deficiencies and malabsorption can be seen in pellagra. This B_3 deficiency disease is actually quite complex.

1. B_2, B_6, and the amino acid tryptophan are also likely to be deficient before pellagra appears.
2. The B_3 deficiency impairs absorption of C.
3. The depletion of C impairs absorption of iron.
4. The iron deficiency induces excessive copper absorption.
5. The excess copper inhibits nickel metabolism.
6. Poor nickel metabolism adversely affects iron metabolism.

Along the way, B_{12}, folic acid, and zinc are also denied to the body in some measure by malabsorption or poor metabolism.

A second block is that certain nutrients are just not absorbed very readily. Only 1 to 3 percent of chromium, less than 5 percent of manganese, and 5 to 15 percent of iron in the digestive contents are absorbed by the normal, healthy adult. Most of the minerals rarely exceed 50 percent absorption. Several of these low rates mean persistent health problems for significant numbers of Americans. Iron is a case in point.

Although plentiful in food, only 5 to 15 percent of dietary iron is absorbed by a well-nourished person. That figure rises to about 20 percent when the body is iron-deficient. The iron in meat ("heme" iron) is absorbed better than the ("nonheme") iron in other sources such as eggs, green vegetables, and beans. And the iron in some of these is absorbed better when the meal includes meat. Further, deficiencies in vitamins C and E seriously impair iron absorption.

Crucial as they are to absorption, proteins themselves are not always well absorbed. Animal protein is more efficiently absorbed (over 90 percent in the healthy individual) than plant protein (approximately 60 to 90 percent). Further, protein is not well absorbed by individuals who lack an adequate caloric intake, since the body must preempt the protein to fulfill immediate energy needs and therefore neglect other protein needs. Vitamin and mineral deficiencies also interfere with the absorption of dietary protein, and for all its benefits fiber decreases the digestibility and absorption of protein.

Another major block to absorption is food itself. Many highly nutritious foods, ranging from eggs to spinach to whole-wheat bread, contain substances that bind themselves to nutrients, forming insoluble salts and preventing their proper absorption. There are several such substances but the two best known are:

- *Phytates.* These phosphorus compounds are abundant in the outer layers of cereal grains and in nuts, seeds, and legumes.
- *Oxalates.* These are naturally occurring toxins (even the human body produces them) found in spinach, beet greens, rhubarb, cabbage, chard, almonds, cashews, cocoa, and tea.

The oxalates bind with calcium and iron, which by nature are already poorly absorbed, further blocking their absorption. The phylates bind with zinc and magnesium, as well as calcium and iron, with the same antinutrient effect.

Iron and calcium deficiencies are common in America, and zinc and magnesium deficiencies are found in certain vulnerable subpopulations, so these malabsorption problems are not negligible. At the same time, such food/nutrient interactions are too complex for laymen to keep track of. The remedy for mineral deficiencies is a highly nutritious and widely varied diet, perhaps with supplementation.

In other cases a particular nutrient is just not absorbed well from a particular food, such as the vitamin C in cabbage. At the opposite extreme, a person's absorption may be defective across the board because of pancreatic insufficiency, for example. And medications and toxins in foods can also inhibit the absorption process. For example, heavy metals such as lead inhibit calcium absorption. And certain antacids, antibiotics, and laxatives, if taken habitually, may lead to chronic malabsorption.

All these blocks reduce the "bioavailability" of nutrients. No nutrient in food is ever 100 percent available for life processes. But, according to Dr. Roger Mazlen, former head of the AMA Council on Nutrition and Heart Disease, middle-class Americans do not choose foods with sufficient nutrients in the first place, and this default is compounded by widespread problems of digestion and absorption.

Utilization

Utilization is the final act in which those missing essentials, the nutrients, lock into their unique slots and the organism functions. Utilization—the actual use of nutrients in life's processes—is not discussed much in the textbooks and nutrition guides. The reason is simple. Utilization is the point at which the targeted process of nutrition flows into and becomes subsumed by ***metabolism.***

Metabolism is—biochemically—the game of life. It is the sum of all the internal processes by which any living organism keeps itself alive and functioning. When we define nutrients as missing essentials, it is metabolism that needs them. Metabolism—body chemistry—puts together tens of thousands of compounds to meet its various requirements; the ones it can't put together are the "missing factors." Once those nutrients have entered the body in food, been released by digestion, and supplied to the cells by absorption, metabolism takes over, utilizing them to help maintain the body's energy level and carry out all its vital processes.

Many factors can interfere with the cells' utilization of nutrients. But at that point—the nutrient having been delivered—the failure is no longer described nutritionally, as malnourishment, but medically, according to the particular ***metabolic disorder*** that prevents their proper utilization. Diabetes, for example, is a metabolic failure of the cells to utilize the nutrients swimming past them in the bloodstream. The failure is due to either a lack of insulin or an inability to respond to insulin, a hormone secreted by the pancreas that promotes the flow of nutrients into the cell.

There are countless other forms of impaired utilization. Among the simplest is the lack of other nutrients needed for the process in question. Protein cannot be utilized—metabolized—without adequate B_3, B_6, potassium, phosphorus, and carbohydrates. Nor carbohydrates without B_1. Nor fat without vitamin E. Nor calcium without vitamin D. And so on. The thousands of ***inborn errors of metabolism*** frequently involve a failure to utilize nutrients properly. Finally, many commonly used medications interfere with the utilization of nutrients. For example, the antibiotic penicillamine can combine directly with vitamin B_6, as well as compete with it at enzyme-binding sites, causing a deficiency.

Increased Requirements and Nutrient Depletion

Many factors—notably adolescence, pregnancy, illness, stress, environmental toxins, medications, excessive alcohol, sugar, and other low nutrient-density foods—make unusually high nutrient demands on the body. Unless the higher metabolic requirements are met, the result over time is chronic depletion of the body's intake and stores of nutrients, leading to malnutrition and eventually one of the deficiency states.

There may also be a link between nutrient depletion and obesity. Some experts argue that in many cases excess poundage may be the result, surprisingly enough, of too few nutrients. The appetite control center in the brain is quite sensitive to the need for nutrients. Given the low nutrient density of the American diet and the nutrient-depleting action of such foods, individuals with high nutrient requirements may become so deficient in certain nutrients that they eat compulsively in an insatiable metabolic drive to obtain them.

The National Academy of Sciences has called obesity the commonest form of malnutrition in the Western nations. If this is so, the American mania for weight-loss programs—further nutrient restriction—desperately needs to be reversed. Instead of dieting, we need ***better nutrition.*** Nationally, that means simple, effective nutrition education and federal policies that raise the nutrient density of our foods.

The Myth of the RDAs

Proper nutrition is unique to the individual. When the diet is fully adequate:

- Dietary protein affords the varying combinations of amino acids the organism needs to build its thousands of structural proteins and operating enzymes.
- Carbohydrate and fat meet its operating energy needs.
- Vitamins and certain fats and fatty acids supply the missing coenzymes and other cofactors its unique metabolism requires.
- Minerals provide the essential earth elements it must have to maintain the skeleton, cellular function, and other basic processes.

The most personal of nutrition questions naturally arises. "What are ***my*** essential nutrients? Are they much different from other people's? And if so, how can I find out what they are? And if I meet these needs, will that lead to optimal health?"

These natural questions, strangely enough, open up a "Great Divide" in nutrition today. On one side is most of the American health establishment, from the National Academy of Sciences (its Food and Nutrition Board), the Food and Drug Administration, and the Department of Agriculture to the American Medical Association, nearly all doctors, most public-health organizations, university nutrition programs, and virtually all dietitians in the country. On the other side, an array of Nobel laureates, research scientists, individual physicians and psychiatrists (some unorthodox), chiropractors, health food enthusiasts, vitamin companies, and up to a quarter of American consumers.

What are these two divergent views of nutrition? And how could such a deep difference of opinion occur over something as basic as the essential nutrients?

The second question first. Several factors converged over the last forty years to create the Nutrition Divide, but perhaps the fundamental one is the scientific lag noted earlier. Actually there are three lags or gaps involved:

- Medical school science has lagged far behind the evolution of scientific understanding in this century.
- Science's institutional establishment moves more slowly and cautiously than individual researchers with their insights and breakthroughs.
- Science itself always falls far short of the immediate, practical needs of people.

The result is that many researchers, along with physicians and lay people who take an interest in the subject, see nutrition playing a primary role in human health that the more conservative bodies and those who follow their lead regard as unproven, unwarranted, and possibly dangerous. These institutional voices—the American nutrition establishment—have developed a fairly monolithic position on most aspects of human nutrition: namely, that it's part of the picture but cannot support the exaggerated expectations many individuals have of it. On the other side, many biochemists, physicians, and others—including Nobel laureates such as Linus Pauling and Albert Szent-Gyorgyi and researchers like Roger Williams and Jonas Salk—find nutrients so basic to human metabolism that shortchanging them over time is bound to involve human illness, particularly chronic conditions such as those today's high-technology medicine can't seem to get a handle on.

Individuality in Nutrition

Since nutrients must fit the system's particular needs at any particular moment, "proper" nutrition is highly variable. Each person has distinctive variations of metabolism, different enzyme efficiency rates, and specific endocrine reactions that yield distinctive patterns of nutrient need. Typically, these needs vary severalfold among individuals, and extreme variations are common, as researchers have repeatedly shown over the last fifty years.

- In 1943, Hans Popper and Frederick Steigmann found a tenfold range of vitamin A levels and a thirtyfold range of carotenoid levels in ninety-two subjects.[10]
- Three years later, a series of studies conducted by F. R. Steggerda and H. H. Mitchell found 450 percent variations in individuals' requirements for calcium.[11]
- In 1948, Bert Vallee and John Gibson (of Harvard University) investigated plasma zinc levels in thirty-one subjects and discovered values ranging from 1.2 and 11.4 mcg per cc of blood.[12]
- In 1951, after a decade of research, Roger J. Williams and a large team of investigators at the University of Texas published the 205-page bulletin *Individual Metabolic Patterns and Human Disease.* In a series of twenty-two articles, these researchers delineated how individual animals and human beings have "distinctive metabolic patterns as judged by numerous criteria."[13]
- And more recently, in 1982, Dr. Michael Colgan—investigating the rates of vitamin C absorption in groups of athletes—found rates that varied up to ten times between individuals.[14]

The distinctiveness of each individual's nutrient needs is basic to understanding the relationship between nutrition and health. Yet conventional science and medicine have largely ignored the individuality of nutrition. Due in large part to the classical-science mind-set of modern medicine, practitioners continue to treat humans as uniform members of a standardized species. The concept of "standard nutrition" (as exemplified by the Recommended Dietary Allowances) arises from this value system—in which individuality and nutrition may be acknowledged, but are not considered significant.

Although most of the public views the RDAs as individual nutritional guidelines, in actual fact they are *not* meant to be measures of individual nutrient requirements, and special nutrient needs are not covered at all. The RDAs are designed for application to *population groups*, and were originally developed as a guide for procuring food supplies for national defense during World War II.

Nonetheless, consumers assume that the RDA for any given nutrient is the level that will assure them good health. Indeed, they are often warned by the FDA, AMA, and other authorities that exceeding the RDAs can be dangerous. In reality, the RDAs are, at best, the level that will assure an absence of overt deficiency disease. But health and absence of disease are two vastly different things.

Criticism of the RDA approach to nutrition goes back to long before the RDAs themselves were devised. In 1919, nutritionist Elmer V. McCollum of the University of Wisconsin noted that "the idea that freedom of choice and variety of food sources for the diet will prevent any fault in the diet from becoming serious is no longer tenable."[15] In the ensuing years, the nutritional quality of the food supply has declined considerably, yet the FDA continues to advise against the use of conventional food supplements, let alone larger doses, despite the fact that a diet that is nutritionally adequate for one person may be critically inadequate for another. Several studies in the late 1970s found tremendous differences in the nutritional requirements of normal healthy men—including twofold to sevenfold differences for calcium and various essential amino acids.

The RDAs, which are based on small and possibly unrepresentative population samples, cannot even hope to address these common and significant deviations from the "norm," nor can they be applied to the real intricacies of malnutrition. The RDAs are based on studies of single nutrients, and malnutrition is never the result of a single nutrient deficiency. Even in classic deficiency diseases such as scurvy there are multiple deficiencies involved. On an individual level, therefore, the RDAs are functionally useless as guidelines.

"What," you may ask, "*are* they good for, then?"

The Recommended Dietary Allowances (although *not* the abbreviated Recommended Daily Allowances) are very useful when applied to the task for which they were designed—evaluating the nutritional status of population *groups*. When used as a baseline measurement for the needs of specific groups of people, both comparatively and over time, the RDAs can pinpoint areas and groups of specific need. They have been well used in a variety of nutritional surveys to draw attention to the needs of special groups such as children, the elderly, and pregnant women.

It is when we confuse the RDA measures of "standard" nutrition for groups with the reality of individual nutrition that we get into trouble. For individuals, the opposite extreme from standard nutrition is optimum nutrition—precisely the right nutrients, in just the right amounts, at exactly the right times. Given the extreme variations in nutrient needs from day to day and moment to moment, optimum nutrition is a lovely but unattainable ideal. But actual nutrition can always be improved, and a functional goal—for nutrition science and individuals—is *optimal* nutrition—the effort to bring individuals' nutrition within the optimum range.

One of the most promising efforts at developing a method for determining the specific nutrient needs of individuals is being carried out by Professor William Shive and his colleagues (also of the Clayton Foundation at the University of Texas). Shive and co-workers have developed a medium that will support the growth of human lymphocytes (immune cells that circulate in the bloodstream).[16] Lymphocytes remain dormant until they are presented with a threat (such as a virus). At that point they carry out most of the reactions required of normally growing cells in the body. Their normally dormant state makes them a sort of circulating record of long-term nutritional status, and their discreet responses to mitogens (outside threats) can be measured with relative ease.[17]

By adjusting the nutrients present in the growth medium, these researchers are able to determine the concentration of nutrient(s) that will encourage optimal growth and responsiveness in the lymphocytes.[18] Since activated lymphocytes carry out most of the same activities as the other cells of the body, the results of this testing can be used to infer the nutritional needs of the body as a whole. For the first time, science can determine the precise needs of an individual person—based not on arbitrary norms but on the actual functioning of his or her cells.

Since initiating this research in the mid-1970s, Shive's group has evaluated the nutrient needs and sensitivities of hundreds of patients. In almost all cases, they found that patients' actual nutrient requirements exceeded the RDAs. One autistic seven-year-old required more than seventeen times the RDAs for riboflavin and vitamin B_6.[19]

Nutrient therapy based on this testing has yielded some truly remarkable results. Patients with multiple sclerosis have found relief from many of their symptoms, including cramps, fatigue, spasms, spasticity, and tenseness.[20] Autistic children have responded to outside stimulation and—in the case mentioned above—have been successfully removed from psychiatric medication.[21] In case after case, Shive and his co-workers have found that individualized nutritional analysis and supplementation significantly improved—if not outright cured—many of their patients' conditions. For these people, biological individuality is more than an interesting theoretical question, it is the difference between health and illness. For the "average" person, it could mean the difference between robust good health and a lifetime of low-grade illnesses.

NUTRITION—in its most basic sense—is the complex of processes by which the organism finds, consumes, liberates, absorbs, and utilizes the nutrients it must have to live. The process of human nutrition is far more complicated than most individuals imagine, but it is also extremely efficient. When fed properly, the body can generate new cells, fight off infection, and carry out intricate metabolic and physical processes with remarkable ease.

Proper feeding is, however, no easy task. As we have seen, everybody (and every body) has distinctly different nutritional requirements. Since nutrients act in concert, it is important to consume not only the proper *amounts* but also the right *balance* to meet the body's needs. Further, nutrients themselves are often fragile substances, and their passage from field and farm to the chemistry of our cells can be risky and fraught with loss. Any diet that relies heavily on only a few foods is virtually guaranteed to be deficient in several necessary nutrients.

In the past hundred years, the nature of our food supply has undergone vast changes, all of which have had an impact on nutritional quality. Although some of the changes have been beneficial, many have not. General guidance for consumers must therefore emphasize nutritional individuality, the value of whole foods and moderate supplementation, the importance of greatly reducing low nutrient-density foods in the diet, and the need for everyone to learn the simple basics of nutrition.

3

Deadly Diet: Nutrition and Disease

IT TOOK NEARLY three hundred years—and the deaths of millions of sailors—for the relationship of scurvy to diet to be recognized, documented, and finally accepted by the world. But scurvy is only one of the many nutritional deficiencies that can disable and kill individuals who seem to be consuming adequate diets. Another striking example is pellagra, which was responsible for the institutionalization of thousands of people in the rural South up until the 1920s.

Characterized by the "four Ds" of dermatitis, diarrhea, dementia (madness), and death, pellagra was the result of a Southern diet high in corn and fatback pork and almost totally devoid of niacin-containing foods such as eggs, milk, fish, and meat. Because of this lopsided diet, these seemingly well-fed individuals were actually massively deficient in niacin.

When improved nutrition (including concentrated doses of liver) was instituted in the mental hospitals of the South, the inpatient population plummeted. It was not until 1937, when niacin was isolated and identified, that the specific relationship between niacin and pellagra was understood.

Scurvy and pellagra are extreme examples of what can happen when a single nutrient is missing from the diet. However, since nutrients are interdependent, these "single-nutrient" deficiencies never really occur in isolation. Although vitamin C and niacin are the limiting nutrients in scurvy and pellagra, their absence damages the body's entire nutritional balance, and full recovery requires a fully balanced diet.

Nutrition research surveys in the last two decades have shown that Americans are eating anything *but* balanced diets, and also uncovered three startling facts. One, there is clear-cut malnutrition in America among certain groups. Two, there are widespread deficiencies in several nutrients among the population at large. And three, these deficiencies are affecting our health, disease resistance, and performance—including school behavior and achievement.

One of the first government studies on the nation's nutritional status was carried out in in 1968 when, in response to growing evidence of malnutrition in the rural poor, the Department of Health, Education, and Welfare (HEW) undertook the Ten State Survey.[1]

The findings were disturbing. Nutritional inadequacy was not limited to the poor, although lower socioeconomic groups were in the most precarious condition. Iron deficiency was deemed a "public health problem," particularly among infants, pregnant or lactating women, adolescents, and the elderly. Deficiencies in vitamins A, B_2 (riboflavin), and B_1 (thiamine) were common throughout the population, regardless of socioeconomic status. In lower-income groups, undersized and underweight children were common, and bone maturation and development of adult teeth were significantly slower in these children, as well. The study revealed the precarious nutritional status of the most vulnerable members of the population—pregnant women, the elderly, and the young. Large numbers of children were malnourished, and this malnourishment began in utero—hence the low birthweights of so many children born in poverty. Since low birthweight frequently correlates with retarded development, these findings boded ill for the children's future in school and society.

Between 1971 and 1974, the first Health and Nutrition Examination Survey (HANES) expanded the Ten State program to the forty-eight contiguous states.[2] Once again, evidence of poor nutrition was found across all classes. While the poor were at highest nutritional risk, it appeared that no segment of the population was without some nutritional deficiency.

- The median for every age category over twelve years was below standard for vitamin A. Similarly, the median value for vitamin C was below the standard for half of the adult population.
- Half of the adult population was below the standard for vitamin C.
- One in seven men from age twenty through forty-four, and one in nine young adults aged eighteen through twenty-four, was below the standard for vitamins B_1 and B_2, respectively.
- Half or more of all women over twenty were deficient in calcium.
- Of women aged ten through fifty-four, 91 percent were deficient in iron.
- Of infants and children aged one through five, 95 percent were iron deficient, regardless of race or income.
- Protein deficiency afflicted the majority of American women and one third of American men.

Both the Ten State Survey and the HANES were carried out when government nutrition programs had barely begun. The Nationwide Food Consumption Survey of 1977 to 1978 showed the effect government action had on nutritional status.[3] While some nutrient intakes had increased (vitamin C and the iron intake of infants, for example), others had gone down or continued to be deficient. And, as before, the problem was not bound by class distinctions.

- Calcium levels for females aged twelve and over were 25 percent or more below the RDA.
- The calcium intake of infants had *dropped* by 40 percent or more.
- B_2 intake had dropped almost 35 percent from the 1965 levels.
- More than half of all Americans were deficient in vitamin B_6.
- Magnesium intakes were below the RDA throughout the population.

Overall, the survey indicated that all was not well with the American diet, since a large segment of the population was consuming less than the RDAs of at least vitamins A, C, and B_6; calcium; iron; and magnesium. And keep in mind that these results made no allowance for individuals with higher than "average" needs for any nutrient.

In 1977, the Senate Select Committee issued a statement that "current dietary trends may be leading to malnutrition through undernutrition."[4] The statement was attacked from several sides, including a few nay-sayers who claimed (incorrectly) that deficiency diseases such as pellagra, rickets, goiter, and scurvy would not recur.

Government studies in the 1980s confirmed that specific nutrient deficiencies continue to afflict most of the population of the United States, and that outright malnutrition is on the rise in many groups. The Total Diet Study (1982 through 1986) evaluated the nutritional content of foods generally consumed by eight different age-sex groups for eleven essential elements.[5] The findings included:

- Calcium levels between 28 and 39 percent below the RDA for teenage girls, adult women, and older women, and somewhat below the RDA for young children and older men.
- Teenage girls 11.5 percent below the RDA for phosphorous.
- Young children, teenage girls, and adult women averaging only 57 to 60 percent of the RDA for iron. Infants averaging 80 percent.
- Zinc levels for young children 25 percent below the RDA.
- Magnesium levels for teenage, adult, and older females 40 to 43 percent below the RDA, and levels for males in these age groups 16 to 28 percent below the RDA.
- Sodium intake 71 percent *above* the safe level in young children, and 23 percent above the safe level in teenage males.

The Continuing Survey of Food Intakes by Individuals (conducted by the U.S. Department of Agriculture in 1985) concurred with several of the Total Diet Study's findings.[6] Deficiencies in zinc, folacin, vitamin B_6, and copper were found in one or more of the three age-sex groups (children, adult women, adult men) studied. In addition:

- Calcium intake in adult women is 22 percent below the RDA.
- Iron intake in adult women is 39 percent below the RDA, and intake in children is 12 percent below.
- Sodium intake by children and men exceeds the recommended safe level, and this finding *does not* include salt added at the table.

The picture is even more bleak for known at-risk populations. For example, a recent study in the *Journal of the American Geriatric Society* found that 30 to 40 percent of noninstitutionalized elderly individuals living in an urban area were consuming diets inadequate in calcium, iron, and vitamins A, C, and B_{12}.[7] Ninety percent were deficient in vitamin B_6 and thiamine. The situation of many lower socioeconomic groups has reached crisis proportions since the cutback of government programs that had provided nutritional support in the late 1960s and 1970s.

The American Medical Association's Council on Scientific Affairs has stated that dietary supplements are not necessary for "healthy adult men and healthy adult nonpregnant, nonlactating women consuming a usual, varied diet."[8] Unfortunately, as the Total Diet Study indicates, the usual American diet fails to provide even the Recommended Daily Allowance for several crucial nutrients, and a significant portion of the population is either pregnant, lactating, or chronically ill. Furthermore, as the Council itself has noted, American dietary practices . . .

> Have changed in ways that may have reduced the overall vitamin delivery from the diet. Since the turn of the century, consumption of processed foods has increased, many more meals are eaten away from home, and a greater portion of the diet is consumed as between meal snacks.

Good nutrition is more than the absence of overt signs of deficiency disease. The fact that an individual's gums are not bleeding from scurvy hardly means that his vitamin C intake is adequate. As Roger Williams has written:

> The whole problem of cellular nutrition is a vast one because there are so many different kinds of cells which are not precisely alike in their synthetic abilities. Furnishing good nutrition to brain cells, retinal cells, digestive cells, heart cells, and kidney cells must inevitably make the processes of thinking, seeing, digesting, pumping of blood, and elimination of waste products take place more effectively.
>
> Contemplation of the fact . . . leads us to recognize a form of pathology which has hitherto been unrecognized—namely, generalized cytopathy [cell sickness]. If the available amount of any essential nutrient is grossly inadequate, the body as a whole may be afflicted with generalized cytopathy, a condition in which every cell in the body is deficient and the whole body may be said to suffer from "cell sickness." In the classical deficiency disease, beriberi, every cell is probably deficient in thiamin. The symptoms of the disease reveal where deficiency is most keenly felt.[9]

Government surveys indicate that levels of several essential nutrients are "grossly inadequate" in a significant portion of the population. The incidence of and deaths from diseases that have been tied to nutritional status illustrate the close relationship between poor nutrition and degenerative illness. The exact biological mechanisms of many of these diseases (cancer, heart disease, and arthritis, for example) are still unclear. But "generalized cytopathy" seems a strikingly appropriate way of looking at the killer diseases of the twentieth century and many of the marginal conditions, from hyperactivity to depression, that are so common. As Williams has noted, "It is probable that cell sickness of one kind or another in varying degrees affects everyone who lacks vigorous, energetic good health."

Beyond the overt deficiency syndromes such as scurvy, malnutrition plays a significant role in most illness and disease. As the *National Academy of Sciences Recommended Dietary Allowances* observes: "Consistent uncompensated deficits, even small ones, will lead to deficiencies over a long period of time."[10] Specifically, poor nutrition leads to:

Lack of growth	Aberrant food choices
Decreased reproductivity	Malabsorption of nutrients
Lessening of sexual desire	Impaired learning ability
Reduced vigor	Loss of memory
Poor stamina	Weakened disease resistance
Diminished appetite	Shortened life span

The data linking susceptibility with poor nutritional status is enormous. The same link is true for accidents, burns, and trauma: The impact varies widely depending on the nutritional reserves and metabolic resilience of the individual, often called "host resistance."

We live in a sea of microorganisms, many of which are potentially harmful. They do not normally infect us because the body's immune system and other defense mechanisms hold them at bay. But when resistance is low—usually because inadequate nutrition isn't supplying the organism's many defense needs—any sudden or prolonged stress (overwork, tension, a chill, emotional shock, an accident, and so forth) overwhelms the body's weakened defenses and illness ensues.

The converse is also true. Acute or chronic infection, accidents, trauma, fear, and other stressors greatly increase the body's need for protein and other nutrients. Studies by the Food and Nutrition Board have shown that protein loss during a fever or infection is substantial and takes about four times as long as the period of infection to return to normal. Parasitic infections typically deplete vitamin B_{12}, further compromising the nutritional state of the patient. On a broad scale this complication is seen in developing countries, where respiratory and intestinal infections lead to acute nutritional disease. The term ***malnutrition-infection complex*** best describes this cycle of disease. Only a sustained, highly nutritious diet can break the cycle.

The crucial role of nutrition in health is most evident in the Third World, where other medical measures often are lacking. The World Health Organization has stated: "For the time being, an adequate diet is the most effective vaccine against most of the diarrhoeal, respiratory, and other common infections."[11]

Perhaps the clearest example of the effects of nutritional inadequacy can be found in the elderly: One of the most basic reasons they catch pneumonia or break bones at far higher rates than younger people is that their resistance and resilience have long been undermined by inadequate nutrition. As we grow older we need fewer and fewer calories but just as many or more nutrients each day. Thus, we all require an increasingly nutrient-dense diet as the years pass—a need that is scarcely recognized and rarely met in contemporary America.

A similar effect among the middle-aged and even adolescents is obesity, which in many cases appears to be the result of a prolonged calorie-excessive nutrient-deficient diet in genetically predisposed individuals.

The earlier the nutrient inadequacy, the more profound the impairment. Malnutrition in children, especially insufficient protein, causes neurological dysfunctions that many experts fear are irreversible. Severe low birthweight associated with malnutrition in mothers is now established as a major cause of brain damage. In all, "seventy-five percent of the mental retardation in this country is estimated to occur in areas of urban and rural poverty."[12] Even lesser malnutrition has neurological effect. Broad behavioral changes "are likely to be among the consequences of marginal vitamin deficiency."[13]

Thus, any significant deviation from the proper intake and utilization of nutrients is considered a form of malnutrition. These deviations are divided into four categories:

1. *Critical.* Extreme malnutrition with threat of death. Common examples are protein deficiency in children (kwashiorkor), abnormal heartbeat (arrhythmia) due to lack of zinc or essential fatty acids, and heat prostration due to lack of water.
2. *Clinical.* A deficiency extreme enough to cause symptoms observable in a routine medical examination. Some of the classic deficiency diseases, such as beriberi, are again turning up in countries with a heavy reliance on rice as a dietary staple.
3. *Subclinical.* An insufficiency of one or more nutrients that results in long-term deterioration, not immediately observable in a doctor's examination. A good example is the recently documented association between periodontal disease and a deficiency of vitamin C without any symptoms of scurvy.
4. *Marginal.* An imbalance of nutrients leading to a lack of well-being or behavioral changes that may not be observable except in controlled conditions. Included here are such generalized complaints as tiredness, anxiety, and depression.

In the day-to-day practice of U.S. physicians, it is assumed that malnutrition is rare. In the light of newer knowledge about nutrition, this assumption seems premature.

Subclinical deficiencies are receiving increasing attention in leading scientific publications. Such widely different maladies as gum disease and postoperative wound complications have been associated with a subclinical deficiency of vitamin C. Other researchers report a variety of vague "subclinical" symptoms that may indicate nutrient deficiencies: decreased feeling of well-being, nervousness, listlessness, frequent minor infections, nonspecific aches and pains, uncharacteristic personality problems. Yet in the absence of classical deficiency symptoms, most physicians will regard the complaints as "subjective." However:

> Their subjective nature is perhaps the most provocative aspect of the disease and would represent a trap for the unwary physician since he would be unable to find any objective physical sign other than variations of normal which would be easily classed as the effects of a chronic state of anxiety.[14]

This "trap for the unwary physician" may include a range of seemingly behavioral problems.

Concentration difficulty	Lethargy
Anorexia	Irritability
Hysteria	Muscle pain or weakness
Headache	Depression
Palpitations	Fatigue
Loss of appetite	Insomnia

Such symptoms are familiar to psychiatrists, who are often the "last resort" of the medical profession. The symptoms are not overt in the sense that they are confirmed by direct observable evidence during the physical exam or measurable by standard laboratory tests. Yet, nearly all practicing physicians will admit they encounter them daily in medical histories and their conferences with patients. This constant flow of symptoms among apparently normal patients tends to be downplayed as so much hypochondriac or psychosomatic complaining. However, studies have shown that vitamin undernutrition that allows a normal growth rate and healthy appearance can have an adverse effect on biological efficiency. Animals (including humans) can look well, grow adequately, and still be "sick" in this broader meaning of the word.

When compounded by risks such as smoking or exposure to lead or pesticides, nutritional deficits can lead to learning and memory disabilities, premature aging, and possibly degenerative disease. Thus, malnutrition may be latent in many complaints for which current medical practice has no clear-cut diagnosis. Indeed, in 1978 Beverly Winikoff of the Rockefeller Foundation and the Senate Select Committee on Diet and the Killer Diseases noted that:

> Over 70 percent of all deaths in the United States in 1973 were caused by diseases linked to the consumption of our diet, including high levels of fat, sugar, and salt. The leading causes of death, heart disease and stroke, are related to the types of food we eat and overeat. If we could eliminate these disorders, we would add 18 years to a baby's life expectancy.[15]

Many scientists question the wisdom of much dietary advice that tends to focus on the macronutrients—the proportions among protein, carbohydrate, and different types of fat—to the neglect of the micronutrients (vitamins, essential fatty acids, minerals, and trace elements) that play such key roles in the regulatory processes of the body. Nutrition scientists such as Roger Williams, Linus Pauling, and others do not make this mistake. To Williams it was crystal clear that suboptimal nutrition at the cellular level is the ultimate cause of heart disease, cancer, diabetes, arthritis, and much of alcoholism. Pauling contends that the vegetarian diet of our early predecessors contained between two and five times the present RDAs for vitamins A, B_1, B_2, and B_6 and reasons that our modern food supply is not capable of sufficiently supplying these and other vitamins, even when we make good food choices. Our bodies excrete most vitamins not needed, and problems of toxic doses are rare and easily correctable. In short, this view weighs the risks and concludes that the most serious danger is not overdosing but chronic undernourishment—an undernourishment that often begins well before we are even born.

Until recently, the fetus was thought to be capable of extracting all the nutrients it needed from the mother's body, even when her diet was inadequate. Consequently, nutrition during pregnancy was not given much consideration.

Evidence emerging during the past two decades, however, has completely reversed the picture. Maternal nutrition is now believed to be *a major determinant* of infant and child health.

Further, *nutrient requirements* rise sharply with pregnancy. The growth of the fetus and placenta, plus the mother's heightened metabolism and added tissues, all require extra supplies of energy and various nutrients. The magnitude of the increase varies with each nutrient. Certain nutrient requirements dramatically increase during pregnancy, particularly iron, calcium, folic acid, and vitamin B_6.

When this demand for more nutrients is not met, a variety of negative consequences results. Severe malnutrition can cause infertility and spontaneous abortion, while lesser degrees of malnutrition have been linked to a variety of disorders.

The earliest connection between a mother's nutrition and the birthweight of her infant was made in 1929 by Dr. Honora Acosta-Sison.[16] Working in the rural Philippines, she observed that the worse her patients' nutritional status was, the lower were both the maximum and the average birthweights of their infants. Most striking, she found that low-weight births were ten times more frequent among the poorest-fed than among the best-fed mothers.

Since these early studies, the causal relationship between nutrition and birthweight has been thoroughly documented. Dr. Benjamin Pasamanick studied the survivors of the 1944–45 famine in western Holland, finding that *congenital defects* of the nervous system and cerebral palsy were elevated and that the rates of severe mental retardation rose significantly in those whose first trimester of fetal life began during the famine.[17] Today, the inadequate nutrition of adolescent mothers is a critical factor in the incidence of low birthweight babies in this group.

In 1982, a potentially momentous study found that pregnant mice fed a diet only moderately deficient in zinc produced offspring with depressed immune function through six months of age.[18] Further, although given a completely normal diet including adequate zinc, these offspring produced similarly immune-depressed offspring—through *three generations.* The authors conclude that such *inherited deficiencies* can only be overcome by extraordinary supplementation.

It is now obvious that the fetus cannot simply tap the mother's reserves for all necessary nutrients. Fetal demands must be met by a much higher than normal intake of nutrients. The mother's failure to do so can have grave consequences for her offspring, ranging from spontaneous abortion and perinatal death to varying degrees of developmental and neurological defects. Provision of optimal nutrition from the start of pregnancy is imperative if the infant is to be given the chance to develop to his or her full potential, and—in later life—avoid the chronic diseases that are now the primary causes of death in the developed world.

SEVERAL THEORIES on this overall increase in chronic disease have focused on the negative effects of widespread dietary change. In 1956, Dr. Thomas L. Cleave (former Surgeon Captain of the Royal Navy and research director of the British Institute of Naval Medicine) hypothesized that many chronic conditions are manifestations of a "master disease" resulting from the rise in popularity of refined carbohydrates.[19] He argued that, allowing for an incubation period of about twenty years, the sudden rise in the popularity of these foods coincided with the emergence of heart disease and disorders of the digestive tract as major killers after World War I.

To illustrate his point, Cleave showed that when Iceland's diet (which consisted primarily of proteins and fats) became Westernized in the 1930s, with a concomitant rise in sugar and refined carbohydrate consumption, it was followed by a precipitous increase in diabetes from the

1950s onward. Similarly, in studies of African nations he found that wherever rapid dietary change introduced refined carbohydrates, heart disease and diabetes began to spread approximately two decades later. Ultimately, he concluded, studies ranging from the Kurds to Yemenites to Zulus indicated that the refining and processing of foods appeared to result in a rise in chronic disease in less than a quarter century.

Although Cleave acknowledged the importance of a genetic predisposition for diabetes, he also indicated that the onset of the disease depended on both the degree of genetic predisposition and the presence of a triggering event. In industrialized society the triggering event appears to be the overload of sugar, white flour products, white rice, and processed fruits and vegetables. This overload—the result of both the frequency and amount of carbohydrate consumption—places an unnatural strain on the pancreas and insulin production.

Modern medicine tacitly agrees with this analysis in its management of diabetic patients. The standard treatment course is to restrict the intake of simpler carbohydrates in favor of complex carbohydrates such as vegetables and whole grains. The assumption is that complex carbohydrates take longer to metabolize, with a steadier effect on blood glucose levels.

This simple explanation has been challenged by new research on patients' actual responses to various carbohydrate foods.[20] The effects of these foods on blood glucose is more complex than was once believed, and the form the food takes may be more important to blood glucose levels than the substance itself. The glycemic response to a food differed based on how it was prepared, what foods it was consumed with, and the presence of other nutrients in the body. For example:

- Processing carbohydrates raises the blood glucose response, and cooking increases it further.
- Table sugar does not have a dramatic effect on plasma glucose when it is consumed in a mixed meal that also contains protein and fat.
- Chromium deficiency causes glucose intolerance in lab animals, and chromium supplementation works well for some diabetics. Refined sugar, meanwhile, actually depletes the body's chromium stores.

Findings such as these indicate the enormous amount we have still to learn about how individuals respond to overloads of carbohydrates. The interacting effects of other dietary components—including fats, proteins, and chromium—have only begun to be investigated. An understanding of these fundamental mechanisms in human energy, functioning, and mood will have far-reaching implications, not only for diabetics, but for the health and behavior of all peoples consuming a Westernized diet. For example, in certain areas of the West Indies atherosclerosis and hypertension are major health problems—yet their diet is virtually devoid of fats. It is, however, quite high in refined carbohydrates.

Both Cleave and his countryman Dr. Denis Burkitt (of the British Medical Research Council) linked the removal of fiber during refining with the negative health effects of refined carbohydrates. Cleave noted that the loss of fiber slows the passage of bowel contents, giving rise to numerous intestinal disorders, including cancer. He further argued that refining left these foods so concentrated in calories that a serious overconsumption takes place, causing obesity and coronary artery disease as well as diabetes. Burkitt, meanwhile, noted that people whose diet was high in bulk (unrefined carbohydrates) were unusually free of gastrointestinal disorders, including cancers of the colon and rectum.[21] His research showed the importance of dietary fiber in gastrointestinal health and cancer prevention, and led to considerable dietary changes and the appreciation of the importance of a "high-fiber" diet. Unfortunately, his admonition that "important though it is, fiber must not be considered in isolation from other components of food" has been largely ignored by many fiber advocates—particularly in the food industry.

Another Englishman, nutritionist John Yudkin, pointed out a positive correlation between sugar consumption and increased levels of cholesterol and triglycerides in the blood.[22] From this, Yudkin inferred that the ingestion of sugar over time may be a factor in the development of cardiovascular disease and some kinds of cancer through its effect on lipid metabolism.

Other researchers have noted the complexity of dietary involvement in cardiovascular disorders, as well. Despite the fact that many authorities, particularly Dr. Ancel Keys of Minneapolis, conclude that excessive dietary cholesterol is the cause of atherosclerosis, findings such as those of Cleave, Burkitt, and Yudkin cast significant doubts on this theory. In addition, research has shown polyunsaturates to be anything but benign, while the evidence linking dietary fat to high serum cholesterol and the buildup of plaque has remained confusing, at best.

As far back as 1946 it was shown that prolonged feeding of cholesterol did not cause atherosclerotic lesions in rhesus monkeys,[23] while the Tecumseh study (1976) found that serum cholesterol and triglyceride levels were independent of any constituent in the human subjects' diets.[24] Even the famous Framingham study, which is often cited as proof of the dietary cholesterol connection to heart disease, failed to come up with a connection between the two. In the words of the National Heart Institute, these researchers concluded that there is "no suggestion of any relation between diet and the subsequent development of coronary heart disease."[25]

There are many peoples that consume far more saturated fats than Americans yet are almost completely free of coronary heart disease. I have already mentioned Eskimos above the Arctic Circle, but the most dramatic example was reported by Dr. George Mann and his colleagues, who studied atherosclerosis in the Masai of central Africa.[26] These people, who live almost exclusively on milk and meat, appear to be almost immune to coronary heart disease. After performing autopsies on fifty Masai who had died of accident or acute illness, researchers were surprised to find that the Masai *did* have atherosclerosis! Their arteries had plaque deposits similar to those found in elderly Americans. But in the Masai the coronary vessels seemed to have enlarged with age to make up for the narrowing.

Data such as these, coupled with the inconclusive results of most of the major studies on dietary cholesterol, argue against any simple cause-effect relationship in the development of cardiovascular disease. While there are obviously dietary factors involved, they are complex and may differ in different persons. As we have seen, dietary elements other than cholesterol—most notably sugar and refined carbohydrates—are definitely in the running as culprits.

It is true, however, that there does appear to be a relationship between high levels of cholesterol *in the blood* and cardiovascular disease. The point of contention is whether or not the cholesterol you eat actually affects serum cholesterol levels. It is known that reduced serum cholesterol levels will reduce the risk of heart disease; the question is, what *really* lowers serum cholesterol?

There are several nutrients that have been firmly associated with lowered serum cholesterol levels, most notably the essential trace element chromium. Chromium-deficient patients characteristically have high serum cholesterol levels, and numerous reports have shown that chromium supplementation both lowers serum cholesterol and restores blood sugar levels to normal in many patients.

Other deficiencies that have been implicated in the development of cardiovascular disease include vitamin B_6, the fiber pectin, iodine, magnesium, selenium, and vitamin E. These nutrients are often deficient in the American diet.

Another popular dietary culprit, sodium, is frequently implicated in high blood pressure (hypertension). Like fats in coronary heart disease, the evidence linking sodium to hypertension is inconclusive. The issue may not be sodium alone but the relative concentration of sodium and its partner, potassium, which work together to maintain the balance of pressure within and without the cells.

Calcium deficiency also raises blood pressure. Oregon Health Sciences University researchers report that approximately half of hypertensive patients responded well to calcium therapy,[27] and Cornell researchers have reported blood pressure decreases in mildly hypertensive patients treated with calcium supplements. Since proper calcium concentration is crucial to the proper functioning of cell membranes and also to the coagulation of blood, Dr. John Laragh of Cornell University has noted that calcium may be more important than sodium in hypertension.[28] These data are particularly interesting in light of the fact that hypertension is more prevalent in blacks, who are significantly calcium-deficient, than it is in whites.

The dramatic increase in refined carbohydrates and other dietary factors, coupled with environmental and lifestyle shifts, distorts the body's integral regulatory systems. These chronic distortions cause problems in all the body's systems—including those that govern our psychological and emotional states.

Unfortunately, many who readily accept the link between diet and heart disease or other chronic physical conditions find it hard to imagine that nutrition could have a direct and determining effect on human behavior and personality dysfunctions. Yet researchers at MIT have shown that there are actually changes in brain composition after a meal. Other researchers have found that brain abnormalities associated with learning and behavioral difficulties appear to be strongly associated with neurotransmitter precursor imbalances, vitamin and mineral deficiencies, and the consumption of refined carbohydrates, toxic elements, additives, colorings, caffeine, and allergens.

Diet therapy has always been a staple of folk medicine. In the 1790s, the Tuke family established a human mental hospital known as the York Retreat, and successfully used diet to calm manic patients. The Tukes would give manic patients meat, cheese, bread, and good porter at bedtime to help induce sleep. Nearly two hundred years later, researchers throughout the world are discovering the links that exist between individuals' diets and their behavior.

In 1980, at the world-famous Cleveland Clinic, twenty adolescents suffering from neurotic dysfunctions that are normally treated with drugs and counseling were diagnosed in laboratory studies as seriously deficient in thiamine.[29] Treatment with thiamine supplements and a better diet brought marked improvement or complete disappearance of the symptoms.

Disturbingly, the majority of the symptoms, including aggressive personality changes, correlated with high levels of empty calories. These teenagers showed the typically American pattern of skipping breakfast, snacking on junk foods, and drinking many cans of soda a day. Their symptoms, which were consistent with the early stages of beriberi (a thiamine-deficiency disease that can be characterized by delusions and disorientation), had failed to respond to conventional therapy. Neither the teenagers nor their parents ever thought that the symptoms might be related to their diet. Yet thiamine is a nutrient that is depleted by sugar, refined flour, and alcohol—all of which were major components of the teens' diets.

This syndrome led the researchers to suggest that many of the personality traits that we attribute to the "phase" of adolescence may in fact be a side effect of the massive ingestion of sugar that is typical of young people today, and that excessive sugar consumption (particularly in beverages) is a significant and unrecognized threat.

Evidence of the importance of dietary components such as various amino acids and the B vitamin choline has led researchers to hypothesize that dietary therapy may be useful in some psychiatric illnesses, including depression. Such strategies have already been used to increase the natural synthesis of neurotransmitters in certain addictive disorders, with some success. Prescribing tranquilizers or other psychiatric drugs, on the other hand, can mask or exacerbate underlying malnourishment and unique nutritional needs. Psychiatrists who ignore nutrition—and most do—may thereby be profiteering off many of their patients, albeit unwittingly.

THE PUBLIC IGNORES the links between poor nutrition and illness out of ignorance. The science/health establishment, on the other hand, tends to discount these connections in its preoccupation with overt symptoms and single-factor causes.

When one considers that three quarters of all nonaccidental deaths in the United States are attributable to heart disease, cancer, and stroke and that crisis intervention is clearly of little help in changing this pattern, a realistic dietary goal might better be to reverse the underconsumption of nutrients.

The resurgence of hunger and malnourishment in this nation carries with it the assurance of ill health, developmental disabilities, and high social cost in the future. Marginal deficiencies, as we have seen, have much more than marginal consequences for overall health. And the deficiencies that are rife among the American public are often far more than marginal. They are prime among the complex factors that are killing us.

> Malnourishment, whether caused by poverty or improper diet, contributes to the alarming health situation in the United States today. Between 1950 and 1970, that portion of the nation's income devoted to health services rose from $12 billion to $70 billion. Yet during the same period, there had been absolutely no increase in the life expectancy of males at age 10, and a very insignificant increase for women.[30]

This trend continues.

What is to be done? The wisest course will be to return to the lessons learned in the late 1960s and *augment*, rather than cut, the nutrition programs that had been launched. Particular emphasis needs to be put on educating the public in the basics of nutrition, since so many of these deficiencies are found even in persons well above the poverty level.

But many policy makers and politicians, knowing nothing of nutrition, regard such programs as economically unjustifiable. These authorities would have consumers rely on the private sector—the modern food-production system—or wait until the economy is in better shape. But for millions of Americans that wait may be too long. In the words of Dr. J. Larry Brown of Harvard University and the Physician Task Force on Hunger:

> We are advised that in the long run the economy will return to normal. But the problem is that a child does not eat in the long run. An elderly person does not live in the long run. From a nutritional perspective, they live now. They are hungry now.[31]

4

The Industrialization of Food

FROM THE Agricultural Revolution until the Industrial Revolution food was produced the old-fashioned way. It was grown, cooked, and eaten. Or, for that minority of townsfolk who didn't produce their own food, it was grown, carted, sold—and cooked and eaten. That was it. What little processing was done nearly always took place in the home kitchen. True, in small pockets of trade, ale was brewed and put up for sale, or milled flour, or salt-cured meat, or coarse bread, or cheese. But mostly the sale of food consisted simply of raw foodstuffs: salt, fresh vegetables or fruits, grain. Without farm machinery or rapid transportation or refrigeration, there weren't any further possibilities.

In 1783, in England, the first factory for making plows was opened; in America Cyrus McCormick introduced his mechanical reaper in 1831, and John Deere's steel plow and the combine soon followed. From those days forward, a whirlwind was unleashed that mechanized, hybridized, fertilized, electrified, industrialized, refined, and processed old-fashioned food right off the farm and the family table. Today we reap that whirlwind in brightly packaged supermarket aisles and fast-food outlets.

The American food-production system has become the largest and most important industry in the world. It is a system described by Professor Ross Hall, former chairman of the Department of Biochemistry at McMaster University, as "a gigantic, highly integrated service system in which the object is not to nourish or even to feed, but to force an ever-increasing consumption of fabricated products."[1] In the scholarly understatement of Jean Mayer, writing in *Science*, "This nation's food products have been virtually transformed under the impact of forces that the public has yet to recognize fully."[2]

It is essential to first acknowledge the system's tremendous benefits. Historically, the three major threats to the food supply were:

1. Scarcity, causing hunger, malnutrition, or starvation.
2. Such a limited diet as to cause acute deficiency diseases (in sailors on long voyages, for example).
3. Decaying or contaminated food, causing disease.

Even when adequate, food supplies used to be highly seasonal and limited to what could be produced locally. Until this century the vast majority of human beings lived on unbelievably restricted (and boring) diets; many people ate primarily bread supplemented with a little meat and, in season, a few vegetables and fruits. Such basics to us as oranges, tomatoes, potatoes, corn, and sugar were unknown just two or three hundred years ago. In contrast, today's abundant food supply includes such year-round variety that hunger and the overt deficiency diseases of the past are almost unknown in advanced societies, except among the very poor and the sick.

Similarly, contaminated or spoiled food was often not apparent or was ignored, and people became sick or suddenly died, cause unknown. Many plagues of the history books were water or food borne. Ergot (fungus) contamination of wheat provoked such bizarre behavior that afflicted individuals were sometimes persecuted or put to death for possession by the devil. Only in this century, by the action of governments, have natural contaminants of food ceased to be a significant problem in industrialized nations.

To its enormous credit, the modern food-production system has eliminated or greatly reduced all of these ancient threats in developed countries, preventing untold deaths, suffering, and developmental problems. Yet, simultaneously, it has introduced two major new problems that society has still to recognize and confront.

First, the system now introduces a new host of man-made contaminants into our food. These include intentional additives as well as chemicals used during the growing process (growth hormones, antibiotics, pesticides) and many risky industrial and other pollutants.

Second, the system intensively handles, refines, and processes our foodstuffs. Each of these steps reduces the food's nutrient content, with a progressive impact that can be denaturing. They are exacerbated by genetics, growing conditions, harvesting, handling, refining, and processing. Moreover, the system has now added the ultimate nutrient insult, fabricating.

Genetics

In industrialized nations, the farmer can only survive economically if he produces high-yield crops. To meet this need, seed companies use their genetic know-how to produce seeds that deliver high yields per acre of plants that will:

- Ripen at the same time, to help the farmer improve the cost-effectiveness of his harvesting and use of machinery and manpower.
- Be uniform in shape and appearance, since the crop that varies greatly in size or coloring is much more difficult to market.
- Be resistant to specific diseases or able to grow in terrains unfavorable because of climatic or soil conditions.
- Facilitate processing and manufacturing; different strains of wheat, for example, have been developed for pasta, bread, and for cakes and cookies.
- Ship better across long distances; some years ago, for example, tomato strains were bred that averaged twice the vitamin C of prevailing varieties, making them equivalent in C to citrus fruits. However, these strains have been displaced by types, with thicker skins and less water, that transport better without bruising. The genetic loss of nutrient value was not a commercial consideration.

All these genetic manipulations have their counterparts in livestock breeding. With an eye to economy, breeders have selected cattle that are specialized for beef or milk production, chicken specialized for either eggs or meat, and even pigs that are specialized to produce pork or bacon. Dairy cows are bred for increased milk yields with high butterfat or protein content, and beef cattle can be bred to produce more tender meat and leaner steaks or roasts. It is even possible to select for such qualities as temperament, disease resistance, food efficiency, and carcass qualities. Hens' egg production has been stepped up, and the use of artificial insemination to produce bigger, meatier turkeys has been so successful that "commercial turkeys can no longer breed naturally. The big-breasted male, even when inclined to do so, finds it physically impossible to mount the female."[3]

So far there is little hard evidence of how much this commercialization of genetic strains has meant in significant nutrient losses. Little or no research has been done on the subject because government and corporate funding has concentrated on developing high-yield, disease-resistant strains. There is plenty of evidence, however, that genetic research could be used just as effectively to improve nutrient values, if sufficient capital were made available.

- As long ago as 1953, Tomes and co-workers raised the provitamin A content of tomatoes by thirty times through genetic techniques.
- In 1963, a team of Purdue scientists developed a breed of corn with 70 percent more lysine than standard corn (lysine is the amino acid deficient in corn that makes it a poor source of protein).
- The Plainsman V strain of wheat was developed to produce not only high yield levels but high protein levels.

Soil Depletion

The soils of the world have frequently suffered, and continue to suffer, at the hand of farming. But our present methods, while correcting some abuses of the past, inflict on soil a variety of new and old insults that diminish its nutrient value. Because of intensive farming, poor crop management, erosion, commercial fertilization, the use of pesticides, and other problematic factors, much of the soil in which our crops are now raised has been depleted, particularly of essential minerals.

Plants draw their nutrients and general health from a complex of inorganic and organic material. Inorganic elements include oxygen and carbon, nitrogen, phosphorus, and potassium, along with iron, calcium, and an array of other minerals. The chief organic substances range from decaying plant material and animal wastes to earthworms and an amazing variety of microscopic organisms including bacteria, fungi, algae, and protozoa. All of these elements are important to the health and nutrient value of the crop—and of the animals that feed on it.

Soils vary widely in each of these factors. Because plants break down or absorb many of them as they grow, and the assaults of farming destroy others, even high-quality soils become increasingly depleted the longer they are farmed. Contemporary farming is intensive in the extreme. The huge yields that are now common mean equally large losses of nutrients from the soil.

A host of strategies has been applied over the centuries to avoid depletion: fallow years, crop rotation, stubble plowing, terracing, contour plowing, irrigation, fertilization, and so on. Contemporary farm managers, focusing on the quantity and appearance of the crop, try to head off the predictable problems by the massive application of commercial fertilizer and pesticides.

Despite these efforts, soil, and therefore plant, depletion of nutrients continues and worsens. This is chiefly because modern farm practices do not take into account the complex chemical and physical interactions within soil. The most common fertilizers today are nitrogen and NPK (nitrogen-phosphorus-potassium) formulas. These applications were developed in the 1830s and 1840s, before nutrition science existed. We now know these wonder fertilizers have serious drawbacks.

These simple chemical fertilizers do produce larger fruits and vegetables; unfortunately, smaller items of produce are usually richer in nutrients. The addition of nitrogen to the soil also dramatically increases crop yields, hence its popularity. But nitrogen also decreases essential nutrients in crops, although not enough research has been done to say how extensive the losses are. We do know, however, that nitrogen depletes ascorbic acid and causes a serious decrease of iron in food crops.

The use of pesticides, which protect crops from devastating blights, can have disastrous effects on soil ecology. Many of these toxic substances are quite tenacious, leaving residues on crops and building up in the soil until they can actually inhibit the growth of plants. In addition, pesticides kill earthworms and soil microorganisms, including nutrifying bacteria, almost as efficiently as they kill pests.

Unfortunately, the food-production system's intense focus on quantity over quality is perpetuating many of these problems. As R. H. Hall has pointed out: "The fertilizer [and pesticide] industry profitably sells a technology based on the scientific discoveries of 1840 and feels no compulsion to change its manufacturing and marketing practices."[4]

IN THE CASE of meat and poultry, growing conditions have been entirely transformed. The best example is chicken production. The birds produced, eight weeks from birth to death, never see the light of day or touch the surface of the earth. In the dark factory of cages where the animal lives so briefly, the feed required to produce a live pound of the bird has been cut (by dint of synthetic hormones and antibodies) from four pounds in 1940 to two pounds in 1980. In 1934, 34 million broilers were produced in the United States—the old-fashioned way. In 1979, 3,940 million broilers were produced, an 11,500 percent increase in sheer meat tonnage. Again, virtually no research has been done on the nutrient impact of these tremendous changes.

Harvesting

The main loss of nutrients during harvesting comes from taking the crop before it has ripened in order to meet marketing and transportation dictates. Harder, greener vegetables and fruits "travel" better and do not spoil as soon during long transportation and storage periods. Yet the ripening process on the plant is often essential to high nutrient density in food. Mineral content increases during the maturing of snap beans, turnip greens, and Merlot grapes, and the vitamin content of many fruits and vegetables rises only when they near the peak of ripeness.

Transportation, Handling, and Storage

Two of the most fundamental advancements of the modern food-production system are the nationwide and year-round availability of all types of foods. What historically were regional and seasonal foods (from maple syrup to strawberries) are now available coast-to-coast at any time.

The highest price paid for this unlimited abundance is in nutrients. Our foods must be transported, often over long distances, and must be stored, often for long periods. Physical stresses such as wide fluctuations in temperature and humidity (the two factors most critical in preserving nutritional values), as well as bruises, injuries, and microbial contamination, each take an enormous toll. These preprocessing losses range as high as 25 percent or more.

- Potatoes lose as much as 78 percent of their vitamin C during long-term storage at 36°F.
- Spinach and asparagus lose 50 to 70 percent of their folic acid if kept at room temperature for three days.
- Kale will wilt and lose 33 percent of its vitamin C when kept at 50°F for two days.
- Harvested lettuce stored at room temperature loses 50 percent of its C within twenty-four hours after picking. Even if refrigerated immediately, it suffers the same loss in three days.
- More stable vegetables like asparagus, broccoli, and green beans lose 50 percent of their C before they reach the produce counter.

Refining

Before being processed into a myriad of food products, several basic food commodities are "refined" into a more workable or (presumably) pleasing form. Refining is a nutrient-devastating series of industrial procedures. Indeed, the term *refining* is actually a cosmetic word for the process of extracting: The industrially workable material is extracted from foodstuffs and, though stripped of most nutrients, is sold as "refined." Commodities most often refined are wheat and other grains (into refined white flour), corn (into cornmeal or corn syrup), brown rice (into refined white rice), sugarcane or sugar beets (into pure sugar), and to a lesser degree, fruits and vegetables (into juices or baby food).

The two predominant refined foods in the Western diet, sugar and flour, have a common birth. In the later nineteenth century, the food industry began applying mechanical technology to the preparation of foods for sale commercially. By their nature, wheat grain and sugarcane lent themselves to this kind of treatment all too well. Both—after extensive extracting—ended up as a fine white powder that went right to the head and heart of the public. It was "addiction" at first taste.

Both products were cheap to produce, easily stored for long periods without decay or infestation (there was little left to decompose or attract vermin), and remarkably adaptable industrial materials from which, it turned out, an endless succession of popular food products could be concocted. Today over 95 percent of the flour used in the United States is white, and sugar consumption (including the new high-fructose corn syrup) is at an all-time high.

WHEAT. The greatest single loss of vitamins from industrial food processing occurs during the milling of wheat down to refined white flour. Almost all the flour we use today is refined through a series of about two dozen processes, including high-pressure steel rolling, scouring, grinding, and magnetic separation. From the original grain of wheat this lengthy extraction separates out the relatively tasteless, colorless, low nutrient-density white flour for human consumption, and discards the very nutritious wheat germ at the center and the mineral-laden high-fiber shell (the wheat bran).

Before this extraction, the wheat grain is genuinely a "staff of life." Whole wheat contains essential amino acids, fiber, vitamins, and crucial minerals and trace elements. But the distribution of these nutrients in the kernel is lopsided—nearly all are found in the germ and bran; the residue—white flour—has few of these nutrients left. Some 82 percent of B_1, 67 percent of B_2, 80 percent of B_3, 83 percent of B_6, 75 percent of folic acid, 80 percent of biotin, and 76 percent of vitamin K are lost. Losses of fat-soluble nutrients include 50 percent of linoleic acid (the basic essential fatty acid) and 98 percent of vitamin E. Total protein losses range from 15 to 20 percent, but the loss of certain essential amino acids reduces the utilizable protein by over 50 percent. The loss of fiber is about 85 percent. There is one gain. Due to the removal of protein, fiber, and minerals, white flour has about 7 percent more calories.

But what about "fortification"? Isn't "enriched" white bread brought back to the level of whole wheat? Unfortunately, there is no comparison. Of the twenty-seven or so nutrients lost during refining, only four were required (in 1941) to be added back, and in minute amounts, at that. The chief effect of fortification and enrichment is antinutritional: It lulls consumers into a false sense of security about some of the most basic foods we eat and feed our children.

White flour is more than merely deficient, however. The missing nutrients have definite depleting effects within the body. The depletion of zinc, for example, results in an increase in cadmium—which can accumulate in the kidneys and blood vessels, causing arterial hypertension. The consumption of white flour products has also been associated with a depletion of pantothenic acid (B_5) from nerve and muscle tissue, pyridoxine (B_6) from the brain, and phosphorous and magnesium from the heart and bones.

RICE, CORN, AND OTHER GRAINS. The refining of rice, corn, and grains such as rye, barley, and oats entails similar losses of nutrients. As with wheat, in rice, corn, and the other major grains most nutrients are concentrated in the layers that are removed during refining.

- Rice loses 79 percent of its B_1 when the outer layers are "polished" off in milling. This simple act of refining is the cause of beriberi, the B_1 deficiency disease that has plagued rice-eating peoples for millennia.
- Corn is low in protein quality (poor levels of the amino acids lysine and tryptophan), and removing the germ by milling further cuts its nutritive value. In the early 1900s, Southern diets heavy in refined cornmeal triggered the plague of pellagra, the B_3 deficiency disease that ends in madness. In addition, the refining of corn oil into corn syrup (mostly glucose) leaves nothing but calories.

SUGAR. Over the last two hundred years, the refined white granules of pure sucrose that we call sugar have become a universal staple of the human diet in developed countries; and as we have seen, sugar's amazing rise has been paralleled by the dramatic rise in arterial disease and other chronic conditions during this century.

The per capita consumption of sugar has risen ever since it was first introduced to our diets in 1751. This includes not just table sugar (which has been declining) but all the "nutritive" sweeteners, including those, like corn syrup, that industry now routinely adds to virtually every processed food from champagne to sauerkraut.

Whereas wheat is almost always highly refined and of low nutrient density, sugar is always highly refined—and of zero nutrient density. That is, it has essentially no nutrients left except calories. Raw sugar is already 96 percent sucrose, 1 percent water, and 3 percent residue. Equally problematic is the fact that all fiber is removed, leaving the immediately digestible pure sucrose. The consequences of such highly refined sugar are mixed: some serious, some uncertain.

Such a high proportion of sucrose in the diet pours virtually pure glucose (blood sugar) into the bloodstream. The long-term effects of this loading are troubling, but not enough research has been done on the question for scientists to know exactly what the deleterious mechanisms are, or what the role of a high-sugar diet like ours is in diabetes, high blood pressure, atherosclerosis, obesity, alcoholism, behavioral disorders, or even cancer (tumors are known to be enormous sugar absorbers). We do know sugar rots a person's teeth, although the sugar industry disputes even that.

Second, there is sugar's effect on the rest of our diet. Sugar-rich, nutrient-poor foods take up a disproportionate share of many Americans' diets, especially children's. Just as bad money drives out good, nutrient-impoverished foods crowd out nutrient-rich foods, leaving individuals in caloric excess, increasingly fat, yet still hungry—and malnourished.

Third, there is sugar's effect on the other nutrients in our diets or bodily stores. Empty calories are really "negative nutrients" since the organism must consume its own nutrients to metabolize them. Sugar (along with its cousin alcohol) is unique among foods—it is not only nutrient-devoid (except for calories), it is also nutrient-depleting. The body requires thiamine, niacin, and riboflavin to oxidize carbohydrates, and sugar contributes none of these vitamins. As a result, these vitamins must come from other foods or the body's reserves.

Together with other sweeteners, the nutrient-depleting calories of sugar now make up over a quarter of the average American's diet; each of us, on the average, consumes some 170 pounds of sugar a year. In the mid-1970s, the Bogalusa Heart Study found that ten-year-olds consume some 48 percent of their calories as refined sugar, and even before a baby is weaned the taste for sugar has been nurtured by commercial baby formulas containing added sugar.

In 1980, the Center for Science in the Public Interest estimated that added sugar amounted to 82 percent of all the sugar we consume. Thus the real problem is not the sugar bowl we see on the table, but the invisible sugar that the food industry adds to processed foods (see table 4). On a per-calorie basis, there is almost twice as much sugar in commercially produced ketchup as in ice cream.

As long ago as 1942, the American Medical Association recognized the health risks inherent in our sugar fetish and stated that the consumption of sugar "presents a serious obstacle to the improved nutrition of the general public."[5] In the strongest terms possible, the report called for "all practical means to be taken to limit the consumption of sugar in any form" in which significant nutrients are not present.

It was a call unheeded. When, in 1981, the FDA approved sugar as a food additive, a group of authorities challenged the decision. Citing thirty-one studies that relate sucrose not only to nutrient deficiencies but to heart disease, diabetes, hypertension, obesity, behavioral disorders, hyperactivity, and other neurochemical dysfunctions, they called for sugar's removal from the list of approved food additives. They were ignored. And today the use of industrially added sugar is increasing at nearly twice the rate the public has been reducing its voluntary use.

Food Processing

The last seventy years have witnessed an exponential growth in food processing: canned goods, frozen foods, frozen prepared dinners, convenience foods at home, fast foods to take out. The technology to deliver these items consists of such nutrient-destroying processes as boiling then freezing the same food, bleaching then dying, dehydrating then reconstituting. It involves thousands of chemical additives and dozens of

TABLE 4

Hidden Sugar in Common Processed Foods

(Average percent by weight reported by industry)

Condiments, relishes, salt substitutes	27
Cheese	25
Milk, milk products	18
Dairy product analogs	16
Beverages, nonalcoholic	13
Processed vegetables, juices	13
Instant coffee and tea	13
Baby processed fruit	12
Seasonings and flavors	11
Beverages, alcoholic	10
Nuts, nut products	8
Baby meat dinners	5
Baby formulas	5

SOURCE: *Evaluation of the Health Aspects of Sucrose as a Food Ingredient* (Bethesda, Md.: Federation of American Societies for Experimental Biology, 1976), p.4.

processes unknown in the history of food—extruding, stabilizing, freeze-drying, hydrolyzing, and so on.

The severe stresses of industrial processing entail many nutrient losses, and factory processing *plus* home preparation usually means extensive nutrient destruction. To cite a few simple examples:

- Dry oatmeal is about 14 percent protein. Cooked oatmeal, on the other hand, is only about 2 percent protein.
- Vitamin B_3 leaches in blanching and washing and is reduced both in frozen and canned vegetables even prior to home heating.
- Canned vegetables lose up to 70 percent of their vitamin C in the canning process and may lose up to 20 percent of their vitamins A and B_1.
- Canning fruits such as apples, cherries, peaches, strawberries, and apricots results in losses of 39 percent of vitamin A, 47 percent of thiamin, 57 percent of riboflavin, 42 percent of niacin, and 56 percent of vitamin C.

Most Americans believe that frozen vegetables are almost the same as fresh, nutritionally speaking, and far better than canned. There is no truth to this. Compare the two processes. Canned goods are cooked, canned, and then warmed again at home. Frozen vegetables are typically blanched first (flash boiled) to help preserve their color and condition, then packaged and frozen, moved in and out of refrigeration units several times, and then boiled again at home. The result is predictable:

> When vegetables are exposed to a freezing process and then cooked, their contents of common vitamins (A, B_1, B_2, niacin, and C) almost invariably will be significantly lower (often 25 percent plus or minus 20) than those existing in comparable fresh-cooked products.[6]

Five major providers of vitamin C, for example, are lima beans, broccoli, cauliflower, peas, and spinach; they lose an average of half their C in the freezing process. Similar losses for other nutrients have been reported by researchers.

The additional nutrient losses when the frozen vegetables are cooked at home are almost as high. In the vegetables mentioned above, loss of ascorbic acid ranges from a quarter to a half. Among the minerals, iron is the most easily lost, and most of the vitamins suffer as much. Length of time in cooking frozen vegetables is a factor, of course, along with the amount of water used. "Underdone" spinach in minimal water suffers about half the loss of "overdone" spinach in water covering the vegetable (two thirds of vitamin C lost, for example).

Nutrient losses in the canning process are generally comparable to those in freezing or a little higher, but canned goods do not have to be boiled in water again at home. Two thirds of B_1 and half of niacin and C are the mean losses of seven common canned vegetables. Vitamin A fares as well in canning as freezing. (These values were calculated *after cooking* both the processed and the fresh vegetables.)

Clearly, "fresh is best." Even in our urbanized society, frozen and canned foods are an impoverishing convenience. As the *Food and Nutrition Encyclopedia* observes, "The appalling processing and preservation losses revealed above underscore the dietary need for whole grains and unprocessed foods of many varieties."[7]

FATS AND OILS. Fats and oils (lipids) contain several nutrients essential to human health. The nutrients in these foods are quite easily destroyed and the processing applied to them is particularly intense.

Where animals store energy in their fat cells, the vegetable kingdom stores energy in "fruits" such as olives and avocados, but mainly in seeds and nuts, from peanuts to sunflower seeds, from the wheat germ to corn kernels and soybeans. In order for manufacturers to use the oils (in products from paint to margarine), they must first be extracted by a variety of mechanical or chemical processes, each of which strips away nutrients in varying degrees.

- In the mechanical extraction process, the seeds are crushed, the resulting pulp is heated for half an hour at 230°F, and the crude oil is then squeezed out at pressures from ten to twenty tons per square inch, generating considerably more heat.
- In the solvent method, the crushed pulp is treated with gasoline, hexane, benzene, ethyl ether, carbon disulfide, carbon tetrachloride, or methylene chloride. (Chemical extraction gets more of the oil out and is the preferred method.) The solvent is then boiled off—except for up to 100 parts per million, which remain in the crude oil.

Then, depending on the manufacturer's objective, the extracted crude oil is usually processed to a lesser or greater extent, removing or destroying many remaining nutrients. At 140 to 160°F, the crude is first treated with a solution of lye; the resulting soap settles and the oil is skimmed off. It is then bleached to rid it of carotene (provitamin A) and other color factors, deodorized by heating it at 330 to 380°F in a partial vacuum for about twelve hours, and finally an ***antioxidant*** is added to stop the oils from turning rancid.

After all this, it is light, clear, has a reasonably long shelf life, and is almost completely devitalized. Vitamins A, K, B_{12}, and E, as well as chromium, manganese, cobalt, and copper have all been destroyed by the heat and oxidation, while the essential fatty acids have become either inactive or toxic as a result of oxidation. Chromium, manganese, and B_6 deficiencies correlate closely with heart disease.

But the worst stage of oil processing is hydrogenation—the hardening of the oil product into solids to serve as imitation butter or lard. In order to harden the oil into this spreadable form, the processors must artificially "saturate" the oil with hydrogen atoms. This is accomplished by mixing the oil with a nickel catalyst and then subjecting it to hydrogen gas in a high-pressure reactor, a process that generates temperatures of about 380°F. The final product is shaped into solid rectangles of margarine or tubs of vegetable shortening, and is now used in virtually all commercial baked goods under the healthful-sounding rubric of "partially hydrogenated vegetable oil." An ideal arrangement, right?

Wrong. Food oil refineries are not nature, and partially hydrogenated vegetable oils are anything but natural. In fact, the molecular structure of hydrogenated oils has been so radically disorganized that it is largely unrecognizable and unusable by the body.

In plants, unsaturated fats occur in a natural form that chemists refer to as "cis-" (as opposed to "trans-"). During artificial hydrogenation, some of the unsaturated points do not link up with hydrogen atoms, but instead are changed to the "trans-" form. Trans-fat molecules are great for keeping margarine or vegetable shortening solid (they have a much higher melting point than cis-fats) but they are devastating biochemically.

Trans-fats are incorporated into cell membranes as if they were cis-fats, but they behave very differently. Only the cis-fatty acids are biologically active, while the trans- forms actually block the body's utilization of essential fatty acids. These blockages throughout the body's biochemistry have disastrous effects.

For example, linoleic acid is an essential fatty acid that is essential for the formation of the vital hormone/enzymes called prostaglandins. The trans-linoleic acid in hydrogenated oil blocks cis-linoleic acid. Prostaglandin deficiencies can result in elevated blood pressure, blood clotting, arterial degeneration, and a host of other maladies including sexual dysfunction. Similarly, trans-fatty acids are associated with increased blood cholesterol (possibly because of disruption of fat transport across cell membranes) and increased concentration of low-density lipoproteins.

Oil processing, therefore, does not result in "heart healthy" foods at all. Instead, oil processing and hydrogenation tend to increase malnutrition and the risk of related illnesses, including heart disease. And food oils are just one of the countless products that are subjected to such physical and chemical manipulations during refining and processing.

The basic materials of food processing are the refined carbohydrates (mainly white flour and sugar) and processed oils. The food industry has taken to sugar and hydrogenated fats not merely because of their taste appeal but because they are the cheapest constituents available for the manufacture of packaged foods.

> One company can't sell a tomato, for example, for much more than another company. But process it into ketchup, add spices and a fraction of a cent of flavor, and bottle it; call it barbecue sauce; advertise it; tout its brand name, and higher and higher profits can be made because the product seems unique.[8]

We might not begrudge industry these manipulated profits if, in return, the purchasers got nutrients they need from the food product. Unfortunately, they don't. The profits are made at the consumers' twofold expense—in purchasing power and in nutrients needed. Probably the foremost authority on the nutrient losses in food processing is Robert S. Harris of MIT, who summed up the nutrient disaster of our food-production system this way:

> By the time that processed foods reach you, they may have been shipped and stored, trimmed, blanched, frozen, canned, condensed, dehydrated, pasteur-

> ized, sterilized, smoked, cured, milled, roasted, cooked, toasted or puffed. What's left of their composition after any combination of those tortures is then liable to be further stolen by heat, light, oxygen, oxalates, antivitamins, acidity, alkalinity, metal catalysts, enzymes, and irradiation.[9]

Given the deterioration of the U.S. food supply, the lack of a public policy on food quality has serious consequences. Yet it is unlikely that attention will be focused on this highly commercial issue soon since both the FDA and the AMA have abandoned their earlier stands and joined the food-production industry in lauding the volume, variety, and value of today's food supply.

Considering that food processing is both the largest industry in the country and fiercely competitive, what do the critics of the industry recommend?

First, that the seriousness of the problem be recognized at both governmental and scientific levels.

Second, that the pat answers fed to the public over the last half century be retired. Consumers are concerned about nutrition, and they know what junk food is. What they don't know is which way to turn or whom to believe. They need better dietary advice than "Eat a balanced diet" and more useful guidance than the RDAs and today's food labels.

Third, that the questions of fortification and labeling of foods must be reopened. As long ago as 1971, an HEW report noted that "changing patterns of consumption have 'made obsolete some of the food fortification and improvement practices initiated by regulations over the last twenty or thirty years.' "[10] A USDA scientist in trace minerals likewise warns: "Soil depletion, increased processing of foods and feeds, and changing eating patterns are forcing us to change our concepts in mineral nutrition."[11] Of the fifty nutrients, labels now list only eight—on fewer than 10 percent of labeled foods.

Fourth, that we face the fact that neither academic research nor federal intervention can be relied on to help reverse the trend of overprocessing. Regulatory agencies and university researchers are closely tied to the food industry. In one year studied, almost half of the leading officials at the FDA had previously worked for organizations the agency was attempting to regulate.[12] Although congressional ties to agriculture and industry are legendary, public opinion holds some sway on Capitol Hill, and elected representatives may be consumers' best allies in their efforts to improve the quality of the food they eat.

WHILE THE small-scale unindustrialized agriculture business was being transformed into a vast food-production industry, consumers have gone through an almost equally momentous change in how, when, where, and what we prefer to eat. Since 1909, the Department of Agriculture has conducted periodic surveys of the nation's overall food consumption. Among the increases from 1909 to 1976, for example: processed fruits, up 913 percent; processed vegetables, up 306 percent; fats and oils (largely processed), up 139 percent.

During those same years, our yearly consumption of *fresh* fruits dropped sixty-one pounds per person. Fresh vegetables dropped forty-one pounds. And butter plummeted from eighteen pounds to four.

In all, these USDA figures trace a sharp downward trend in four major components of the traditional diet: fresh produce, whole grain products, natural fats and oils, and fiber-rich foods. Meanwhile, our intake of treated fats, sugar, and highly processed foods has skyrocketed. Intake of food colors, alone, jumped 1,006 percent between 1940 and 1981. Soft drink consumption rose 182 percent between 1960 and 1981, and corn syrup intake increased 291 percent during that same period. American children now drink more soft drinks than milk, and 95 percent of all flour and 35 percent of red meat eaten in the United States are processed. Processed meats such as salami, bologna, frankfurters, and other sausages derive 85 percent of their calories from fat.

In addition, a revolution in our lifestyle has crowded out our eating pattern of three homemade meals a day. More than 35 percent of U.S. food dollars are now spent on meals away from home. Not counting the untold millions who subsist on snacking, we as a nation are existing on either "institutional" or "fast" foods.

The nutritional deficits of institutional food result from the additional factory processing involved and then the longer storage, cooking, and holding times in the institution's kitchen and steam tables. Fast-food outlets specialize in eliminating the waiting times between ordering and eating by offering foods that are cooked ahead of time and kept hot and processed items that are ready to eat.

Nutrient losses in fast foods are magnified by the extremely limited menus at most fast-food restaurants. Processed fats, extracted flour, and sugar (and therefore calories) predominate; up to 40 percent of calories in fried and grilled items are from fat, while sodas' calories are 100 percent sugar. Fast foods' sole plus is the hardiness of protein. And although some of these outlets are installing salad bars, many of the prepared salads are also commercially produced, while the "fresh" vegetables continue to lose nutrients as they sit in large serving bins.

Vitamins lose out the most in fast food. A and C are virtually unknown in these outlets. In 1980, a study of seven popular combinations sold at McDonald's detected vitamin E at only 2 to 8 percent of the USRDA, while pantothenic acid and folic acid averaged less than 15 percent each. Fiber is also low to nonexistent in fast foods.

Even meals eaten at home have changed tremendously since the turn of the century. The proliferation of "convenience foods"—factory-made dishes or meals that consumers can "heat and eat" or "just add milk and serve"—has caused further nutrient losses as well as steep increases in the chemical additives in our meals. Artificial colors, flavors, enhancers, stabilizers, and preservatives are all needed by the processor to make these products (of unknown age and industrial history) seem like appetizing foods.

But the worst case, on the homefront, is the disappearance altogether of meals, which have been replaced by that nonpareil of convenience—the snack food.

Snack foods are immediately ready to eat, have a high "satisfaction quotient" (courtesy of all that fat and sugar), and are virtually, but not completely, devoid of nutrients. Made mostly from refined sugar, extracted flour, and processed fats, snack foods skirt the limits of low nutrient density. And although they are billed as quick pick-me-ups between meals, these addictive and highly available products tend to nudge full meals out of the picture. Replacing meals, they displace the essential teamwork of nutrition.

THE TRANSFORMATION of our food-production system and our eating patterns is the result of twentieth-century forces beyond any one individual's control. There was no conspiracy to dilute the nutrient density of our diet, but it has happened. The proportion of empty and near-empty calories has risen steadily, matched by the decline in whole foods and other nutrient-rich sources. The result is a double-edged loss in nutrient density: fewer nutrients being delivered by more calories.

In 1971 at Dartmouth, Dr. Henry Schroeder painstakingly analyzed 723 foods to ascertain whether losses in storage and processing were such that Americans were failing to achieve the RDAs even on a relatively "adequate" diet. His conclusion? Individuals who subsist on refined, processed, and canned foods have no assurance of getting adequate amounts of the nutrients studied.[13] Twenty years later, Americans have increased their reliance on just these foods.

The near scarcity of vegetables and fruit (the chief source of many vitamins and trace minerals) spells trouble in itself. Thus, together with a food-production system that constantly reduces the nutrient density of our food supply, our own eating habits further limit the quality and variety of what we eat. For many of us, fewer and fewer essential nutrients reach our cells. With nourishment undermined in this fundamental way for so long, it is not surprising that, especially among adolescents, obesity, hyperactivity, concentration, and behavioral problems have been spreading, and that, among the general population, chronic disorders have increased.

5

Our Toxic World

THE RAPID SPREAD of industrialization and technology has affected not only our diet but the entire environment in which we live. We are now exposed daily to chemicals in our food, air, water, homes, and workplaces that either didn't exist or were barely used a hundred years ago. Despite the perils of altering the environment to which the earth's species have adapted over thousands of centuries, scientists have only begun to trace the impact of these changes on the web of life.

In *Silent Spring*, published in 1962, Rachel Carson vividly described the impact of DDT and other new pesticides on plants, animals, birds, and fish. Her portrait of a ghostly springtime in which no birds sing started the worldwide environmental movement. Although she was ridiculed at the time by industry and scientists, events confirmed her fears that what kills fish and birds is not good for humans.

- Air pollution "inversions" in New York and London in the 1960s killed many with heart and respiratory ailments.
- The abrupt 1975 shutdown of Life Science Products' Kepone pesticide plant on the James River, Virginia, and the subsequent findings of symptoms of Kepone poisoning in some 80 former employees.

- Buried toxic wastes at Love Canal in Niagara Falls poisoned a whole neighborhood.
- The entire town of Times Beach, Missouri, was abandoned in 1983 due to traces of dioxin in its road dust.
- In 1985, over two thousand residents of Bhopal, India, died from pesticide gas escaping a Union Carbide plant.

From the 25 percent rate of fatal cancers in groups of asbestos workers to the "deficits" in behavior and IQ of seemingly normal second-graders exposed to common sources of lead, humans are vulnerable, just like all other living things. As the Special Commission on Internal Pollution noted in 1977:

> It could hardly have been foreseen [in the 1930s] that the industrial production of chemicals was to grow so fast, and even less foreseen that within a generation the chemicals produced would affect every area of human and natural life. Just as there is no square inch of the earth's surface without its DDT molecules, there is no industrialized nation which does not depend absolutely on chemicals for the maintenance of its living standards, with the rest of the world aspiring to that dependence . . .
>
> What cannot be overlooked are the unknown consequences—among them the teratogenic and conceivably mutagenic effects—of the unremitting barrage of chemicals to which the populations of the industrialized world are subjected.[1]

Our health is threatened not only by individual chemicals—deadly or toxic—but even more by the overall chemical load the human organism now has to sustain.

- It has been estimated that the annual production of chemicals grew from 8 million tons at the end of World War II to more than 108 million tons in 1985.
- More than 4 million chemical compounds (at least sixty thousand of which are commercially produced) are now recognized, and new ones are continually being synthesized.
- In 1979, the Surgeon General noted that new chemical substances are being produced at a rate of one thousand each year—three each day.

- Over two hundred chemicals have been conclusively demonstrated to cause cancer in animals, and approximately thirty of these are officially recognized as human carcinogens. Some experts estimate that there are up to fifteen hundred carcinogens extant in our modern environment.

Only a small fraction of these chemicals have been adequately tested for their impact on our health. We have become technology's guinea pigs in a worldwide, uncontrolled experiment. On the one hand, it is now recognized that people can be made sick by their environment, that there are "ecological illnesses." On the other hand, we have little scientific understanding of either environmental toxins or ecological illness—for the most part we are still learning from our own tragic mistakes.

The environment is an encompassing biological system, one in which all living beings coexist in ever-shifting balances. The underlying rules of capability and need are defined by genetics and supplied by nutrition in ways scientists are only beginning to understand. But as to how the intricacies of genetics and nutrition interact with the environment, researchers have made only preliminary soundings. In particular, medicine has a very limited understanding of the burgeoning caseload of environmental illness. But in the emerging picture, two principles of environmental illness are critical.

In the first place, most environmental agents do not cause a specific disease or syndrome but a range of symptoms and diseases that vary from individual to individual. This principle—rooted in genetics—is important both in public health and for the clinicians trying to diagnose a patient.

The second principle reflects the first: Much ecological illness is not a reaction to a single agent but an accumulated response to many combined factors, or "stressors." This is technically known as the "total body load principle."

Even nonchemical stressors, whether a virus or a divorce, can finally trigger the illness that brings underlying chemical disorders to the attention of the patient and physician. Often reactions to synthetic chemicals are accompanied by allergies to ordinary foods or other "natural" substances that are used extensively in contemporary society.

These and other principles emerging in environmental medicine give hope that someday many diseases that now baffle us may be prevented or treated effectively—from cancer, the major environmental disease of our time, to some of the chronic debilitating conditions that have been called "the diseases of civilization." Moreover, there is growing evidence, beginning with lead poisoning and food dyes, that environmental factors play a role in learning and behavioral difficulties.

To understand the challenge of environmental illness, we must explore the complexity of host and agent interactions. Environmental chemicals are taken into the body by many routes—food, drinking water, the air we breathe, skin contact—and their particular toxic effects often depend on the route. Further, toxicity varies not only with different individuals' genetic predisposition and nutritional status but also with their lifestyle, level of stress, whether or not they drink or smoke, and so on.

Understanding and finally relating all these factors in ways that make compelling medical sense will prove an enormous challenge. But every step of progress in environmental medicine is welcome at a time when more and more people are becoming allergic to the twentieth century.

Food Contaminants

Extraordinary efforts are made by food producers to select, dye, flavor, texturize, and preserve their food products so they seem as ideal as possible. It is almost unnatural to think that our handsome, modern foods are contaminated with pollutants, pathogens, and toxins. Surely it never occurred to the 14,316 people struck by the 1985 Illinois salmonella outbreak that their supermarket milk was poisonous. In fact, the salmonella strain had become genetically resistant to both penicillin and tetracycline, killing an apparently healthy Rockford man and causing the largest such outbreak on record.

Even worse, in more ways than one, are the countless cases of invisible poisoning, the steady feeding of traces of potentially cancer-causing or nerve-destroying substances like PCBs, now found in many fish, or lead, which is at critical levels in the blood of 40 percent of children to the age of five in some cities.[2]

In all, there are four main kinds of food contaminants threatening us today.

1. Pesticides and other agricultural contaminants added to the food crop while it is growing.

2. Toxic industrial metals and synthetic compounds that contaminate water or soils (and thereby foodstuffs).
3. Packaging chemicals that leach into the food product.
4. Natural (biological) toxins, such as the Illinois salmonella, that can infect foods during storage, processing, or kitchen preparation.

Agricultural contamination enters the food chain right from the start. As noted earlier, the soil in which contemporary crops are grown has been altered chemically with commercial pesticides and fertilizers. The growing harvest is then sprayed with additional herbicides, insecticides, and other pesticides. In raising animals, many drugs and other chemicals are routinely added to the feed or injected into the flesh—penicillin, for instance, or hormone drugs like DES. After harvest or slaughter preservatives and still more pesticides are added to these foods.

The first pesticide/food scare was the great cranberry recall of 1959, when, just at Thanksgiving, the government found huge supplies contaminated with the herbicide aminotrazole. The cranberry producers argued that a little bit of herbicide never hurt anybody. But as Rachel Carson was then writing, these poisons aimed at simpler forms of life are also toxic to higher orders such as birds and fish . . . and humans. Yet, despite its historic impact, *Silent Spring* had little effect on its principal target, the blanket use of pesticides. Although there has been a shift away from compounds like DDT that persist in the environment indefinitely, the total volume dispersed in the United States continues to rise every year.

Pesticides are made up of a wide variety of toxic substances. They are used in both agriculture and indoors—in very large amounts. In California in 1980, for example, 268 million pounds were applied to food crops, of which 7.8 million pounds were substances found carcinogenic in test animals. Over 90 percent of all U.S. households use pesticides in the home, garden, or on lawns, many of which remain active for long periods. Chlordane, for example, lasts up to twenty years. At Bhopal, more than 2,000 people died and another 150,000 were injured in a single release of the pesticide methyl isocynate.

One enormous unintended side effect is that these poisons surface in our food supply. Today 94 percent of commercial foods contain pesticides, a constant source of low-level exposure to some of the most toxic chemicals ever made. Available evidence suggests that low-level pesticide exposures over time have wide-ranging toxic effects. Indeed, pesticides may be our worst single environmental health problem.

- Charles Benrook, head of the agricultural board at the National Academy of Sciences, says simply, "The weight of evidence is clear: exposure to pesticides is a cause of cancer."[3]
- Infants and children are susceptible to pesticide toxicity, as are adults with certain chronic illnesses.
- Once in the body, pesticides accumulate in target organs and tissues. Autopsy reports in a 1968 study of individuals who died from liver, brain, or neurological diseases showed significantly higher concentrations of pesticide residues in brain and fat tissue than control patients.
- Chronic pesticide exposures also appear to increase vitamin needs (particularly A and C), causing chronic deficits that may lead to general ill health or lowered resistance to other stresses.

In 1979, the House Subcommittee on Oversight and Investigations found that the EPA's pesticide tolerance program was inadequate to protect the public health.[4] That same year, EPA administrator Douglas Costle noted in a letter to the Senate Committee on Agriculture, Nutrition, and Forestry that "the scientific foundation of the tolerance program has not been systematically reexamined during the more than twenty years of federal experience in establishing pesticide tolerances."[5] Finally in 1986 the EPA, in a new ranking of priorities, put first on the list, ahead even of toxic wastes or chemical plant accidents, *pesticides already in use.*

After pesticides, the routine use of "subtherapeutic" doses of antibiotics in animal feeds and the injecting of hormones to promote growth present the most alarming agricultural risk. Their effectiveness has led to wide abuse. As Orville Schell wrote about the meat industry:

> Some farmers heavily overdose their animals with antibiotics to control diseases brought on by filthy and poorly heated barns. Others, desperate to get weak or even sick animals to market, will continue to administer a variety of drugs to their stock right up to the day they are shipped to the slaughterhouse. Still others will use illegal or banned drugs. More often than not, these violations will go undetected by the Department of Agriculture's meat inspectors.[6]

Even the moderate use of antibiotics in animal feed can result in the development of antibiotic-resistant bacteria and the subsequent transfer of these bacteria to humans (as occurred in the Illinois salmonella epidemic), or prompt an allergic response in individuals who are allergic to antibiotics.

Toxic metals and industrial compounds form the second largest class of food contaminants. The toxic elements include aluminum, arsenic, cadmium, copper, and nickel, but especially the highly poisonous mercury and lead. Once such toxins leach (or are dumped) into the water cycle, they start their climb up the food chain. Many of them, not being biodegradable, become increasingly concentrated at each higher level of consumption, accumulating in the fatty tissues instead of being excreted, particularly heavy metals like lead and mercury and chemicals like DDT.

Mercury wastes dumped by local chemical plants into Japan's Minimata Bay in the 1950s were converted by marine organisms to methyl-mercuric-chloride, which accumulated in fish that were a staple of the town's diet. Children born during that period had grotesque deformities as a result of the concentrated methyl-mercury poisoning they suffered in the womb.

Lead poisoning is far more extensive in America, particularly among the very young. As in the case of paint chips eaten by children, ingestion is a main route. Our food is contaminated by lead solder in tin cans, lead pipes in the water supply, and leaded gasoline emissions in air and soil that make their way into the food chain. The average American has 100 to 1,000 times more lead in his body than his prehistoric ancestors. In urban areas approximately 100 to 2,000 micrograms of lead are ingested with food every day.

High levels of body lead cause brain damage and, ultimately, death. Lower dosages involve permanent neuropsychological difficulties, behavior disorders, and anemia. More immediate symptoms include dizziness, nausea, and irritability. Follow-up studies of children who were overtly lead-poisoned have found the adults, ten to forty years later, with a range of serious conditions, including kidney disease, gout, arthritis, and psychological disturbances, as well as mental retardation. It is a most serious matter, then, that lead levels are so high in the U.S. food supply today. In the eyes of some experts, there are no demonstrably safe levels of lead in the human body.

In addition to toxic elements like mercury and lead, thousands of *industrial compounds*, known to be toxic or of dubious safety, are prevalent in the environment today and find their way up the food chain. The General Accounting Office has identified 143 drugs and chemicals that are likely to leave residues in raw poultry and meat, 42 of which are suspected carcinogens, 20 of which may cause birth defects, and 6 of which are suspected mutagens.

Packaging is the third major source of food contamination. Lead in soldered tin cans is hardly the only container pollutant. Plastic wraps and packages are often made of polymers that contain stabilizers, plasticizers, fillers, and colorants that can be toxic. Unreacted monomers in many of these substances may be released into food, including such toxic substances as acrylic acid, toluene, styrene, and vinyl chloride.

Natural toxins, chiefly bacteria and molds, are the fourth major contaminant.

- The commonest form of food poisoning is staphylococcal contamination. Staph germs are everywhere, but only build up toxic concentrations in foods that are not handled with proper hygiene, refrigeration, or heating. Symptoms usually subside within twelve hours.
- Salmonella poisoning is typically caused by infected chicken or pork—in the United States 3 to 4 percent of pork sausages are infected. Fortunately, salmonella are readily killed by heat. The familiar symptoms of diarrhea, cramps, and fever abate within a day or two, although critical illness can develop, as happened in the 1985 Illinois outbreak.
- The gravest form of food poisoning is botulism. The causative toxin is the single most potent biological poison known. Improperly canned low-acid foods (such as home-preserved fruits and vegetables) as well as canned meat, meat products, fish, and honey can be contaminated with spores of the bacteria. Symptoms include nausea, vomiting, blurred vision, and severe difficulty in breathing, swallowing, or speaking. The death rate from food-borne botulism, once as high as 60 percent, has been reduced to 10 percent.

Fungus or mold contamination, at low levels, is widely present in foods. Poisonous mushrooms are the most obvious example, but critical levels of mycotoxins, as they are called, including neurotoxins that attack the central nervous system, can build up on grains and other stored foodstuffs, especially when dampness and overlong storage permit the omnipresent fungi to thrive.

The most fabled is ergot, the mold on rye that is chemically related to LSD. In the Middle Ages bread made from the moldy grain reportedly sent whole villages rushing out of town in a hallucinogenic madness known as "St. Anthony's Fire." In the 1950s an outbreak occurred in France. So far virtually nothing is known about the behavioral dysfunctions and low-dose effects of these dietary poisons.

AGE-OLD CONTAMINANTS native to foodstuffs have always posed a variety of risks. To these *biological toxins* technology has added a host of others: *agricultural residues* (pesticides, antibiotics, hormonal agents), *toxic metals* (lead, mercury, and others), and questionable *packaging materials* (like PVC) that pass into the food.

Grossly toxic effects are usually recognized in muscular or central nervous system damage. But we know little about low-dose effects over time, particularly on delicate neurological, hormonal, and immune systems that are crucial to daily functioning and long-term well-being.

Anyone wondering about chemical treatment of foodstuffs before they reach the family table should remember that every serving of processed food has been treated with one or more of the following: acidifiers, alkalizers, anticaking, and antifoaming agents; artificial colors, flavors, and sweetners; bleaches, buffers, conditioners, curers, defoliants, deodorants, desiccants, disinfectants, emulsifiers, extenders, flavor enhancers, flavor fortifiers, hydrogenators, hydrolyzers, maturers, moisturizers, neutralizers, preservatives, thickeners. Ingredient labels often list three times as many artificial chemicals as real food components in the products we eat. These food additives fall into two very different groups.

- *Preservatives* are the basic additive because they meet an important biological need, preventing food-borne disease. In fact, it was biological food contaminants that originally gave rise to additives and additive processes such as salt curing and pickling, sugar curing, and smoke curing.
- All *other additives*, starting with the dyes, merely cater to what the producer hopes are the consumers' qualitative preferences.

The use of additives requires weighing risks versus benefits. Preservatives can afford a powerful benefit that offsets some level of risk, whereas other additives that increase the look or sales potential have much less substantive benefit to justify any risk they entail.

A good example of this is nitrites, which are almost always added to ham, luncheon meats, sausages, and bacon. Nitrites are both a preservative and a cosmetic. When nitrite-treated meat is heated, botulinum spores are destroyed. At the same time, by reacting with the iron-containing pigments in meat, nitrite produces a pink or red color that makes the meat appear fresh.

The health risks of nitrites are also twofold. In the human bloodstream, nitrites convert hemoglobin to methemoglobin, which cannot carry oxygen. Nitrites also combine with elements of saliva, tobacco, medications, and certain foods to form ***nitrosamines***, which are potent carcinogens.

Measures are now being taken to reduce the level of nitrites allowed in meat processing. Despite industry claims that nitrites are primarily used to kill bacteria, the desirability of pink, fresh-looking meats is the industry's prime motive in defending nitrites.

> A preservative may . . . be necessary in thick foods, such as ham, because these offer an oxygen-free environment, the kind in which botulinum can grow. The toxin would be destroyed in cooking. Laboratory studies demonstrate clearly that nitrite ***can*** kill botulinum, but whether it actually does in commercially processed meat is now being questioned. In a few foods, the level used may be too low to do anything but contribute to color.[7]

In 1966 the average American ingested three pounds of chemical food additives annually. By 1974 the figure had risen to five pounds, and today, it exceeds nine pounds.

Obviously the sheer bulk of food additives is disturbing—and yet, under current laws and regulations, it is almost impossible to control. Food additives are legally permitted in the food supply at the discretion of manufacturers so long as no positive demonstration has been made that they harm animals or humans. Despite the public's risks in consuming them, the law does not require that they be shown to benefit the public in any way.

Both the FDA and the USDA appear to be content to regulate specific additives only when powerful evidence against one arises, often at the insistence of outside scientists or consumer groups. Even as our ingestion of additives tripled in less than a generation, these agencies have not addressed such crucial issues as (1) overall additive exposures, (2) interacting exposures, and (3) very-low-dose effects over a lifetime. James Crow, chairman of the Genetics Department at the University of Wisconsin, has written:

> Special attention should be given to the danger of very low concentrations of highly mutagenic compounds that might be introduced into foodstuffs. . . . Even though the compounds may not be demonstrably mutagenic to man at the concentrations used, the total number of deleterious mutations induced in the whole population over a prolonged period of time could nevertheless be substantial.[8]

Despite the government's sleepiness, the number of food additives that have had to be banned in recent years is disturbing (see table 5). Most additives banned so far have been implicated in cancer. By contrast, even though there is increasing evidence that a much larger number of people are being harmed or put at risk, it remains extremely difficult to get additives banned on the grounds of allergic reactions or sensitivities to them, however widespread.

An example is the sulfite controversy. Certain sulfite compounds prevent fresh fruit and vegetables from browning—for instance, precut potatoes or the lettuce greens at restaurant salad bars. These compounds also trigger acute reactions in some individuals, including many asthma victims. Yet restaurants' use of sulfites, which increased rapidly in the 1980s, is mostly unknown to consumers. Moreover, many sulfite-sensitive individuals are not aware of their reaction potential. And the reactions can be extremely serious—fifteen sulfite fatalities were documented from 1983 to 1985. Indeed, sulfites are the only food additive in the last twenty years known to have killed anyone. For years the FDA, while admitting these agents provoke attacks in an unknown number of people and 5 to 10 percent of asthma victims, refused outright to consider a ban. Finally, in 1985 it agreed to review the matter and banned sulfites a year later.

Although most additive bans have occurred on the narrow but urgent issue of cancer, the evidence is growing that additives undermine human

TABLE 5
Partial List of Additives That Have Been Banned[9]

Additive	*Function*	*Source*	*Last Used*	*Reason for Ban*
Agene (nitrogen trichloride)	Flour bleaching and aging agent	Synthetic	1949	Dogs that ate bread made from treated flour suffered epilepticlike fits; the toxic agent was methionine sulfoxime
Dyes	Artificial coloring	Synthetic		
Butter Yellow			1919	Toxic, later found to cause liver cancer
FD&C Green 1			1965	Liver cancer
FD&C Orange 1			1956	Organ damage
FD&C Orange 2			1960	Organ damage
FD&C Red 1			1961	Liver cancer
FD&C Red 4			1976	High levels damaged adrenal cortex of dog; after 1965 used only in maraschino cherries and certain pills; still allowed in externally applied drugs and cosmetics

health more broadly. Whether in chronic conditions such as asthma or allergy, mood disturbances or nervous system dysfunctions like migraine or hyperactivity in children, additives have to be given much more scientific and official attention. Until now the government has tended to face the issue only after great public pressure, only very slowly with much hemming and hawing, and only focusing on the one additive then in dispute. Meanwhile, the number of additives and the sheer tonnage being mixed into the food supply continue to rise.

TABLE 5 *(Continued)*

Additive	*Function*	*Source*	*Last Used*	*Reason for Ban*
FD&C Red 32			1956	Damages internal organs and may be a weak carcinogen; since 1956 used under the name Citrus Red 2 to color oranges (2 ppm)
Sudan 1			1919	Toxic, later found to be carcinogenic
FD&C Yellow 1 and 2			1959	Intestinal lesions at high dosages
FD&C Yellow 3			1959	Heart damage at high dosages
FD&C Yellow 4			1959	Heart damage at high dosages
FD&C Violet 1			1973	Cancer
FD&C Red 2			1976	Possible carcinogen
Cobalt salts	Stabilize beer foam	Synthetic	1966	Toxic effect on heart
Coumarin	Flavoring	Tonka bean	1954	Liver poison
Cyclamate	Artificial sweetener	Synthetic	1970	Bladder cancer
Diethylpyrocarbonate (DEPC)	Preservative (beverages)	Synthetic	1972	Combines with ammonia to form urethan, a carcinogen

TABLE 5 *(Continued)*

Additive	*Function*	*Source*	*Last Used*	*Reason for Ban*
Dulcin (p-ethoxyphenyl urea)	Artificial sweetener	Synthetic	1950	Liver cancer
Ethylene glycol	Solvent, humectant	Synthetic		Kidney damage
Monochloroacetic acid	Preservative	Synthetic	1941	Highly toxic
Nordihydroguaiaretic acid (NDGA)	Antioxidant	Desert	1971*	Kidney damage
Oil of calamus	Flavoring	Root of calamus	1968	Intestinal cancer
Polyoxyethylene-8-stearate (Myrj 45)	Emulsifier (used in baked goods)	Synthetic	1952	High levels caused bladder stones and tumors
Safrole	Flavoring (root beer)	Sassafras	1960	Liver cancer
Thiourea	Preservative	Synthetic	c. 1950	Liver cancer

SOURCE: M. F. Jacobson, *The Complete Eater's Digest and Nutrition Scoreboard* (Garden City, N.Y.: Anchor Press/Doubleday, 1985), pp. 361–62. Used by permission.
*NDGA was banned by the FDA in 1968, but the Department of Agriculture did not ban it until 1971.

Water Pollution

In the late 1980s millions of Americans paid more for a quart of clean water than for a quart of oil. This is understandable, since the public water supply has been increasingly contaminated with various levels of toxic chemicals that have been shown to cause illness, birth defects, or cancer.

Water pollution first surfaced as a major problem for society in the nineteenth century when, with the growth of dense cities, raw sewage, leaching into nearby wells, increasingly contaminated the public drinking water. Cities across Europe and America responded by constructing separate underground systems for *pure water supply* coming in and, going out, *waste water sewerage.* The second phase of water pollution control, which is still being constructed, adds treatment to both of these systems: Drinking water is filtered and then purified with chlorine, and waste water is subjected to one or more levels of sewage treatment. Yet sophisticated cities like Los Angeles and New York, not to mention countless smaller towns, still dump raw sewage into waterways or the ocean. The massive program to build municipal treatment plants across the nation, launched by the Water Pollution Control Act in 1972 and costing hundreds of billions of dollars, may someday bring this, the original pollution problem, under control.

The twentieth-century proliferation of industry and the dawn of the chemical age have introduced new, far more complex, subtle, and sometimes lethal pollutants into the water cycle. The municipal systems of upgraded treatment plants—despite their staggering cost—do not detect, much less detoxify, the majority of these chemical pollutants. Many of our waters are now as badly tainted with chemicals as they were with bacteria before chlorination.

As numerous as oil spills have become, synthetic chemicals pose a greater problem of both detection and management. Our waters are polluted by any combination of more than sixty thousand synthetic chemicals produced annually in America. For example:

- *Polychlorinated biphenyls* (PCBs) are found in hydraulic fluids, plasticizers, adhesives, printing products . . . and in many parts of the Great Lakes, the Hudson River, the Mediterranean Sea, in fish, humans, and mother's milk. More than two hundred types have been manufactured, and different types have different properties. As the Surgeon General noted in 1979: "Not until tens of millions of pounds were produced and released into the environment was there any realization of how toxic and persistent these substances are."[10]
- *Dioxin*, one of the most potent carcinogens known, arises in the manufacturing of defoliants (such as Agent Orange) and may be a product of simple combustion. Dioxin achieved notoriety in the latter 1970s as the most lethal of the toxic wastes dumped by Occidental Petroleum into Love Canal at Niagara Falls; as the

contaminant of white fish in the Great Lakes; and as the parts-per-billion trace in the road dust that turned Times Beach, Missouri, into a ghost town.

- *Polybrominated biphenyls* (PBBs) are manufactured fire retardants. As reported in the *Journal of the American Medical Association*, "Studies of maternal-infant pairs of blood specimens showed that PBBs cross the placenta. They concentrate in the fat of breast milk. A survey of breast milk specimens indicated that about 96% of the people living in the lower peninsula of Michigan have PBBs in their body fat."[11]
- *Ethylene dibromide* (EDB) is a pesticide widely used in the citrus industry. In the early 1970s, animal tests warned that EDB was a potent carcinogen, but it was only in October 1983 that most of its agricultural uses were finally banned. By that time, EDB had contaminated groundwater in Florida, Hawaii, California, and Georgia.

In theory, these threats to our water supply and health should be curtailed by the Water Pollution Control Act of 1972, with its scheme of effluent standards, self-reporting by facilities, and governmental spot checks. Unfortunately, the act is a regulatory latticework. Small plants are not regulated or effectively monitored, and large companies are known to falsify reports, engage in midnight dumping, bribe government officers, and cut deals with shady disposal companies that are often linked to organized crime.

The system is also quite vulnerable to the winds of political change. The first Reagan administration brutally subordinated the nation's environmental programs to suit special interest groups. The EPA was crippled in its task of inspecting, testing, enforcing, and even in releasing congressionally allocated funds. The federal construction grants that had allowed many municipalities to establish or upgrade sewage treatment plants (which were passed in the 1970s and began to have an environmental impact in the 1980s) were cut shortly before Reagan left office and have not been restored.

The case of General Electric and the Hudson is a classic example of the conflicting interests that are involved in controlling industrial water pollution. When the Hudson's PCB problem was discovered—crippling the region's commercial fisheries—General Electric never contested that it had been releasing PCBs into the river. But it held that the releases were within the legal limits prescribed in the permit it had secured from the state. When the state's environmental commissioner commenced proceedings against G.E., pressing for substantial penalties against the company, a storm of protest broke out, not only from General Electric but from other companies in New York State. Indeed, in April of 1976, the Associated Industries of New York State (which claimed to represent 2,000 companies) filed a petition at the state hearings stating that action against General Electric would have "far-reaching and serious economic consequences" to its members—prompting General Electric to express gratification that the other businesses in the state had "recognized the importance and impact" of the hearings.

Faced with a potentially serious blow to its economy, the state eventually arrived at a settlement in which G.E. paid a total of $4 million and was then absolved from further liability. But not before the total cost of cleaning the river was estimated at $20 million, G.E. itself had proposed paying only $2 million, and the incumbent environmental commissioner felt compelled to resign from office—in part over his tough stand against G.E.

General Electric is only one of the myriad industrial polluters who continue to compromise the nation's waterways and water supplies. The difficulties inherent in monitoring and regulating such pollution are only compounded when the culprit stands outside the already limited range of the Environmental Protection Agency. But the Justice Department has consistently denied the EPA the right to police or intercede with one of the nation's worst polluters—the Defense Department.

The American military establishment generates nearly a ton of toxic pollutants every minute, ranging from the residue of chemical weapons tests to tons of radioactive materials. Unchecked by EPA inspections and out of sight of most environmental activists, the poisonous by-products of the military establishment have been mishandled for decades, and they are surfacing in the water supplies of neighboring civilian communities.[12] For example:

- In Mountainview, New Mexico (a community downstream of the Kirtland Air Force Base), well water has been contaminated by nitrates and nitroaromatic compounds such as nitroglycerine and nitrobenzene—both of which are used in the manufacture of explosives.

- At the Lakehurst Naval Air Station in New Jersey, more than 3 million gallons of carcinogenic aviation fuel and other toxins have leached into the underground aquifer that supplies much of South Jersey's water. Toxins have been found in water in concentrations as high as ten thousand times above the state's "safe" levels.
- At the Cornhusker Army Ammunition Plant in Nebraska, army officials waited a full year to inform local residents that at least eight hundred wells had been contaminated with explosive compounds.

Even in cases where the EPA *can* gain access to possible pollution sources a number of factors continue to impede the effort to clean up the water supply, including: identifying pollutants, controlling discharges, regulating production, and dealing with wastes.

The *identification of pollutants* entails isolating and testing the tens of thousands of chemical compounds produced in the United States each year, as well as their interaction with each other. Given the fact that there are more than 4 million recognized chemical compounds, with approximately one thousand new ones produced each year, comprehensive testing is virtually impossible. The time and money involved in animal testing, coupled with ever-changing technologies, make it impossible to keep up with production. In 1988, shortly before taking over as the head of the EPA, William Riley noted that we have information on the human health effects of less than 2 percent of all man-made chemicals. As a result, many harmful chemicals are not recognized as a public danger until an animal or human disaster occurs, and many other substances continue to pervade the environment at subthreshold levels.

Controlling the discharge of pollutants is hampered by the fact that the Clean Water Act covers only "point" sources of pollution—identifiable industrial discharge points such as pipes and sewers. But "nonpoint" sources such as agricultural and urban runoff and the leaching of industrial and military wastes from storage sites and landfills pose a tremendous (and unregulated) risk to waterways, reservoirs, and groundwater. The once widely used pesticide Temik, for example, is known to have contaminated more than one thousand wells on Long Island, where it was used extensively by potato farmers.

While the *regulation or outright banning* of known toxins is an increasingly popular alternative among environmentalists, it is also vehemently opposed by those who manufacture and use these chemicals—

including thousands of farmers. Temik, for example, was popular because it is an extremely effective pesticide. Since the Clean Water Act does not regulate these sources of pollution, a federal ban is often impossible.

While Temik was withdrawn from agricultural use on the North Fork of Long Island in 1980 (and several years later the state of New York decided to ban its use throughout the state), it continued to be used by Florida citrus growers until 1983, when a temporary ban was imposed after its neurotoxic active ingredient was found in at least eight Florida wells. In 1984, after extensive research, Florida once again allowed the use of Temik, under stringent limits and careful monitoring.

The current methods for dealing with known point sources of pollution consist of filtering noxious substances out of liquid wastes. While this seems a good compromise, the fact remains that many newer pollutants escape our current filtration systems. In addition, we have yet to figure out what to do with the thousands of tons of toxic sludge that are screened out of industrial effluents. Much of this deadly glop is simply shifted to a nonpoint source, like a landfill or toxic waste dump, where it leaches into the water supply over time, and a significant portion is illegally dumped in the ocean.

New York State is still trying to devise a way to clean PCB-contaminated silt and sludge out of the Hudson River, but the most recent cleanup proposal (presented in 1980) has been stalled by economic questions. Simply removing the sludge from "hot spots" in the river will cost at least $280 million and present the problem of where to safely dispose of or store the toxins. Technologies have been developed that can break down toxic compounds into less harmful or mobile forms—but using these techniques will take an undertermined amount of additional funding. With General Electric absolved of any further responsibility for the PCB mess, New York State must either fund the cleanup itself or involve the EPA, which can force General Electric to fund the cleanup under Superfund.

Ultimately, these chemicals and wastes *will* surface in our drinking water. The problem of maintaining a safe water supply, which we thought was resolved with the advent of modern sewer systems and sewage treatment plants, has returned with a vengeance. And it will not be easily solved.

Tests on the underground water supplies of 954 cities found that nearly 30 percent were contaminated, while seventeen pesticides (including the known carcinogens aldicarb and ethylene dibromide) have been found in the groundwater of twenty-three states. The purification systems that remove biological contaminants have proved ineffective against many of these chemicals.

The groundwater problem is exacerbated by a rising demand that is depleting many groundwater reserves faster than nature can restore them. In the words of Rep. Mike Synar of Oklahoma (chairman of the House Environment and Natural Resources subcommittee): "We are sitting on a time bomb."[13]

In many areas the groundwater is not only contaminated, it is falling too rapidly to meet the future needs of agricultural and domestic use. The Ogallala aquifer, which supplies water to eight states in the Great Plains, supplies water to 20 percent of America's irrigated cropland. At the current rate of water use, the groundwater supply beneath Texas will have dropped by more than two thirds—and the groundwater beneath New Mexico will be completely gone—by the year 2020.

Air Pollution

The problem of air pollution, like water pollution, has been with us for centuries. In 1273 a foggy and increasingly smoky London passed the first air pollution law. Thirty-three years later, in 1306, a local man was tried and executed for illegally burning coal. While we have yet to impose capital punishment on convicted polluters, the modern problem of our filthy atmosphere has been driven home by many notorious air pollution incidents, including:

- The 1930 air emergency in an industrialized valley in Belgium (sixty dead, six thousand sick).
- The 1948 air inversion in Donora, Pennsylvania, that left twenty people dead and more than six thousand sick.
- The suffocating smog that wrapped London in 1952, killing four thousand people and sickening tens of thousands of others.

These early incidents have been followed by hundreds more in which cities such as New York and Los Angeles have been held virtual prisoners by the dangerous levels of carbon monoxide, sulfur oxide, and other pollutants that hang in their skies. Citizens are warned to stay indoors, and hundreds of people with respiratory problems sicken or die from the toxic effects of the gaseous chemical soup known as "smog."

Smog is the deadly by-product of sunlight combining with hydrocarbons, nitrogen oxides, and particulates (minute particles of soot and other solids) to form a photochemical mixture of secondary pollutants, including the highly irritating and toxic chemical formaldehyde. When a temperature inversion (high warm air seals in cooler air near the ground) occurs, this stagnant soup not only damages trees and human lungs, it can corrode steel buildings.

When evaluating our current crisis, it is useful to compare our modern air pollution problem with the "natural" polluters of our world—most notably volcanoes. In 1815, the volcano Tambora spewed 220 million tons of particulates into the stratosphere, and in this century, the most recent eruption of Mount Saint Helens dumped up to thirty tons of sulfur dioxide into the air each day it erupted. The industrialized world, on the other hand, expels more than *74,000 tons* of sulfur dioxide into the atmosphere *every day of the year.* And that is just one of the thousands of compounds released each day. Others include particulates, nitrogen oxides, hydrocarbons, carbon monoxide, lead, and ozone-destroying fluorocarbons.

When we breathe these substances they bypass the normal detoxification mechanisms of digestion and are absorbed directly into the bloodstream via the lungs. While some are excreted through the kidneys, most (particularly toxic metals such as lead) accumulate in the body's cells, where they cause untold and often permanent damage. A recent study at the University of Southern California illustrated just how damaging these airborne pollutants can be to individuals.[14] In autopsies of one hundred youths who had died from nonmedical causes (violence, accidents, and so forth) they found that 80 percent had significant abnormalities in their lung tissue and 27 percent had serious lesions. As the primary investigator, Dr. Russell Sherwin, put it, these young people were literally "running out of lung."

The federal clean air strategy was meant to curtail the release of these toxins, and it focused on the most obvious sources of pollution—smokestacks and automobiles. Ambient air quality standards were set as goals for each urban area, and the auto industry was compelled to install catalytic converters that would reduce car emissions. These measures did have some effect, but the problem of airborne lead and lead poisoning has persisted. Although the EPA in 1984 ordered a further 90 percent reduction in lead emissions from gasoline, the consequences will haunt this society for decades into the future. For example, more than half the children living near a major roadway display toxic levels of lead in their bloodstreams.

Air pollution has proven to be even more intractable than water pollution, and it took the EPA and state agencies a decade to show improvement in cities' air quality. In the interim, other air pollution concerns began to rear their heads, including acid rain and snow, the depletion of the atmosphere's protective ozone layer, and a frightening number of toxic leaks from chemical plants.

Acid precipitation was first observed in Canada. It is formed when pollutants (particularly sulfur dioxide and nitrogen oxides) change chemically in the atmosphere and fall to earth in rain, snow, or dust. Its effects on plants and aquatic life are horrifying. In Ontario and the Adirondack mountains hundreds of lakes have been rendered lifeless, while forests throughout eastern Canada, the Pacific Northwest, and central Europe have been decimated. In West Germany alone, thousands of acres of woodland (including some in the Black Forest) have died, and more than 200,000 acres are seriously damaged. And with the fall of the Iron Curtain the atmospheric and environmental toll of industrial air pollution in Eastern Bloc countries has been revealed.

The pollutants that are infiltrating precipitation are also causing extensive and possibly permanent damage in the atmospheric envelope that protects the planet and its inhabitants from the more harmful effects of the sun. Although there have been heated debates over global warming and the health significance of the depleted ozone layer, such arguments are extraneous and foolish. Global warming *will* occur if we continue to pour carbon dioxide into the atmosphere at the current rate of *5 billion metric tons* each year. These gases absorb the infrared light emitted by the earth and trap it in the atmosphere—warming the earth's surface. If the planet warms by only five degrees in the next hundred years the polar ice caps could melt (raising the sea level by up to twenty feet), and now-fertile lands will become desert.

The ozone layer, meanwhile, has developed a hole the size of the United States, courtesy of the depredations of such ozone-destroying chemicals as chlorofluorocarbons, halon, methyl chloroform, carbon tetrachloride, and hydrofluorocarbons. These chlorine-containing chemicals are used in everything from fire extinguishers to Styrofoam coffee cups. Although fifty-nine countries have committed themselves to stop production of most of these chemicals by the year 2020 (at the latest), many others—particularly economically disadvantaged nations such as China and India—continue to resist for economic reasons.

Economic reasons are also at the root of the progressive destruction of the earth's forests—from the rain forests of Brazil to the woodlands of the Pacific Northwest. Less than 55 percent of the world's rain forests remain intact, and if deforestation continues at its present rate they will be gone by 2035. Each year, an area the size of Washington State is cleared of forest.

These trees and plants are more than just pretty areas featured on nature specials. They are the homes of countless endangered and unique species of plants and animals, and also the "glue" that prevents erosion. Rain forests exist in a remarkably thin layer of topsoil (the bulk of nutrients are maintained in the forest itself), and when they are cut down the remaining land is only marginally fertile and quickly depleted. Even more important, the world's forests are the lungs of the planet, and they are suffering from progressive emphysema. Trees and plants cool the air and convert carbon dioxide to oxygen—a fact that has led some urban planners to suggest that more trees be planted in cities to help diminish smog.

Beyond the risks of acid rain, smog, and the depleted ozone layer, *toxic emissions* from chemical plants top the world's list of unaddressed air pollution problems. The accidental releases of toxic gases at Union Carbide plants in Bhopal, India, and Institute, West Virginia, and at a Sequoyah Fuels facility at Gore, Oklahoma, exposed a dangerous world of toxic emissions that the Clean Air strategy never addressed. They fall into four general groups:

1. Synthetic organic chemicals such as benzene and many pesticides.
2. Naturally occurring chemicals like chlorine, ammonia, and the hydrogen flouride that killed one young man at Gore.
3. Fibers such as the carcinogenic asbestos.
4. Toxic metals such as mercury, cadmium, and nickel.

Setting standards to prevent tragedies such as Bhopal and Gore is hampered by many factors, including the fact that many companies set up their factories in Third World countries precisely so they can avoid strict regulations and government inspections.

Even in the United States, the regulation of these chemicals is influenced by economic considerations. For example, EPA pollution standards have generally permitted risks to human life of no more than one in a million to one in a hundred thousand. While Anne McGill Burford was administrator of the EPA in the early 1980s, the agency adopted rules for formaldehyde and several pesticides that permitted risks of one in one thousand or higher. Commenting on these higher risks, Robert E. Yuhnke (a regional counsel for the Environmental Defense Fund) noted that such decisions showed a "pattern of sacrificing human health for the economic well-being of industry."

Sometimes these health risks are posed as a macabre trade-off for economic gains. In 1983, for instance, 575 jobs at the ninety-three-year-old Asarco copper smelter in Tacoma, Washington, were imperiled by the threatened closing of the plant, which fills the surrounding air with about thirty micrograms of arsenic per cubic yard of air. The EPA asked Tacoma residents which they would prefer—a health risk of two deaths per hundred citizens exposed to the arsenic, or the loss of 575 jobs when the plant closed. In the politics of air pollution, it is almost always the average citizen (and his or her lungs) who loses out.

Indoor Chemicals

When smog alerts, ozone alerts, and temperature inversions render the outside air dangerous, weathermen and health experts advise us to stay indoors to avoid the bad air. But today even the indoors—like the mountaintops scarred by acid rain—is not safe from pollution.

Reports are more frequent every year of office workers or shopping mall customers coming down with "unexplainable" eye and skin irritations, headaches, or respiratory problems. In Encino, California, for example, bank customers complained of headaches, nausea, and vomiting after transacting business. Testing found that the concentration of carbon monoxide *in* the bank was twenty times higher than the national ambient air quality standard for *outdoor* air.

In the long run indoor pollution may pose a more serious health threat than outdoor air pollution. Board-certified allergist and ecologist Dr. Alfred Zamm found that the air in a sample of typical American homes contained carbon monoxide, nitric oxide, and nitrogen dioxide in concentrations up to four times the maximum recommended by federal guidelines.[15] These findings are particularly disturbing since newer homes are increasingly airtight, so that air exchange is limited and noxious vapors can build up to even greater toxic levels. It is possible that indoor carbon monoxide levels could rise to three times that of heavily polluted urban air outdoors, nitric oxide to five times peak outdoor levels, and nitrogen dioxide to ten times the ambient levels in inner cities.

Preventing, as well as detecting and treating, ailments arising from indoor pollution is frustrated by both the declining quality of our indoor environment and the dearth of information on indoor environmental hazards. Health effects, emission-control technology, techniques for measuring ambient concentrations, interactions among pollutants, and ways to protect a population are not well understood. Even when a problem is well defined—as in the cases of formaldehyde, asbestos, and lead—remedies are not always implemented.

Formaldehyde vapors in homes and offices emanate from urea-formaldehyde foam insulation, from resin adhesives in particle board, and from formaldehyde found in textiles, plywood, carpeting, and molded plastics. Formaldehyde is also used in antiperspirants and as an antiseptic in dentifrices, mouthwashes, germicidals, and detergent soaps. It is found in hair-setting compounds and shampoo and is included in air deodorizers.

Surgical instruments and sickrooms are disinfected with formaldehyde. As a preservative, it is an ingredient in embalming fluids and such products as waxes, fats, oils, polishes, and adhesives. It is also used to make natural and synthetic fibers crease resistant, wrinkle resistant, shrinkproof, mothproof, and more elastic. It is a resin in nail polish. And since combustion produces significant amounts of formaldehyde, tobacco smoking, gas stoves, wood stoves, and kerosene space heaters increase its concentration in indoor air.

Asbestos compounds are prized for their resistance to heat and chemicals, high tensile strength, and flexibility. As a result, they are used in thousands of commercial products including thermal insulation, floor tiles, and heat-resistant textiles. For all its remarkable properties, however, asbestos has been known to cause lung and related cancers. There has been a soaring caseload of asbestos illnesses beyond the factory gate. Asbestos was freely used in construction from 1946 to 1973, when its spray application was severely curtailed by EPA's new Standards for Hazardous Air Pollutants. Other applications of asbestos have since been banned, but the 500,000 tons of asbestos-containing materials already sprayed remain a serious problem.

An estimated 15 million children are exposed to asbestos at school. A 1983 EPA report estimated that 66 percent of the nation's schools had failed to report asbestos conditions threatening the health of students, as required, to say nothing of remedying the peril. The U.S. Department of Education has estimated the cost of removing the asbestos at about $100,000 *per school building.* And the EPA has projected that because of prevalent (nonpeak) exposures, at least 1,100 people (and possibly as many as 6,800) will die prematurely of cancers from the asbestos now in schools.

Lead is also an indoor health hazard, principally in lead water pipes and, among newer homes, in lead solder used on copper water pipes, as well as in cigarette smoke, plastics, and the lead paint used for many years in homes and buildings. Soft and acidic water has been implicated in the breakdown of cadmium, copper, and lead from pipes. The result is a steady low-level exposure.

The case against the older lead-based paint is well known. A main cause of lead poisoning in children, the paint has been banned for most uses, and a massive campaign to remove older paint wherever there are children has been under way in many cities in hopes of preventing the devastating effects of lead on child development.

Combustion (in stoves, heaters, clothes dryers, automobile exhaust, fireplaces, and tobacco smoking) is the source of many additional indoor pollutants: carbon monoxide, nitrogen oxides, carbon dioxide, formaldehyde, and sulfur oxides. As home insulation has improved and wood stoves and kerosene space heaters have become more popular, low-level toxic gases in the home are on the rise.

Occupational Exposures

Chimney sweeps in eighteenth-century England hold the dubious honor of being the first patients ever diagnosed with a disease caused by their working environment. Percival Pott, a surgeon, noted the high rate of cancer of the scrotum of young men who had been chimney sweeps in their childhood. He correctly traced the cancer to coal tar exposure.

In the eighteenth and nineteenth centuries, hatmakers used mercury in the preparation of felt. The resulting toxic psychosis was immortalized in Lewis Carroll's frenetic character the Mad Hatter. Today these illnesses and others ranging from migraine to sterility threaten many of the approximately 100 million workers in this country. The Public Health Service, in 1980, summarized the health implications of occupational exposure:[16]

- Occupational exposure can produce acute or chronic lung disease, cancers, sensory loss, skin disorders, degenerative diseases in a number of vital organ systems, birth defects, or genetic changes.
- Exposure to some agents can also increase the frequency of stillbirths, spontaneous abortions, reduced fertility, and sterility.
- Skin diseases are the largest group of occupational illness, followed by repeated trauma.
- About 15 percent of coal miners exhibit some chest X-ray evidence of coal workers' pneumoconiosis, and black lung disease may be responsible for four thousand deaths each year.

While there have been improvements in the field of occupational safety and health, the latter half of the 1980s showed significant declines. In 1989, the Public Health Service's report, *Health, United States*, noted that between 1983 and 1987 there were increases in the rate of work-related disabling injuries, the incidence of occupational skin diseases, and the rate of lost workdays from injuries (which was higher in 1987 than at any time in the previous decade).

The same chemicals that are implicated in indoor pollution in homes are culprits in occupational exposures. In all, nearly 34,000 chemicals found in the workplace have toxic effects, and over 2,000 of these are potential human carcinogens. Asbestos, for example, is the single most carcinogenic substance known. By the end of this century, an estimated 10,000 people a year will die from asbestos-caused disease. That is the price for exposing 27.5 million workers (and countless schoolchildren) to asbestos over the last forty years. As many as 30 percent of exposed workers succumb to asbestosis, mesothelioma, and other cancers of the lung, oral cavity, larynx, esophagus, colon, stomach, kidney, and of the linings of the thoracic and abdominal cavities. These diseases can result from a brief exposure and have latency periods of up to thirty years.

Ethylene dibromide (EDB), a pesticide, had been suspected of causing cancer for at least ten years before any action was taken to protect workers and consumers. In 1983 eight different risk assessments by EPA and OSHA showed excess cancer death ranging from seventy to ninety-nine for every thousand workers regularly exposed to the *legal* limit of EDB in air.

Dioxin and Agent Orange (a defoliant that contains dioxin) have been linked to cancer, liver damage, neurological problems, loss of sex drive, dizziness, and problems in breathing. Dioxin has been documented as 150,000 times as toxic as cyanide and up to 670 times more lethal than strychnine. Yet Rita Lavelle, former head of the EPA's toxic waste cleanup (before she was indicted for perjury), complained that it got her "mad that some scientists are saying that dioxin is the most deadly chemical known to man. That's not true. It depends on the concentration. In the right concentration, table salt is just as deadly."[17]

It has been shown that a dose of dioxin of a mere 5 parts per *1,000 billion* is carcinogenic. The concentration of dioxin in the homes near Love Canal was as high as 17.2 parts per *million.* Even by Ms. Lavelle's dubious standards, the concentration at Love Canal was considerably more deadly than table salt.

Because of the prevalence of these and other pollutants and toxins, the workplace is where individuals most quickly demonstrate the effects of chemical exposures, particularly behavioral and reproductive problems. For example:

- Manganese miners in the early stages of toxicity exhibit "locura manganica" or managense madness, characterized by pathological laughter.
- Within a few months of starting use of a foaming agent called Lucel-7, four Texas workers developed dysfunctions of the central and peripheral nervous systems including neuromuscular problems, loss of memory, decreased attention span, and loss of peripheral and color vision.
- In 1977 several men engaged in the manufacture of DBCP consulted physicians after discovering that none of them was having any

> luck conceiving a child. Tests revealed that all the men had abnormal sperm counts—some with no sperm at all and others with levels well below that necessary to conceive children.

A hundred years ago, coal miners took canaries with them down into the shafts. When the canaries stopped singing and/or died, they knew it was time to get out. Today, millions of American workers are serving as our canaries, and they are clearly telling us that many of our work environments are not all that safe.

At labor's urging, the government has become acutely aware of the health hazards in the workplace, but what constitutes a safe workplace often gets lost in the conflicting interests of management and labor. Employees (and their insurers) want to know which chemicals they handle and breathe at work. Management says that such disclosures would reveal trade secrets.

Management, in turn, wants to conduct genetic screening to identify employees predisposed to illnesses that can arise in particular workplaces. Critics of genetic screening say it would place the blame for illness on the worker's "faulty" genes. Consensus is not in sight. As long as this is the case, there are implications for both public and private health practice that demand special attention. With more than one quarter of the work force potentially at risk, physicians must consider on-the-job exposures in diagnosis and treatment, and integrate questions about workplace conditions into their usual patient histories.

Toxic Wastes

The controversies that plague the field of occupational safety are only magnified when dealing with the problem of toxic wastes. There are an estimated thirty thousand toxic dumps across the nation, as well as fifty thousand "unofficial" sites in an inestimable array of ponds, creeks, roadbeds, landfills, lakes, warehouses, mines, and abandoned factories. There are at least twenty thousand such sites on land that is (or was) owned by the military. The Office of Technology Assessment has estimated that for every individual in the country, a ton of hazardous waste is added to the environment each year.

As was noted earlier, the federal government itself, principally the

Defense and Energy departments, is the leading offender against waste storage standards. The Pentagon is predictably tight-lipped on the subject, but the *Wall Street Journal* reported in 1983:

> Around the country, hundreds of federal facilities spew out more hazardous chemicals each day than the three or four largest chemical companies combined. According to some estimates, the armed forces alone must dispose of more than 400,000 tons of liquid wastes annually. . . .
>
> By any yardstick, the extent of the government's pollution problem is staggering. At the Energy Department's Oak Ridge laboratory in Tennessee, for example, since 1950 a total of 2.4 million pounds of toxic mercury used in nuclear-weapons production have leaked into the nearby ground and waterways. The state contends some of the discharges were 3,000 times above legally permitted levels, but the responsible federal and local environmental officials weren't notified.[18]

Virtually no community is safe from these hazardous materials. It is estimated that more than 90 percent of the hazardous waste in the United States is handled improperly, including enormous quantities dumped illegally into the oceans. By the end of the century there will be 265 million gallons of high-level nuclear waste (and more than a billion of low-level waste) in permanent and "temporary" storage, including the waste from the construction of the Hiroshima and Nagasaki bombs.

Unlike industrial exposures, which primarily affect working adults, toxic dumps and wastes are encroaching on a growing list of residential areas, taking their major toll on the health of children. Miscarriage rates among women living closest to the Love Canal waste site were triple the national average, and a study by the homeowners' association showed that 56 percent of children born in the vicinity of the canal had physical or mental disabilities. Among the other, more visible, damages due to toxic wastes are greatly increased rates of respiratory ailments, birth defects, reproductive disorders, and various forms of cancer.

At present, the famous Superfund—revenues from a tax on chemical stocks—is the main strategy for cleaning up waste sites. However, the Superfund accomplished virtually nothing in its first five years, and the EPA has estimated it will take at least $16 billion just to clean up the country's most hazardous sites.

An alternative strategy is to ban the worst of these chemicals. Dioxin, for one, is too dangerous to be anywhere. In another approach, some companies are finding that they can actually make money by detoxifying their wastes.

- Allied Chemical's plant in Metropolis, Illinois, recycles calcium fluoride, a toxic by-product that had accumulated at the plant for seven years. By investing $4.3 million in a "recovery plant" that turns out safe raw materials for fluorine-based chemicals, Allied saves $1 million annually.
- The 3M Company estimates that forty projects in its Pollution Prevention Pays program have eliminated fifteen thousand tons a year of hazardous wastes, yielding a total of $13.2 million in first-year savings. A central incinerator in Saint Paul, for example, burns eighteen thousand tons of hazardous waste a year, leaving a non-hazardous residue less than one tenth the volume of the original and saving a million dollars a year in storage and fuel costs.

Although the federal government has begun to tighten up its laissez-faire attitude toward the handling of toxic wastes, so far this most urgent priority continues to be a stepchild of politics.

Radiation

About half the radiation we take in our lifetime is "man-made." (The other half derives from the natural radioactivity in the planet Earth's soil, water, and atmosphere.) Of the man-made half, nine tenths comes from medicine and dentistry's use of X rays and radioactive materials used in treatment. The remaining tenth (5 percent of the total) is generated by nuclear power, fallout, consumer products, and industries related to the nuclear fuel cycle (from uranium mining to nuclear waste disposal).

The damaging effects of radiation are primarily the result of ionization—alterations in the electrical charge of the atoms and molecules of the body's cells. Whether the effects are manifested within hours or years depends on the amount of the exposure, as measured in REM (roentegen equivalent man) units. Exposure to 600 rems or more produces acute radiation sickness. Lower doses can cause leukemia five years after exposure or other cancers twelve to fourteen years later, as well as genetic diseases and abnormalities in offspring. Even the smallest dose (measured in millirems) can affect us, since radiation's effects are additive. Multiple small exposures can, over time, be as damaging as a single large dose. According to Dr. Helen Caldicott, president of Physicians for Social Responsibility:

> Studies conducted over the past forty years have shown that many people irradiated in infancy and childhood for such minor maladies as acne, enlarged thymus, bronchitis, ringworm, tonsillitis, and adenoids have developed cancers of the thyroid, salivary glands, brain, pharynx, and larynx as much as thirty years later. Studies of uranium miners and people engaged in commercial activities, as well as of Japanese survivors of atomic explosions, have yielded enough evidence to demonstrate beyond doubt that cancer of the blood, lung, thyroid, breast, stomach, lymph glands, and bone occur in human beings as a result of exposure to radiation. Today, therefore, it is an accepted medical fact that radiation causes cancer.[19]

The modern problem of radiation has become a matter of weighing limited benefits against uncertain risks. In 1984, ten days after the EPA banned the agricultural use of ethylene dibromide (EDB) as a pesticide and fumigant, the FDA proposed replacing it with low-level irradiation of fruits and vegetables. There were protests, but one food processor who had long been irradiating products for export assured nightly news audiences that the health threat was no greater than that of an ordinary X ray. Unfortunately, the threat of an "ordinary" chest X ray is considerable, particularly when multiplied over a lifetime.

The incident reflects our many uncertainties today about the use and misuse of radiation:

- The deep disagreement on the effects of low-level exposure.
- Industry's and the government's proclivity for replacing a known danger with an unknown one.
- The public's acceptance (and ignorance) of medicine's widespread and many times unjustified use of radiation.

Follow-up of the Hiroshima and Nagasaki victims has confirmed the worst: from small head size and depleted brain cells among children in utero to high cancer rates as the overall population ages. But the effects of even low-level exposures have recently come to light in studies of workers in the nuclear industry and people exposed to the fallout of above-ground atomic bomb tests—studies undertaken a generation after the advent of both nuclear weapons and nuclear power. It is these lower-level exposures, whether they're the result of a chest X ray or a clerical job at a nuclear plant, that must concern us all.

In 1964, Thomas Mancuso, a professor at the University of Pittsburgh, studied 35,000 current and former employees of the Hanford, Washington, atomic facilities and 112,000 workers at three atomic installations in Tennessee. Mancuso found that 6 percent of the cancer deaths of Hanford employees could be attributed to low-level radiation. These figures corroborated those of Washington State Health Department epidemiologist Samuel Milham and threw the Atomic Energy Commission, the Department of Energy, and the EPA into a tailspin. The permitted levels for low-level exposure were clearly dangerous to workers' health.

Indeed, according to Edward Radford, past chairman of the National Academy of Sciences' committee on ionizing radiation, the cancer risk of low-level radiation may be ten times worse than that generally accepted by the nuclear power industry; and lower doses of radiation may produce a greater incidence of disease than higher doses (which at least kill off both damaged *and* reproductive cells, preventing spread). Dr. Katherine L. Kahn, of the Massachusetts Medical Center, has noted that the development of radiation-induced disease "depends upon the type of radiation, the body organ exposed, the length of exposure, and the latency period"[20] as well as the absolute dose of radiation.

The government's policy on allowable radiation exposure received another blow with the publication of Dr. Carl Johnson's findings that radioactive fallout from nuclear bomb tests in Nevada has caused an excess of cancer among Mormons living in southern Utah.[21] These findings were a bombshell because the excess cancer rates were found among Mormons, a group known to have much lower than average cancer rates because they eschew such known risk factors as caffeine, alcohol, and smoking. However, when exposed to even low-level fallout, their rates for several types of cancer zoomed.

The effects of radiation exposure are not limited to cancer. Headaches, allergies, muscle deterioration, lung problems, mental retardation, and various internal disorders have also been linked to various degrees of exposure. Worse still, radiation is *teratogenic* (a cause of birth defects), via its effect on vulnerable reproductive cells.

Before radiation shielding was as sophisticated as it is today, a study was carried out on the families of two thousand radiologists. Researchers found a 2 percent higher rate of fetal deaths among their children and a consistent trend of more abnormalities among their live-born infants than among the children of other physician-specialists. And changes in sperm morphology have been observed even among nuclear physicians well protected with modern shielding. Recently, the International Commission on Radiological Protection recommended drastic reductions in the limits for exposures to ionizing radiation, noting: "Radiation is more risky than we thought in 1977—a factor of three more dangerous."[22]

In sum, evidence from lab animals and humans alike has shown that there is no level of exposure to radiation that can really be considered "safe." Long-term low-dose exposure can be just as deadly, over time, as single massive exposures.

THE BENEFITS and conveniences of today's technology, medicine, energy production, and agriculture have come at too high a price—birth defects, neurological disorders, cancer, and degenerative ailments. Any inquiry into the biological roots of learning and behavioral disorders of the young, or this era's rapid rise in chronic conditions, cannot ignore this pervasive fact of twentieth-century life. Even the Centers for Disease Control in Atlanta are now worried. During a 1983 press conference, Dr. James O. Mason, the CDC's director, declared: "I don't think we can turn our backs for a moment on risk assessment in the field of environmental and occupational health. . . . That's an area where I think the public deserves a lot more information than it has had in the past. What is the risk of low-level radiation? What is the risk of toxic chemicals? I think that there's almost a fear and dread of some of these environmental hazards, and in many cases, it's justified."[23]

6

Ecological Illness and the Individual

MOST PEOPLE ARE by now familiar with the notion of ecology—the network of relationships between a species and its environment. Whether it's bald eagles in the Rockies, stray cats in the inner city, or human beings on a crowded planet, ecology always involves a balancing act if a species is to survive. What is true of a whole species is also true of individuals. The fact that each of us is genetically unique means not only that our nutritional needs are ours alone but that we react to the environment, even toxins, in our own ways. The minority of individuals who are "overtly" allergic to substances in the environment is only the surface expression of this universal reality.

It is a popular delusion that the body is a shield protecting us against the outside world. If a child's balloon crosses our path, it will gently bounce against us and float away. But there is no such barrier between us and the invisible array of microorganisms and molecules in our environment. Many of them move through us as freely as we do through the air. These invaders are hostile, parasitic, or toxic. We survive as healthy individuals because our bodies recognize intruders or external changes and mount a defense or controlling action.

While the organism's leading survival strategy is homeostatis, homeostatic mechanisms alone cannot counter the innumerable biological and chemical agents that enter and circulate through our environment and the body itself. Beyond homeostatis, the organism depends on two specifically targeted defense mechanisms: the liver/enzyme detoxification system and the immune system. The former is a remarkable chemical-processing facility. The latter is an intricate, widely dispersed surveillance network.

The immune system is located throughout the body to maintain immediate contact with our changing ecology. The various elements of this far-flung system are able to distinguish between "self" and "non-self"—attacking invading organisms and "learning" from the experience. Once you've had the measles, for example, your immune system will prevent you from developing it again. It has learned to recognize the virus and is continually "armed" with the cells (antibodies) to destroy it.

Each individual carries over a million different antibodies against invaders encountered during the course of his or her life. Each complex, with its built-in strengths and weaknesses, is as unique as a fingerprint.

Integral to the immune system's success is its intricate communications-regulatory network, by which the system's millions of cells transmit information and maintain a delicate system of checks and balances. This network insures that an immune response will be fast, appropriate, and self-limiting. The detoxification system, on the other hand, defends the body against environmental chemicals through a group of processes called "biotransformation." Specific enzymes alter the molecular structure of toxic substances, transforming them into metabolites that are often nontoxic. When the enzyme action does not actually render the chemical harmless, it has prepared it for excretion from the body (an equally important defense maneuver). These enzymes—collectively called the microsomal enzyme system (MES)—are active in several tissues and organs, but are primarily active in the liver. In all, the MES can metabolize an incredible variety of substances across virtually the entire spectrum of foreign organic chemicals, including: nicotine, alcohol, many barbiturates, many food preservatives, many dyes used as coloring agents, DDT, certain herbicides, and PCBs.

Although these systems make our survival possible, their defense capabilities are ultimately limited. Both can be irritated, overtaxed, or damaged outright by the many pathogens (natural and unnatural) that they are forced to fend off. Moreover, the immune system can overreact, causing disease on its own—as in the case of rheumatoid arthritis. The more new challenges that attack the immune system, the more likely it is to become falsely reactive, "allergic" in the broadest sense of the word. The human body, for all its amazing adaptability, is still limited by the inherently slow pace of evolution.

Twentieth-century technology, with all its chemical creativity and exploitation of radiation, poses extensive new challenges to each individual's personal ecology. The effects of these cumulative pressures on our physical and mental health are complex. There have been strong associations between the contaminated world in which we live, eat, and breathe and this century's endemic rise of chronic, debilitating conditions. Based on a growing body of clinical and experimental evidence, many researchers and clinicians are coming to believe that worldwide chemical contamination, from the ozone layer to the kitchen table, is implicated in the increase of chronic conditions and vague symptomatology among us. Unfortunately, diagnosing these disorders—and their causes—is difficult, at best.

Each individual's vulnerability to environmental illness is different from anyone else's—some are more resistant, others a lot more susceptible. This is basically because of our innate genetic differences: variations in enzyme patterning that leave one person predisposed to allergies or some form of cancer and another peculiarly resistant to organic toxins or even radiation exposure.

In addition, nutrients play a central role in how the body resists, attacks, detoxifies, and metabolizes harmful chemicals. This means that poorly nourished persons are more reactive to, and more susceptible to damage from, environmental substances—just as they are with viruses and other biological causes of disease.

The other side of the story is that pollutants—including a surprising number in everyday use—destroy nutrients in the body, interfere with their absorption or utilization, and make sky-high demands on existing nutrient stores.

The result comes full circle: Ecologically assaulted individuals—unless they eat very well—gradually become malnourished in one or more respects, and malnourished people are more susceptible to ecological illness. The more contaminated one's environment or the more reactive one is, the better one's nourishment should be to head off potential chronic illness down the road.

In part because of these factors, most environmental agents do not cause a specific disease or syndrome but a range of symptoms that vary from individual to individual. And these symptoms are not necessarily caused by a single agent. They can be a response to the accumulated impacts of many stressors—a concept that is known as the "total body load principle." It is believed that the most common cause of ecologic illness is this total body load of environmental stresses. Even when a single event (such as an acute chemical exposure) sets off a patient's illness, it is generally the whole spectrum of underlying stressors that turn out to be the "cause" of the disease.

In this respect, environmental or ecologic illness does not fit the standard definition of poisoning or toxicity. In general, a substance's capacity for harm to humans is defined as its "virulence." The toxin that causes botulism, for instance, is so virulent that it can be fatal if not treated quickly. Most flu viruses, on the other hand, are not virulent enough to withstand the body's immune defenses for more than a week or so. In cases of acute poisoning, such as snakebite, the size of the dose is as crucial as the inherent toxicity of the poison, since the poison does not multiply within the body.

In exposures to the chemical environment, however, virulence is more complicated. Chemicals such as DDT are toxic because of their long resistance to breakdown, which permits them to accumulate in the body to toxic levels. Others, such as lead, selectively destroy vital functions. Still others do not follow a simple dose-response curve, so that low doses can be more dangerous and reactive than higher doses. In the world of environmental illness, a low dose or no immediate response does not mean no effect.

The end product of environmental exposure, whether the result of total body load or acute exposure to a single toxin, is often a quagmire of vague symptoms that are easily misdiagnosed. Research and clinical reports are linking syndromes such as rashes, gastrointestinal disorders, fatigue, migraine, generalized aches and pains, and a number of mental and behavioral disorders to environmental reactions. The responses of environmentally sensitive patients are neither neat nor predictable. It is known, however, that these patients often display general characteristics that are good "clues" for physicians. These include drug sensitivity, food sensitivity (often unrecognized), odor sensitivity, fatigue/weakness, chemical sensitivity, and weather sensitivity.

Because of the inherently vague nature of environmentally induced symptoms, it is important to consider environmental toxicity in all cases of "inexplicable" symptoms and behavioral abnormalities—particularly in children, whose systems are least able to fend off toxic assaults. Evaluation of the home, work, and school environments needs to be integrated into the diagnostic process.

To understand the challenge of environmental illness, we must explore the complexity of the interactions between the host (the human body and mind) and the agents (the countless chemicals we encounter each day). Environmental chemicals are taken into the body by many routes, and their toxic effects often depend on their route of entry into the body. Further, toxicity varies not only with individuals' genetic disposition and nutritional status but also with their lifestyle and stress levels. In the intricate relationship between the human organism and the environment, we are at our most vulnerable in the earliest stages of development—in the womb and childhood.

Reproductive Effects

The human embryo is extremely sensitive to toxic substances in the environment, particularly during the early stages of gestation, when vital organs are being formed. In fact, concern about the dangers of environmental agents now extends back to the reproductive cells prior to conception. Carcinogenic chemicals are most probably also teratogenic (producing birth defects) and mutagenic (damaging the genetic material). Such substances may therefore be partly responsible for the rapid rise in physical and mental disabilities in the last twenty-five years—an estimated 7 percent of all newborns now suffer some defect.

One of the most notorious teratogenic agents is ionizing radiation. Its effects were definitively demonstrated in the birth defects of children who were in utero when atomic bombs were dropped on Hiroshima and Nagasaki—who suffered mental retardation, small head size, seizure disorders, and poor performance in school and on standardized intelligence tests.

The effects of very low-level radioactivity are more difficult to determine. According to present knowledge, even the smallest amount of intense radiation (one particle) is capable of damaging the nucleus of a cell. Medical procedures that were once thought to be benign (such as the irradiation of children's tonsils in the 1930s through the 1950s) have now proven to be dangerous or even deadly. In a study of adults who had been irradiated for neck conditions in childhood, it was found that these individuals had two and a half times the incidence of hyperparathyroidism than the general population, and 31 percent of them subsequently developed thyroid cancer.[1]

For the thousands (and possibly millions) of individuals in the United States who have grown up downwind or downstream of military installations such as the Hanford Reservation in Washington State (where the stuff of the first atomic bomb was produced), the risks are even greater. Up until 1971, Hanford routinely expelled radioactive water into the Columbia River. Between 1944 and 1956, more than half a million curies of iodine-131 were released from stacks of Hanford's plutonium separation building. That's more than *twenty thousand times* what was released during the Three Mile Island fiasco. And during those years of constant exposure more than twenty thousand babies were born in the area surrounding Hanford. Today, many of those born and raised during those years are suffering from a range of disorders—including thyroid and other cancers—that are known to be prompted by radiation exposure. But until recently the government hedged on the possible relationship of the operations at Hanford and the later illnesses of its civilian neighbors.

Many heavy metals are also highly toxic to the developing fetus. Cadmium, lead, and mercury can all cross the placental barrier and do devastating damage. Lead has been linked to stillbirth and birth defects. There is now evidence that the fetus can also be injured through the father, since lead has toxic effects on sperm.

Among synthetic chemicals, PCBs produce hyperactivity in primates whose mothers were exposed to it during gestation and for the first four months of nursing. And dioxin has been proven to cause birth defects in laboratory animals. In 1986 the government reported that nursing mothers in the West were passing the most toxic form of dioxin on to their offspring at levels up to thirteen hundred times the daily exposure level regarded as acceptable by the Centers for Disease Control.

Insecticides like DDT accumulate in body tissues. Repeated inhalation or ingestion of pesticides by pregnant women is a distinct health hazard. A report by the California Department of Consumer Affairs cited the case of a woman in her first trimester of pregnancy who typed in an unventilated basement treated for termites with 1 percent chlordane.[2] She gave birth to a daughter later diagnosed with a cancer of the adrenal gland.

Many chemicals used in consumer products have also been associated with birth defects, including Tris and formaldehyde. Mutations that occur in the gametes before conception can lie undetected for several generations.

The intrauterine environment is not the protective cocoon that it was once believed to be. Many environmental pollutants and toxins in the workplace have been shown to be teratogenic. These substances can injure the sperm or egg prior to conception, or they can penetrate the placental barrier and damage the embryo or fetus. Damages range from death, to physical or mental defects, to a predisposition to chronic diseases. These mutations are being passed along to future generations at an increasing rate.

Immunological Effects

Even in adults, the effects of environmental exposures can be subtle and insidious. At low levels, we rarely notice the impact of exposure to environmental toxins. With the exception of obvious responses to acute irritants (a rash, itchy eyes, and so on), few of us know how, if at all, our bodies are reacting to the toxins and contaminants in the world around us.

For many environmental patients, however, ecologic illness is all too overt: rashes, headaches, stuffy nose, depression, anxiety, tiredness. And it is now being recognized that these chemical effects are by no means limited to classically allergic individuals. The California Department of Consumer Affairs manual observes that people prone to environmental sensitivity who report reactions to low amounts of environmental pollutants also generally report that they were in good health and without allergic reactions prior to that point in their lives. This group, representing almost half the sample, becomes sensitive after an illness (such as mononucleosis, viral hepatitis, or Epstein-Barr virus) renders them highly reactive to chemical exposure. From this newfound reactivity, multiple sensitivities often arise at the same time.

In acute reactions, or after repeated exposures, symptoms can be wide-ranging, both emotional and physical. Central nervous system symptoms can range from relatively minor manifestations such as weakness, dizziness, blurred vision, anxiety, and depression to major psychiatric symptoms such as catatonia, disassociation, paranoid delusions, and hallucinations. Physical symptoms that commonly afflict these patients include tension, hyperactivity, weakness, sleepiness, insomnia, gastritis, diarrhea, colitis, constipation, high or low blood pressure, itching, hives, psoriasis, and disturbances in the rhythms of the heart.

Symptoms such as these indicate how the body's immune and detoxification mechanisms, for all their intricacy, can be evaded and undermined. For example, immune functions can be suppressed or exaggerated by inadvertent exposure to immunotoxic agents. Although the AIDS virus is the most notorious example, many chemicals can damage the system less dramatically. Symptoms such as hay fever, asthma, and hives are among the most common types of environmental reactions that can also be caused by synthetic incitants. Although a number of chemicals (including sulfites and some pesticides) appear to directly alter immune system activity, the immune effects of most synthetic chemicals have yet to be investigated and made known to doctors.

In many cases, the role of the environment in the burden of allergic disease is obvious. For example, as air pollution has increased, pediatricians have noted a steep rise in the incidence and severity of childhood asthma. The death rate from asthma has increased by 31 percent since 1980, particularly among minorities and children. The death rate from asthma in nonwhite males was nearly five times the rate among whites of both sexes, and asthma mortality increased most rapidly in children five to fifteen years old. In addition, increasing numbers of children below the age of fourteen are being hospitalized for asthma.

These trends are disturbing, particularly in light of the distribution of mortality. Strikingly high mortality rates are found in urban areas (particularly New York City and Chicago) among economically disadvantaged youngsters. Findings such as these raise serious questions about the impact of the urban environment on health.

Foods are also sometimes a cause of allergic reactions. Although allergic reactions to a few foods are recognized, medicine in general looks askance at the idea of food allergies. The bone of contention is whether food reactions are only by specific IgE immune mediated cells (and thus a strict allergy) or some other kind of reaction.

In a 1989 article in the *Proceedings of the Mayo Clinic*, two physicians from the Massachusetts General Hospital noted that food allergy "may be defined as an immunologically mediated clinical syndrome that develops after the ingestion of a dietary product."[3] They also noted that the immune response need not be strictly IgE mediated, and that more than one type of immune reaction might be involved in an individual allergic response.

A second controversy is over what methods are reliable in testing a food reaction. Since symptoms are so common and nonspecific, and since diet is so complex, it is not easy to establish hard-and-fast links between a given food and a given response. Nevertheless, there is little doubt that many people do react to specific foods—and that they rarely suspect the culprit. This is certainly true of the food allergies or sensitivities that are most widely reported, such as those to eggs, milk, wheat, corn, pork, and chocolate.

Food allergists say that patients are most likely to react to foods that they like best and eat almost constantly. In theory, this phenomenon is a variation on the classical allergic mechanism of sensitization. In the first step of this process, the immune system mistakenly recognizes some harmless substance (the allergen) as a threat and prepares an immune response (an IgE antibody) in case the substance is encountered again. Step two occurs when the individual next encounters the allergen. The antibody, which is attached to specialized cells in the bloodstream (basophils) and tissues (mast cells) signals these cells to release powerful chemicals, including histamine, that attack the allergen and attempt to drive it out of the body. The wheezing, sneezing, runny nose and eyes, and itching of an allergic reaction are the result of this biochemical attack on the invader. Sometimes the reaction can be so powerful (as in the case of a penicillin or bee sting reaction) that the individual goes into shock.

Oddly, the individual may have come into contact with the substance many times before, but at sensitization—because of stress, a concurrent infection, or some other factor—the immune system suddenly perceives it as an enemy and will continue to do so from that point on.

In chemical reactivity and food allergies, sensitization appears to be the result of repeated exposures to a food or chemical. It is thought that the body ultimately reacts to the unrelenting supply of the same substances by mounting an immune response. Some experts suggest that intestinal infections, parasites, and toxins (including excessive alcohol consumption) can damage the intestinal lining and permit undigested substances to escape into the bloodstream, where immune bodies perceive them as foreign invaders and attack. Many autoimmune diseases such as rheumatoid arthritis and systemic lupus erythematosus may be triggered by environmental agents. In these diseases it is thought that the immune system begins mistaking the body's own cells as foreign and attacks them—the joints in arthritis, for example, or nerve sheaths in multiple sclerosis.

In the case of food allergies, in particular, the immune reaction frequently goes unnoticed, and the body continues to be flooded with the offending food. In these cases, a process of adaptation goes into effect, in which the body progressively dampens its immune response to subsequent exposures. It literally shifts its homeostasis to accommodate the repeated stress. While this may seem like an ideal arrangement, it is extremely unhealthy in the long run. This type of adaptation progressively depletes the body's resources, leading to exhaustion that masks the underlying toll of the repeated assaults on the body. A chronic smoker, after all, may feel perfectly fine while consuming twenty to thirty cigarettes a day, while a malignant cancer quietly grows in his lungs.

Behind the apparent "return to normal" of adaptation, the pathological metabolic and cellular changes continue, unchecked by any immune interference. If the exposure persists or is quite intense the effects on the system grow progressively worse. A good adaptation, if prolonged, can completely mask the inroads of disease.

There appears to be an interplay between genetics and environment as well—approximately 20 percent of the population suffer from some sort of allergy and may transmit an increased susceptibility on to their offspring. Frequency of exposure (along with virulence) then plays a major role in the development of sensitivity to a substance. Once sensitization has occurred, frequency of exposure plays a similar role in the development of adaptation. In the words of Iris Bell, then of the Langley Porter Institute:

> Adaptation dulls acute responses but causes low-grade chronic problems. For example, an individual might tolerate corn well until the age of 35 without acute or chronic symptoms. Then, with age and a high stress load, he might develop a sensitivity to corn while eating it often in various forms. Because the sensitivity developed while he was ingesting corn on a daily basis, he simultaneously develops an adaptation to corn and consequently does not experience acute symptom flares. Instead, he begins to suffer from chronic dull headaches all day, everyday, and never associates them with a clear-cut cause. Thus, adaptation masks the onset of chronic sensitivity to the offending food.[4]

Oddly enough, the first experience of an inciting substance may cause "symptoms" that actually feel pretty good—similar to the response to stimulant drugs. Later, when the reaction passes, sullenness, fatigue, and depression may ensue. If the two sets of "symptoms" are sufficiently separated in time, the reactive individual may not even make a connection between the substance and the withdrawal reaction. In time, however, reactive individuals establish a working relationship between the exciting substance and their cyclic responses. As the discomfort of withdrawal comes on, the individuals experience craving for the substance, just as in the addictive cycle.

Medicine's Answers

In general, environmental agents and illnesses are relegated to the fields of allergy and toxicology. Toxicology deals with acute dosages of poison (like a rattlesnake bite) that affect all humans in the same way. Allergy deals with harmless substances (dust, fur, pollen) that happen to provoke an idiosyncratic reaction in certain individuals.

Toxicology's methodology is focused on single compounds delivered in large doses, and is unprepared to deal with an environment that affects individuals at subthreshold levels over decades. As noted earlier, the virulence of many environmental agents is not dependent on the size of the dose.

The field of allergy ("different effect" in Greek) was born of the hypothesis that allergic reactions are actually mistaken immune responses, in which the individual's system identifies an innocuous substance as a hostile invader. This theory of allergic response led to research into the immune system and its role in cancer, rejection of organ transplants, and probable "autoimmune" disorders such as rheumatoid arthritis.

The field of allergy, for all its growing sophistication, is not prepared to address patients' reactions to today's polluted environment, even though many of these reactions seem just like allergic reactions. In many cases, however, these reactions are not mediated by classic IgE antibodies. As a result many physicians have wanted to broaden the field of allergy to include these types of reactions, but resistance is still quite strong.

For the great majority of environmentally ill patients, who are neither poisoned nor allergic, these existing branches of medicine will not be of help. Despite the fact that environmental toxicity is a major force in the rise of chronic illness and the debilities flowing from prenatal and childhood exposure, medicine's current forces are not adequate to respond to the threat, and frequently deny that such problems exist. Many physicians simply refer these patients to psychiatrists or psychologists and disparage the work of doctors who take a more biological approach. Even more unfortunately, many insurance companies share this attitude and refuse to pay for food allergy testing or treatment, despite the growing body of evidence from institutions as prestigious as the Mayo Clinic that food allergies are a legitimate clinical entity.

DESPITE the difficulties inherent in identifying, treating, and preventing environmentally induced damage (in the womb and beyond), there are some glimmers of hope on the horizon. In the last twenty years research has begun on nutrient-pollutant interactions, and the findings have major implications for the modern struggle against chronic illness. For example:

- As long ago as 1969, injections of vitamin A in quick absorbing formula were used in treating 2 cattle poisoned by the pesticide Ruelene.[5]
- In workers exposed to toxic fluorine, even modest supplements of vitamin C (50 to 150 milligrams per day) enable the body to excrete the toxin more quickly—the more C, the greater the excretion—with a marked decline of symptoms.[6]
- Doctors have reported cases of patients asphyxiated with carbon monoxide in which the usual treatment (administration of oxygen and intravenous glucose) was improved considerably by intravenous doses of up to 50 grams of C.[7]
- In mice, C protects against doses of alcohol that are ordinarily lethal[8] and in humans speeds up the clearance of alcohol from the blood. (Vitamin C also protects against toxic cadmium, whether in the kidneys of exposed industrial workers[9] or in filters used to protect chromium workers, which are far more effective when impregnated with C.[10]
- Zinc reduces the notorious liver damage caused by carbon tetrachloride.[11]

- When exposed to ozone, rats on a diet deficient in either selenium or vitamin E exhibit greater lung damage than rats on an adequate diet.[12] Selenium also appears to prevent toxic effects of chronic benzene exposure.[13]
- The more calcium rabbits are fed, the less strontium they retain in their bodies after exposure,[14] and the same appears to be true of humans.

The role of nutrition in modifying pollutant toxicity is particularly critical in occupational health, for many of the most damaging encounters with the environment take place on the job. True worker protection will include good nutrition and straightforward education about the on-site risks, including early-warning signs of toxic exposure.

We are far from having any full or clear picture of just how the chemical environment interferes with human health, but the methodologies of traditional medicine are not well equipped to protect us from contamination. Once the narrow focus of both toxicology and allergy are modified and better integrated into physicians' diagnoses of chronic disease symptoms, we will be better equipped to manage the risks to our health. Given the evidence of widespread contamination, however, and the research evidence already in hand, there can be little doubt that many citizens suffer overt or covert reactions to a world of increasing toxicity.

During any twenty-four-hour period virtually every American is exposed to a variety of potentially harmful environmental agents. The omnipresence of these agents has raised questions about the role of our contaminated environment in the rise of chronic disease. The scientific and medical research communities recognize that the environment is a key factor in human illness. But among most practicing physicians there is a lack of interest, disbelief, or overt hostility regarding the health effects of specific environmental agents. Few physicians consider environmental diagnoses for familiar conditions, even though there is strong evidence of ecologic involvement in, for example, high blood pressure, gastrointestinal disorders, arthritis, and depression. While the traditional scientific approach is inclined to respect specific cause-effect relationships, such isolated relationships are rare in the field of environmental health. As a result, increasing numbers of patients find themselves going from doctor to doctor, clinic to clinic, or alternative practitioner to alternative practitioner in search of relief from symptoms that many people claim are psychosomatic.

Approximately a century ago, the physician and medical theorist William Cullen made the following observation about hypochondriacs:

> It is said to be the manner of hypochondriacs to change often their physician; and indeed they often do it consistently. *For a physician who does not admit to the reality of the disease cannot be supposed to take much pain to cure it, or to avert the danger of which he entertains no apprehension* [emphasis added].

As recently as 1940, the "safe level" for lead in humans was set at 80 micrograms per decaliter of whole blood. By 1985 the level had dropped by nearly 75 percent to 25 grams per decaliter of whole blood, and many experts are calling for even greater reductions. Radiation once seemed so benign that people drank patent medicines containing distilled water and radium as a cure for rheumatic disease, hypertension, and metabolic problems. Today the "safe" level of radiation exposure is dropping like a brick. These and other historical lessons are telling examples of just how little we know about what is "safe," "normal," or "allowable" in the world of environmental reactions. Rather than discounting or ignoring the claims of environmentally ill patients and their physicians, we should make every effort to reduce known chemical risks and prevent the development of new ones. In today's world, environmentally ill patients may well be the canaries in the coal mine of our contaminated environment.

7

We Are How We Live

OUR LIFESTYLE as a society is the repertoire of behavior patterns that we have developed to feed, clothe, house, reproduce, and enjoy ourselves. Our food sources, weather, environment, economy, information, and culture are all components of this broad lifestyle, in our case "the American way of life." It is a powerful force that is difficult to resist.

The central reality, notwithstanding, is that it is the individual's lifestyle—not everybody else's—that shapes happiness and long-term health. Yet the power of society is always at hand, and if we want to change our behavior we almost certainly must fight these prevailing forces that often conspire against us. These forces may be the fact that all our friends drink a lot too, or that we have sedentary lives or stressful jobs.

Sadly, a fair portion of human behavior shades off into a morass of self-destructive habits. Although many components of our present lifestyle are reasonably healthy, others, such as smoking, overeating, alcohol and drug abuse, and physical inactivity, are literally killing many Americans. What in our overall lifestyle elicits and reinforces these lethal behavior patterns?

It is not an easy question to answer. Yet one of America's leading anthropologists, Marvin Harris, observed: "Over the years I have discovered that lifestyles which others claimed were totally inscrutable actually had definite and readily intelligible causes."[1] As potentially "intelligible causes," this chapter selects seven components of the contemporary American lifestyle that play major roles in shaping individuals' health: physical activity (or lack of it), psychological attitudes, living patterns, stress, chemical dependencies, sexual behaviors, and violence.

Physical Activity

The notion of a "sound" body has been a cornerstone of classical medicine for thousands of years. In the past, most Americans hunted, farmed, and produced most of life's necessities on their own. The lifestyle was active, and classic "farm breakfasts" and the big midday dinner were worked off the same day in the course of hard work.

The Industrial Revolution gradually choked off that rigorous outdoor activity. Commodities once produced in the home are now made in factories, and the office has replaced the field as our place of work. We no longer walk, we drive. Even much of our recreation is sedentary—watching television, reading, playing board games, drinking and talking, going to the movies, playing video games. We are a nation that spends a great deal of money to expend as little energy as possible. We look for external sources of passive pleasure, such as drinking or drugs, television, and other technical artifacts. And, as Jean Mayer has pointed out, while "it is only in the past generation that most people have become sedentary . . . man has inherited an organism which is not adapted to such a life."[2]

To be sure, we are currently witnessing a lot of interest in physical fitness. Thousands of exercise books, videos, and records are now in the market. Health clubs, gyms, salons, and spas are sprouting like mushrooms after days of rain. Yet, despite this boom, the data on our lack of fitness are overwhelming.

The health spas, weight-reduction salons, and exercise videos that are currently in vogue have made barely a dent in our sedentary lifestyle. Going to the gym periodically is an isolated event in an otherwise passive life. The same person who diligently works out twice a week is likely to take the elevator instead of the stairs and drive instead of walk. These passive attitudes, with their attendant health risks, have been passed on to our children, and they are as unfit as we are.

At this time, approximately 23 percent of the children in the United States are obese. Among six-to-eleven-year-olds there has been a 54 percent increase in obesity since 1963. Among twelve-to-seventeen-year-olds the increase was 39 percent. This sharp rise in obesity has been accompanied by a sharp fall in physical activity. Our children are no longer running, jumping, and playing—they are sitting in front of video and television screens. Most school-age children spend between twenty and thirty hours a week watching television, and this sedentariness is not limited to the home front.

At last count, less than one third of all children in fifth through twelfth grade attended daily physical education classes. (The Public Health Service's 1990 goal was 90 percent). During the Amateur Athletic Union's most recent four-part fitness test (in 1989), only 32 percent of the children and teens tested were able to complete all four parts. Less than a decade earlier 43 percent had completed the test. Not only are our children out of shape, they're getting progressively worse.

All age groups in our society share this lack of fitness. According to the Public Health Service, only one in ten men between the ages of twenty and forty-four is a jogger or runner, despite the publicity spotlighting this group; and the fitness boom has completely bypassed most women, the elderly, and most inner-city and rural populations.

There are several health risks to this widespread inactivity. Most, if not all, of the variables known to affect heart disease can be controlled to some extent by exercise. A 1977 study by Stanford Medical School researchers found that as little as two thousand calories of additional energy expenditure a week can reduce the risk of heart attack by 64 percent.[3] This amounts to a total of three hours of brisk walking, running, or cycling a week.

Lack of exercise is correlated with heart and vascular disease. The Masai discussed earlier are at their most active when consuming a diet of meat and milk from ages twelve through thirty (muranhood). Serum cholesterol levels are higher before and after this period (when the Masai have more access to processed foods and refined carbohydrates). Researchers have speculated that the aforementioned compensatory increase in coronary vessel size is a result of intense activity during muranhood.

The benefit of exercise was underscored by a recent British study of men who had emigrated to the Falkland Islands, where the primary occupation—sheep farming—required lots of activity covering miles of rough, roadless countryside.[4] These men had a lower prevalence of obesity and significantly lower blood pressure than their peers in Great Britain.

The benefits of exercise extend beyond the prevention of heart disease, however. Research on the physiological effects of exercise has found that regular exercise can:

- Enhance overall immune function.
- Dissolve blood clots.
- Slow the effects of aging (slower nerve impulses, reduced oxygen utilization, demineralization of bones).

Overall, it is clear that exercise is more than just a way to burn calories, although its effects on metabolism are equally impressive. Vigorous exercise suppresses appetite and also lowers the body's metabolic set point, or resting metabolic rate. This means that the well-exercised individual burns calories at a higher rate than a sedentary person even while at rest. Hence, exercise is a crucial tool for anyone seeking to lose weight.

There are also psychological benefits. The phenomenon of the "runner's high"—a feeling of euphoria after a long run or a grueling race—has been known for years. So has the general "good" feeling that follows a strenuous physical workout. It is now thought that these pleasurable side effects are caused by the body's release of endorphins, natural opiates the body produces to deal with sudden stresses.

These psychological components of exercise are key to changing one's general attitude and may prove to be a major factor in bringing about fundamental changes in lifestyle. If activity becomes more attractive, both psychologically and physically, than situation comedies or video games, exercise becomes something more than a twice-a-week ordeal.

Psychological Attitude

Our state of mind is as much a part of our style of life as our level of physical activity. It shapes how we react to what befalls us in everyday life and plays a major role in health and illness.

As far back as the second century, Galen thought that women with melancholy dispositions were more likely to develop breast cancer than their more contented peers. More recently, the late editor Norman

Cousins in his *Anatomy of an Illness* recounted how laughing at old movies helped cure him of a life-threatening disease. Unfortunately, orthodox medicine, with its reliance on technology and its specific pathogen/disease orientation, has led medical schools and practicing physicians to ignore or minimize the role of psychological variables in disease. Medicine has become increasingly aware, however, that the chronic conditions that occupy most of its time simply do not—and may never—fit such a simple model. One consequence is that the importance of the mind in the development of chronic conditions is receiving greater attention among researchers.

The earliest and most tenacious indicator of the mind's power over bodily health was the so-called placebo effect. In its strict meaning, the effect is the relief an inert substance produces "not by reason of specific pharmacologic action but solely by reinforcing the patient's favorable expectancies of the treatment."[5] The key to the success of any placebo is the patient's *expectation*, or attitude, regarding the treatment.

In the testing of drugs, placebos have long been used as neutral "controls" to delineate what level of improvement is due simply to subjects' expectations or desire to please. Half a study's subjects (the experimental group) will be given the drug and half (the control group) an identical-appearing "sugar pill"; the extent to which the experimental group improves more than the control group shows the effectiveness of the drug. Surprisingly, placebos rarely, if ever, have no effect and often are remarkably effective in relieving symptoms and even illnesses. A 1980 review of eleven double-blind studies of pain relief found that 36 percent of the patients received substantial pain relief from the placebo pills.[6]

Prior to the development of antibiotics, most "medical" treatments (from bleeding to powdered eels) succeeded to the extent they did thanks to the placebo effect. Indeed, the main impact of the physician was to stimulate patients' belief that they could get well. Medical science still experiences these unexplainable effects. Patients recover from fatal illnesses. Tumors disappear. Burns heal "overnight."

Americans today (and too often their physicians) place more faith in pills than in their own minds and bodies. Every year we consume billions of dollars worth of basically useless drugs. Antihistamines, for example, do nothing to cure a cold, yet they are among the most popular of over-the-counter "remedies." One out of every eight prescriptions filled in the United States is either ineffective or unsafe by government standards.

The perceived efficacy of these clincally useless drugs is largely due to the placebo effect: Patients assume they will work. Still, billions of dollars seems a high price to pay for faith in a pill and a positive attitude. Particularly when the evidence keeps growing that we can alter our psychological outlooks, and neuroendocrine and immune systems, all on our own. Researchers like Leonard Derogatis of Johns Hopkins have shown that patients who are "fighters" have a better prognosis than those who accept their illness as a death sentence.[7]

Lawrence LeShan—the controversial researcher on mental aspects of cancer—has suggested that there are psychological characteristics that contribute to the development of the disease.[8] He claims to have found feelings of despair present in many cases of cancer well before the onset of the illness. In addition, LeShan notes that most of his patients had suffered the loss of a crucial person at some point in their lives. Such life stresses, as we shall see, do correlate with the development of many illnesses besides cancer.

The classic example of a psychological state or attitude associated with illness is the "type-A" personality. Type-A persons have two very distinct characteristics: They are always trying to do too much in too little time, and they tend to be unusually hostile. In other words, they are engaged in a constant struggle against time and other people. Type-A behavior, as measured by several psychological scales, has been positively correlated with the development of heart disease. Hostility seems to be the most important factor.

Recent evidence indicates that the type-A pattern may start as early as childhood and adolescence, with serious social and physical ramifications. In a three-year study, some schoolchildren already exhibited its physical as well as psychological characteristics.[9]

The children also exhibited insecurity about their relationships with others and high levels of hostility and frustration. Characteristics commonly observed included:

- Insecurity about how others perceive them.
- Fear of alienating others through their success.
- Lower self-esteem.
- Worry about proving their worth.

It is not yet clear that such children will grow into adult type-A people or be more coronary-prone than their peers. But the presence of a behavior pattern associated with serious health problems in adults is sobering.

On the other side of the behavioral coin, good morale and satisfaction with work have been found to be better predictors of longevity than physical fitness, smoking status, or even parental life span. Research in neuroimmunology has begun to explain such phenomena by delineating the hormonal and neurochemical events that accompany different psychological states. Researchers have found that the secretions and chemical changes of the brain directly affect the body, and that there are biological links between the immune, central nervous, and endocrine systems. Since emotional states are linked to nervous system, endocrine, and immune changes, it is not surprising that twentieth-century scientists are confirming Galen's second-century observations of greater illness in the melancholy. For example, at the Mount Sinai School of Medicine in New York, Dr. Marvin Stein and colleagues have found that hospitalized depressives, as well as hundreds of patients with advanced breast cancer, show suppressed lymphocyte activity.[10]

The evidence of the healing effects of emotional states is less clear, but there are indications that techniques such as imaging, biofeedback, and relaxation exercises reduce the neuroendocrine activity that suppresses immune function, and it therefore seems logical that if negative emotions can impair immune function, positive emotions may enhance it.

Living Patterns

We are, biologically and psychologically, creatures of habit. Like other forms of life, we're subject to rhythms that govern our basic behaviors, notably sleeping, eating, and working. These rhythms are governed by an internal clock that is thought to be centered in the brain's suprachiasmatic nuclei, tiny twin structures located in the hypothalamus. These marvelous structures serve as the coordinators for a variety of regulatory circuits that handle the different rhythms of our daily lives—rhythms that apparently do not require outside input.

Inborn rhythms have been demonstrated in experiments with subjects in "sensory-deprived environments" (such as caves or laboratories) who lacked the environmental cues that usually determine behaviors such as sleep. In these individuals, a natural rhythm emerges of approximately twenty-five-hour cycles. In the "real world" we feel the force of our internal clock whenever we experience jet lag. No matter what the sun or the local clocks tell us, our bodies know when it is bedtime.

Our physical health and psychological well-being depend on honoring these rhythms. Since we are "programmed" to follow certain living patterns, persistent disruptions can result in scores of problems. Given the tremendous disruptions that are characteristic of our urban, industrialized world, it is not surprising that sleep and eating disorders plague millions of Americans.

Prior to the development of efficient artificial light, the workday extended from sunrise to sunset. With the advent of round-the-clock schedules and cities that never sleep, however, the sun was no longer the manager of our work schedule. Today, countless individuals are working during the night and (hopefully) sleeping during the day. While the pay is better, the shift worker is still operating within the confines of a body programmed to obey its natural rhythms. The result? The shift worker is most prone to sleep disorders and the associated motor, digestive, and social problems that arise when traditional work/rest/food schedules are disrupted.

Sleep disturbances go far beyond the shift worker, however. The Institute of Medicine estimates that 29 to 39 percent of Americans over age eighteen have significant difficulties sleeping each year. That means up to 60 million people tossing and turning each night.

There are dozens of reasons why an individual will experience sleep disturbances or insomnia—stress, lack of exercise, overeating, excessive drinking, depression, anxiety, immune dysfunctions, loneliness. Conversely, lack of sleep can itself become a cause of stress, anxiety, and motor difficulties. It is a circle that is difficult to break, and as a result, it has proved difficult to clarify the degree to which sleep problems are an independent health risk.

It *is* possible, however, to quantify one aspect of sleep disorders—the volume of drugs we take to counteract them. Americans consume huge quantities of coffee, cigarettes, and other stimulants (legal and illegal) to stay awake and then take comparable quantities of liquor, barbiturates, benzodiazepines, and sleep aids (both prescription and over-the-counter) to fall asleep.

These drugs—which sidetrack our natural rhythms and force the body to keep functioning when it needs to rest or to rest when it is ready for action—produce a variety of ill effects, both mental and physical, many of which affect other behavior patterns—including eating.

The body metabolizes food differently at different points in its daily cycle. For this reason, nutritionists have long held that the most substantial meal should be eaten early in the day, when the body will directly burn the food's calories for its concurrent energy needs. Such an eating pattern is still the norm in agricultural societies.

In today's urbanized societies, by contrast, most people eat late. They settle for a cup of coffee and a donut after a possibly restless night, then a quick, less-than-nutritious lunch, and a big "hearty" dinner often followed by one or more alcoholic drinks and possibly a snack just before sleep. The pattern runs contrary to the body's energy and nutrient rhythms, experts say. Even alcohol appears to be metabolized according to a circadian rhythm, disappearing from the blood most quickly in the early evening.

On the other hand, there's still a great deal we don't know about metabolism. The fact that so many individuals don't get hungry till late in the morning—or even late in the day—may be the wisdom of their bodies speaking. It's hard to argue against something as elementary as eating when you're hungry. Dietitians reply that it's yesterday's late eating that leaves one uninterested in food this morning—that eating late is a disordered, not a natural, pattern. Stop eating late, they say, and eating early will emerge as the body's real preference. It is also claimed that weight loss is easier on the early eating cycle. And it's true that the bane of most dieters is eating again between dinner and bedtime.

Given these uncertainties, many nutritionists recommend eating several small, nutritious meals a day. The worst pattern, they say, is the all-too-common habit of irregular eating. Missed meals, skipped meals, fast foods gobbled on the run, junk-food snacks strung together with frequent cups of coffee, soft drinks, or alcohol—all high in calories, low in nutrient density, or both—lead inevitably to malnutrition and a disordering of the body/mind's rhythms of appetite, nourishment, digestion, and satiety.

GIVEN the tyranny of our natural rhythms and the widespread imbalances in our eating patterns, it is not surprising that obesity is one of this country's major health problems.

However one classifies obesity, excess poundage is a disorder principally of affluent societies, characterized by stress, a sedentary existence, and high intake of sugars, refined carbohydrates, and processed fats. There are few obese Eskimos, bushmen, Sahara nomads, or animals in the wild. It takes domestication—and the sharp drop in activity and passive feeding and overfeeding that accompany it—to make an animal fat.

There are, however, plenty of fat Americans. According to the National Institute of Health Statistics, more than one quarter of the American population is overweight, and the percentage has been increasing for the last thirty years. Between 1960 and 1980, for example:

- The number of overweight black men (aged thirty-five to forty-four) increased by 43 percent, and the percentage for white men in that age group rose by 28 percent.
- There was a 101 percent increase in the number of overweight black men in their late middle years (forty-five to fifty-four).
- Young women (twenty to twenty-four) showed very sharp increases—67 percent among blacks and 43 percent among whites.

These weight increases come with significant health risks. Mortality rates are 20 to 40 percent higher among overweight persons (and the rates rise with increasing weight). Overweight individuals are more likely to succumb to heart disease, stroke, diabetes, and a host of other illnesses and disabilities secondary to their weight gain. Given these facts, the question remains, why are so many Americans significantly overweight?

The simplistic answer, of course, is that they eat too much. In fact, it is not that simple at all. As was already seen, every organism has its own "thermostat" setting that determines the rate at which the body burns calories, as well as the ratio of body fat maintained. This regulating system is not easily bypassed—hence the phenomenon of thin people who can "eat anything and never gain an ounce" and fat people who cannot lose weight no matter how little they eat.

Diets that drastically limit caloric intake may work for a time, but eventually the body will reduce its resting metabolic rate so that fewer calories are burned in order to conserve energy and fuel stores. When the diet is ended, on the other hand, the body automatically strives to restore the weight balance that it has "learned" (or is genetically programmed) to perceive as the norm. Unless the thermostat is "reset" (usually by increasing the activity level) the body will revert to its "default setting"—which is generally the prediet weight (often with a few extra pounds for good measure).

Both the thermostat's main control switch and the appetite control center are located not in the stomach but in the glands and circuitry of the brain. In order for the behavior of overeating to be halted, the brain must receive a clear signal that enough food has been eaten. These signals to halt originate at various points in the process of digestion, in response to various components of the diet (glucose, amino acids, protein, and so on). It is a delicate, efficient, and little understood system; and it can be overridden by several factors, the most common of which is social eating.

Animals in the wild do not have business lunches and dinner parties. For them, eating is a functional activity governed by the intrinsic objective of getting enough energy to operate efficiently. Similarly, under most circumstances, the human body is perfectly capable of telling us when its needs have been met. Our difficulty is that the stresses of urban, industrialized life, a superabundance of appetizing (and sometimes addictive) food and drink, and the tendency to center our social life around food corrupt our natural eating patterns.

Despite the fact that many Americans are anything but thin, American culture places a high value on thinness—as is exemplified in the media and our various cultural icons. Some believe that this cult of leanness is at least partially responsible for the flip side of eating disorders—made up of those who eat too *little* of any foods (anorectics) and those who binge and then purge (bulimics). In wealthy, developed nations these disorders are rising at a baffling rate. It is estimated that anywhere from 2 to 5 percent of adolescent or young adult women suffer from one or both of these disorders.

In anorectics, the nutritional problems are quite clear—they are starving to death, and generally look it. Mortality rates for this disorder range from 5 to 20 percent. Bulimics, on the other hand, frequently appear perfectly healthy, despite the fact that their purging methods are generally stripping them of crucial nutrients. Instead of obviously wasting away, bulimic individuals tend to develop secondary problems such as dental decay, gastrointestinal damage, and skin damage on the hand used to induce vomiting.

The rise in anorexia and bulimia is generally attributed to social/

psychological factors—from our cultural obsession with thinness to societal pressures to achieve. As John Sours writes in *Starving to Death in a Sea of Objects*: "The Western madness about slimness is good soil for food-phobic obsessional characters."[11] In a world where "thin is in," these individuals are suffering the backlash of affluence, the dark side of the fitness boom.

In both anorexia and bulimia, the normal biological function of eating is fraught with negative connotations. The body image is generally so radically distorted that the individual is likely to "feel fat" even when she (or he) is frighteningly emaciated. The body becomes an adversary to be controlled, so that normal hunger pangs are a threat, and eating a failure of will. And, over time, these disordered eating patterns cease to be a matter just of willpower.

Like the obese, anorectics and bulimics have radically altered their internal thermostats, so that their bodies "believe" that their drastically lowered body mass is the norm. Further, the state of starvation is known to trigger the release of endorphins, and it is likely that anorectics and bulimics are suffering not only from malnutrition but from an addiction to their bodies' natural opiates. In part because of these changes, anorexia and bulimia—like obesity—are extraordinarily resistant to treatment.

In all three of these eating disorders, food and its consumption have slipped out of their proper context and rhythms, with devastating results. Food is consumed in the wrong way, at the wrong time, and in the wrong amounts, overriding the organism's natural regulatory signals and often falling far short of the body's fundamental nutrient needs. In the case of overeating and obesity, food often becomes a panacea for a variety of ills, including our next topic—stress.

Stress

Stress is a "cause célèbre" nowadays—a river of books, articles, and television programs tell us how to recognize it, avoid it, use it, alleviate it. The sheer volume of ideas on the subject is enough to confuse most of us. Worrying about it may even be stressful.

Despite all this media attention, few people understand what stress is or how it is defined. Dr. Hans Selye, the pioneer of stress studies, defined stress as follows:

> In its medical sense, *stress is essentially the rate of wear and tear in the body.* Anyone who feels that whatever he is doing—or whatever is being done to him—is strenuous and wearing, knows vaguely what we mean by *stress.* . . . But stress does not necessarily imply a morbid change: normal life, especially intense pleasure and the ecstasy of fulfillment, also cause some wear and tear in the machinery of the body . . . We define stress as *the nonspecific response of the body to any demand.*[12]

Any demand. The jitters we experience in love, winning the lottery, the shock of jumping into a cold lake—all are "stressful" and prompt the same physiological reaction. Similarly, unpleasant events, such as the death of a loved one, a stormy argument, the loss of one's job, a car crash, or surprising a bear in the woods, will also prompt the stress reaction. The *physiological experience* is the same—even though the subjective experience is radically different.

The idea of a stress reaction was first articulated by Harvard physiologist Walter Cannon in his "fight-or-flight" syndrome. The response is vital to the survival of the organism. It gives us the needed burst of strength and energy to fight off or (prudence being the better part of valor) run from the bear in the woods. The stress response, each time it is provoked, is an essential physiological event.

For tens of thousands of years human beings were often faced with crises—obtaining food, finding shelter, and simply staying alive in an environment filled with hostile predators. The rigors of such a life did not destroy the species; they forced it to develop weapons, tools, and new ways to avoid scarcity.

Given these facts, it may seem puzzling that stress is such a cause for concern today. The current concern over stress is not about the reaction itself (which is essentially healthy, or at least functional), but its frequency and duration in our era. The fight-or-flight reaction is designed to be a short-term response to a specific event—one that terminates when the event is passed. If the reaction continues, the wear and tear on the body continues as well.

Selye and later researchers traced many of the biochemical reactions of the "stress syndrome." Although it can be induced by a thousand stimuli, the syndrome is singular, entailing a specific set of physiological responses, including temporarily increased circulation, heart rate, and other processes.

The pivotal word is *temporarily.* Like other adaptations, the stress response is designed to be short-lived, an alarm that fades when the stressor has passed. In investigating stress illnesses, Selye recognized that organisms undergo a "general adaptation syndrome" when stress is prolonged. In this syndrome the alarm phase of the stress reaction is followed by an adaptation phase, when the body adjusts itself to the hyperactivity prompted by the stressor. Unable to keep up the new pace indefinitely, the organism finally enters an exhaustion phase—flooded regulatory organs shut down with a concomitant lowering of natural defense systems. The body's response systems "wear out," and the end result is bodily damage—ranging from ulcers to depression to a heart attack.

- In severely injured patients serum vitamin A levels drop sharply, leading to gastro-duodenal ulcers without treatment.
- In a 1983 study of over one thousand apparently healthy individuals, University of Nebraska researchers found that one in five has elevated blood pressure due to stress.
- Lawrence LeShan's work with cancer patients suggests a strong correlation between severe life stresses, such as the loss of a loved one, and the onset of physical illnesses.

Stress-related illnesses are common today because the stresses we face are more intractable. In the past, humans dealt mostly with immediate, concrete crises. The challenges involved were direct and had to be dealt with directly. Modern life, in contrast, entails a plethora of impalpable stresses that are less readily dealt with—and many of which are completely beyond our control.

According to Jay Weiss of Duke University, a leading researcher on stress, the predictability of a stressful situation (knowing when it will start and end), as well as having some control over it and an outlet for one's feelings, reduces its damaging effects, and lack of foreknowledge, control, and an outlet aggravate them.[13] Not only are most modern stresses much less predictable or controllable, our opportunities to vent frustration are severely limited. We get upset about taxes, the job, traffic jams, but there's precious little we can do about it. The inborn stress response will give us a jolt of energy to fight or flee, but these options—perfect for chance encounters with large unfriendly animals—are both useless when dealing with the boss or the IRS. As a result, the stress is not relieved.

In 1967, Thomas Holmes and Richard Rahe designed a Life Event Rating Scale to quantify the impact of major events on our health.[14] Not surprisingly, the loss of a spouse (by death or divorce) ranked highest, followed by serving a jail term and the death of a close family member. Marriage, pregnancy, and outstanding achievements also precipitate significant stress. In our Western culture, stressful events seem to involve a perceived loss of control, the anticipation and occurrence of physical or psychic pain, the loss of close emotional and social supports, and efforts to avoid adverse stimuli or conditions. The common theme of all stressful life events is that they tend to prompt some sort of adaptive or coping behavior on the part of the individual experiencing the event.

Subsequent studies support the view that the stress of such life events is a contributing factor in many illnesses:[15]

- The three most popular drugs in the United States are tranquilizers, high blood pressure drugs, and ulcer medication. Dr. Joel Elkes, director of behavioral medicine at the University of Louisville, has characterized the way we live as today's principal cause of illness.
- Lack of closeness to parents and family was one of the strongest prognosticators of cancer, mental illness, and suicide among thirteen hundred medical students studied between 1948 and 1964.
- Over a twenty-five-year period beginning in the late 1940s, heart disease and cirrhosis have directly correlated with unemployment.
- After adjustments for a history of smoking and previous illness, people with "few close contacts" had a mortality rate two to three times higher than that of others in a sample of seven thousand individuals in Alameda County, California.

Although prolonged stress takes a heavy toll on the body, stress alone is not necessarily sufficient for the development of illness; an event that prompts a damaging stress reaction in one person may have little effect on another. The beneficial or damaging effects of stress are highly dependent on the individual, with genetics, nutritional state, and psychosocial history playing roles. The extent to which the stress is maladaptive and becomes a risk factor is contingent upon the health of the organism. When the physiological pattern of stress is prolonged in an organism that is already metabolically deranged by a history of nutritional, environmental, and behavioral abuse, the result can be disease or even chronic illness. Hans Selye, in discussing this point, noted:

> If a microbe is in or around us all the time and yet causes no disease until we are exposed to stress, what is the "cause" of our illness, the microbe or the stress? I think both are equally so. In most instances the disease is due . . . to the inadequacy of our reactions against the germ."[16]

The modern impact of stress results most often from our emotional responses to life events. The perception of an event as threatening is what causes the stress response. We can reduce the ill effects of stress to the extent that we can change our perception of stressful situations. We can achieve this in a number of ways.

- Physical exercise.
- Having someone to talk to (anxiety shared is anxiety halved).
- Improved nutrition.
- Decreased immunological stress (avoidance of allergens).
- Counseling.
- Relaxation and meditation techniques (such as biofeedback).

Relaxation and meditation, the last factor, are ways in which an individual can control physiological reactions to psychological pressures. These measures appear to produce a "relaxation response" that is the opposite of the fight-or-flight syndrome and can be used to counter the negative effects of stress.

The relaxation response is a hypometabolic state characterized by decreased heart rate, respiration, muscle tension, and respiratory rate. It has been amply demonstrated in adepts at meditation techniques such as Zen, transcendental meditation, and Yoga. Taking as little as twenty minutes a day, several different methods can be used to induce this state.

Social supports (whether friends or family) also relieve the negative effects of stress by helping us keep things in perspective and providing an outlet for emotions such as fear, anger, and frustration. Friends and family provide guidance for coping, help us identify resources (both in ourselves and socially), and give feedback that can help us become more competent at handling stress. Studies have shown that social support can:

- Reduce the number of complications of pregnancy for women under high life stress.
- Aid recovery from surgery and heart attacks.
- Reduce the dosage of steroid therapy needed in adult asthmatics during periods of life stress.
- Protect against depression during adverse events.
- Reduce psychological stress and physical abnormalities after bereavement or job loss.
- Protect against emotional problems associated with aging.
- Encourage compliance with therapeutic instructions.

Conversely, the absence of social support and encouragement may be a key factor in the persistence of many stressful and deadly behaviors, such as drug and alcohol abuse. It is known that the presence of a support network greatly improves the success of behavior modification programs that seek to change such behavior.

Chemical Dependencies

Despite the evidence on the role of meditation in reducing stress, most Americans do not meditate. Despite the importance of physical activity, most Americans don't exercise. Despite the need for a good night's sleep and nutritious, regular meals, many Americans all but skip breakfast, snack on junk foods, and don't get enough sleep.

Not surprisingly, a lot of us don't feel all that great. And how do we cope with this lack of wellness?

We get high.

All humans want and need to get high—children spin themselves breathless and dizzy, the surfer cruises atop the perfect wave, Evangelicals speak in tongues. Humans in all cultures have sought and enjoyed euphoric experiences. However, when coca leaves that people in some cultures chew for a pleasant high are refined into pure crystalline powder and inhaled onto delicate mucous membranes again and again, or when fermented beverages are distilled to 50 percent pure alcohol and drunk by the glassful night after night, the euphoric effects are sooner or later short-circuited by breakdowns in one or more systems of the body or mind.

Like the stress response, these higher states are not built for the long run. The frequent introduction of powerful, biologically active (and potentially toxic) substances into the body will eventually upset its natural homeostases. Then, when we ignore its distress signals—such as headaches, sleeplessness, irritability, anxiety, or malaise—we are setting ourselves up for addiction and chronic illnesses, from cancer to cirrhosis of the liver to acute paranoia.

Masking these physiological signals by taking another drug only complicates the biochemistry being violated. And once the abuse has become chronic, the result is a maladaption that depends on the addictive substance for maintenance. The substance no longer brings euphoria but is simply necessary to feel all right again.

Addiction is a chronic disease of the worst kind. There is no long-term cure. Once it is triggered, addiction is a chronic, recurring illness that has to be controlled for the rest of one's life.

The United States is a nation of addicts. From the responsible business person who "can't get started in the morning" without a cup of coffee to the ragged crack addict wandering through an urban bus terminal, vast numbers of Americans are addicted to a plethora of psychoactive substances. Some are legal, others are not, but all disturb (and sometimes permanently alter) the delicate balance of biochemistry. In the modern world of constant availability, constant promotion, and constant stress, most human beings are susceptible to addiction.

The most popular drugs of abuse can be broken down into four basic groups: the depressants (which include alcohol and tranquilizers); the stimulants (which include cocaine, nicotine, caffeine, and a variety of amphetamines); the opiates (such as heroin, morphine, Percodan, or Dilaudid); and the hallucinogens (including LSD, PCP, mushrooms, and peyote). Some drugs, such as marijuana, produce a range of effects that cover several categories. But all "work" because of their impact on already existing neurochemical pathways. Drugs only have an effect if they mimic or interfere with chemicals the body produces naturally, and it is this interference that eventually produces addiction.

Stimulants and depressants are by far the most popular classes of drugs—with caffeine, nicotine, and cocaine heading the list of stimulants, and alcohol leading the pack of the depressants.

- Americans consume 450 million cups of coffee a day. Half the population between the ages of thirty and fifty-nine are coffee drinkers, and at least 15 million are addicted to the tune of six or seven cups a day.

- Of American adults, 30 percent smoke cigarettes, and 12 percent of youngsters aged twelve to seventeen smoke at least half a pack a day.
- Cocaine addiction afflicts at least 2.2 million persons, with one in one hundred Americans using cocaine (or the more potent crack) at least once a week. The percentage in urban areas can be almost twice as high.
- At least 10 percent of the population are "problem drinkers" and millions of individuals are suffering poor health as a result of alcohol abuse.
- Anywhere from 24 to 33 percent of the population consume four to thirteen drinks each week; up to 14 percent admit consuming at least one ounce of ethanol daily.
- One third of high school seniors report "binge drinking" (five or more drinks in a row) at least once in the last two weeks.
- Every year Americans swallow more than 5 billion highly addictive "minor" tranquilizers such as Valium and Xanax. In 1982, researchers reporting in the *Lancet* stated that they observed withdrawal symptoms in patients on Valium after only six weeks of standard therapeutic treatment.[17] Overdoses or fatal mixtures of drugs and alcohol kill approximately fifteen hundred individuals each year.

Addictions are illnesses with a strong social/behavioral component, but the addictive power of drugs rests in their ability to distort our fundamental biology. Some individuals—such as the children of alcoholics—are at particularly high risk genetically, while others seem almost immune. An understanding of these human/drug interactions is imperative if prevention measures are to succeed.

In addition to their addictive properties, alcohol, cigarettes, and caffeine cause systemic damage and may in themselves be carcinogenic. The dangers of these substances are recognized by many Americans, but we continue to consume them at record rates, and at dangerously young ages. Millions of addicts remain undiagnosed and untreated, battling chronic medical problems that they do not even associate with their intake of caffeine, alcohol, or other addictive and dangerous substances that are routinely promoted by manufacturers or even prescribed by physicians.

For the most part, Americans' quest for new ways to feel good is not the pursuit of pure sensuality. We're looking to feel good because frequently we *don't* feel good: We're physically out of shape, improperly fueled, and leading a stressful existence, often out of sync with our own biological rhythms and needs. In many of us, the health of the human organism has become deranged.

Given the many mood-altering substances available, most attempts to ease the symptoms come down to ingesting too much of something that briefly disguises the discomfort while further burdening the body's metabolism. These substances provide short-term release and long-term dependency, increasing the already excessive stress load on our bodies and setting the stage for the breakdown that is addiction.

Part of the blame for the cycle of chemical dependency that is now pervasive in American life lies in passive consumerism, the expectation that health (and happiness) can be had from outside substances or experts—the doctor, the prescription, the drink. We do not trust our own innate capacity to be happy. We "go for the gusto" in too many frosty beers or seek peace of mind in a pill. The "wisdom of the body" is unknown.

This attitude is steadily reinforced by advertising from the drug, liquor, tobacco, and food industries, by peer pressure, and by parents who set the example of their own substance abuse. Public health organizations attempt to counter this flood of propaganda with advertisements of their own, stating the risks involved in America's favorite addictions. Paradoxically, most know the risks . . . and ignore them.

Individuals continue the unhealthy behavior because they feel "okay," get quick gratification from the act, and are addicted to it to one degree or another. Although it's reassuring to tell friends we can "stop anytime" or point out that ninety-seven-year-old Uncle Henry has "smoked all his life," the fact remains that—for most people—the cumulative effects of stress, smoking, drinking, medications or drugs, a sedentary existence, a poor frame of mind, and our happenstance diet are physically disastrous. We need, as individuals and as a nation, to become more realistic about the long-term consequences of these factors. Unlike a lot of things, health, if we ignore and abuse it, *will* go away.

It is important to remember that there is no such thing as a safe drug.

All drugs, from aspirin to penicillin, are contraindicated for many people in certain circumstances. Yet we continue to pour an amazing array of substances into our bodies—substances that alter emotional states, nerve responses, muscular coordination, immune function, and metabolism. Eventually and inevitably, individuals become dependent on these substances to maintain the altered homeostasis they have brought about. At that point they are, for all intents and purposes, addicts.

This cycle has created whole populations of substance abusers: 50 million smokers, 40 million caffeine dependents, eighteen million alcoholics, 5 million tranquilizer and sleeping pill addicts, and uncounted millions of adults and young people dependent on illicit drugs. The behavioral patterns flowing from these dependencies have been implicated in the social dysfunctions that plague our society—learning disabilities, alienation, welfare dependency, suicide, crime.

The effects of these dependencies can be particularly devastating in the young. By the time children reach young adulthood, the lifestyle of chemical dependency has become a debility in and of itself. They are prey to any substance that will alleviate, however briefly, even normal stresses of school, family life, and work. Ironically, the eventual outcome of this deep need to "feel good" is social failure and chronic disease.

For a significant number of Americans, drug use must seem like a reasonable response to dead-end lives. Young men and women who have developed in malnourished, toxic wombs, grown up in poisonous environments on inadequate diet, and received marginal or worse education have little to hope for in today's society. It is this pervasive malnutrition, toxicity, and social disenfranchisement that fuels the drug epidemic. Millions of the nation's young people will never "just say no" until they have something viable to "say yes" to, instead. In failing to recognize this most basic underpinning of the addiction epidemic, the war on drugs is missing the chance to have a real impact on the crisis, and is indirectly fueling two of America's other serious behavioral problems—unsafe sexual practices and violence.

Sexual Behaviors

In an age when many of the infectious diseases have been eradicated in the Western world, several persist with frightening tenacity. This persistence is related not to their virulence but to the fact that they are associated with one of the most basic of human behaviors—sex. And here, in "educated, enlightened" America, irresponsible and unsafe sexual practices continue to be at the root of some of the most deadly infectious diseases known to man.

Sexually transmitted diseases (STDs) are skyrocketing, and they are not limited to the most dreaded STD—AIDS. Syphilis, that ancient scourge of the sexually active, increased 34 percent between 1981 and 1989, and the incidence among blacks more than *doubled* between 1985 and 1989. These increases in adults were matched by a rise in the number of infants born with congenital syphilis—up by 223 percent between 1985 and 1989.

As syphilis has risen, absolute incidence of gonorrhea has decreased—a hopeful statistic that is offset by an alarming rise in the number of antibiotic-resistant strains. In all, as of 1987, the United States was still well below the Public Health Service's projected 1990 goals for these preventable infectious diseases:[18]

- Pelvic inflammatory disease was 38 percent above the 1990 goal.
- Gonorrhea was 9 percent above.
- Syphilis was 140 percent above (and rising).
- And congenital syphilis was *1,027 percent* above the 1990 goal.

These discouraging statistics have been largely overshadowed by America's newest plague—acquired immune deficiency syndrome. Since 1983, the number of reported AIDS cases has grown by more than 1,000 percent. In 1989, 35,238 new cases of AIDS were reported to the Centers for Disease Control, and it is estimated that at least 1 million people in the United States have been infected by the virus but have not developed AIDS symptoms. In 1988 more than 17,000 people died of the disease (including 251 children under age thirteen)—a 1,109 percent increase since 1983.

Far from being a "gay disease," AIDS is now an integral and deadly part of American life. As the rate of new cases drops among gay men (who have caught on to the importance of prevention), it continues to rise among women, children, and—ominously—teenagers. Yet only 77 percent of teenagers receive any education on sexually transmitted disease by age eighteen, and most know little to nothing of symptoms, signs, and preventive measures. Less than 20 percent of all sexually active women use condoms as their contraceptive method of choice—a shockingly low number in an age when an incurable disease is sweeping through America. And even those who do use condoms frequently use them incorrectly or intermittently. Worse yet, the Centers for Disease Control have noted that sex-for-drugs practices are now the leading vector of transmission of STDs, including the AIDS virus.[19]

Despite the acknowledged severity of this epidemic, the bulk of the nation's at-risk population either does not know or does not fully comprehend the importance of preventing the spread of sexually transmitted diseases—of all kinds. Indeed, many young people persist in believing that "it can't happen to me," or that the first sexual experience is magically "safe" from the risks of pregnancy and disease.

It is attitudes such as these that almost guarantee the continued rise of the AIDS epidemic. The AIDS virus, like the syphilis spirochete and the tubercle bacillus, isn't interested in the morals or sexual orientation of its host, it just wants an anaerobic environment in which to grow and multiply. And millions of Americans are proving only too willing to provide such an environment through unsafe sexual practices and naive attitudes about their own risk profiles. One cannot help but wonder what the American public is thinking.

Violence

Among the things the American public is *doing* is shooting, stabbing, and maiming each other—at increasing rates. America's homicide rate is the highest among twenty-one developed nations, including strife-torn Israel.[20] It is more than four times higher than the next highest nation (Scotland). If our rate could be reduced to that of Scotland, more than three thousand lives a year would be saved. In the majority of these cases, young men (between the ages of fifteen and twenty-four) used handguns to kill someone they knew, usually of the same age range and race.

Perhaps the most distressing of all the statistics on violent crime are the drastic increases in homicide among children. In the thirty years between 1950 and 1980, the mortality rates for homicide have risen at an appalling rate:

- For black females aged one through four: up 324 percent.
- For black males in the same age group: up 182 percent.
- The overall rate for children under one year: up 69 percent.

In general, black children of all ages stand a greater chance of being murdered than their white peers. For example, the death rate for homicide is 978 percent higher for black males younger than one year than it is for white males of that age.

The links between the epidemic of violence and the epidemic of drug abuse—like those with the rise of STDs—are clear. Alcohol abuse, alone, is implicated in 86 percent of murders, 72 percent of assaults, and 50 percent of rapes. These interrelated scourges could be viewed as symptoms of an underlying disregard for (or unappreciation of) human life, or simply as a fundamental lack of awareness of the real dangers of unsafe sex and the unregulated use of handguns. In whatever case, there is obviously something amiss in America.

THE IMPORTANCE of our daily patterns of behavior throughout our lifetime is obvious. What is not so obvious is how to go about changing habits that are unhealthy. Among the biological systems that condition health, both genetics and environment are largely beyond our personal control. By contrast, nutrition and lifestyle lie within our power to change—in theory, at least. In practice, personal habits are often so ingrained, or even addictive, that these behavioral factors may seem impossible to change. Everyone knows smokers who cough all day long: They have repeatedly tried to quit and failed, yet genuinely vow—as they tap out another cigarette—that they loathe their own behavior.

This is the lifestyle dilemma, the intransigence of the organism and psyche when it comes to personal habits and preferences. Short of a crisis, we are typically impervious to even the most obvious need for reforming our ways, following instead the path of least resistance—a path that society tacitly encourages.

"Society is giving all of us a double message," says Dr. Robert Gould of New York Medical College.

> On the one hand, we are told, "Don't take illegal drugs." At the same time, this is a drug-taking culture and a drug-encouraging culture. Look in anyone's medicine chest and see how many drugs Americans rely on. Drug

taking is often portrayed in the media as glamorous and chic. And the message the commercials give is: If you have a problem, take a pill.[21]

Health or illness flow both ways in the human organism—from mind to body and body to mind, yet these interactions are only beginning to be explored.

Ancient and naturalistic medicines have recognized these interacting variables for millennia, but today's medicine abandoned such "unscientific" approaches. To modern science's credit, there is a growing awareness of the importance and interconnections of psychology and behavior to physical health. But until medical practice has fully integrated these variables it is up to us—as individuals—to take control of how (and how well) we live.

8

The Next Generation

PERHAPS THE MOST basic measure of a civilization is its capacity to reproduce itself successfully. Childbearing and child rearing are the ways in which societies continue their achievements and meet the demands of the future. Therefore, when reproduction fails, the society—be it a colony of ants or a nation of humans—inevitably fails as well.

In the United States today, the crucial process of reproduction is being compromised at many levels, and the effects are all too apparent. Of the nearly 4 million children born in the United States in 1987:

- More than 19 percent were born to unwed mothers.
- Approximately 15 percent were born to women not yet out of their teens.
- More than 25 percent had mothers who did not receive prenatal care until the second or third trimester of pregnancy.
- Approximately 10 percent were born to mothers who used addictive drugs during pregnancy.
- About 7 percent (more than a quarter million) weighed less than five and one half pounds at birth.

In part because of these factors, more than forty thousand of these infants did not live to see their first birthday. Of those who did survive,

20 percent are not covered by any form of health insurance, and more than 40 percent will not be immunized for measles, mumps, rubella, or polio by the time they are four years of age.

These statistics, appalling as they are, tell only part of the story. The numbers given above are averages that fail to express the even more desperate situation of many lower socioeconomic and minority groups. If the measure of a society is the success of its reproductive performance, America is in sad shape, indeed.

Successful reproduction is more than the delivery of a live baby, of course—it is the physiological, neurological, psychological, and social development of that baby as a healthy new member of our species, from the time it is conceived all the way through to its maturity as an independent adult. On this front, as well, Americans are losing ground. The chronic diseases that are taking an increasing toll among the adult population are also emerging in our children—in the form of declining physical fitness levels, early signs of heart disease, cancer, increased asthma mortality rates, and the steady rise in violent behaviors. These changes are reflected in the increasing number of children whose activities are limited due to acute and chronic conditions. For example, according to a 1989 Public Health Service report:

- Between 1983 and 1988 the number of children under age fifteen with chronic-disease-related limitations in activity rose by 4 percent.
- The number of children with restricted activity due to acute conditions rose by 29 percent between 1985 and 1988—after two years of steady declines.
- The overall incidence of acute illnesses in children under fifteen has risen 3 percent since 1983.

The deteriorating health of our children is a result of their impaired development both within and without the womb. For although reproduction is the most fundamental factor in our civilization's future, it is also the most vulnerable. Ova, sperm, zygote, embryo, fetus, infant, and child are all extremely susceptible to disruptions in development, whether from toxins or a lack of nutrients at critical junctures.

The changes in our world—from the food supply to the air we breathe to the way we lead our daily lives—are having a major impact on our children and our children-to-be. Some of the changes have been beneficial—infant mortality is down (although it should be lower), and we are capable of saving the lives of many children who would have died of their illnesses only a few years ago. But there are millions of children who, from conception onward, are growing up in a toxic environment and receiving an inadequate food supply. And they are exhibiting the effects of this inadequate development in a variety of scholastic, social, and physiological failures.

Fertility

Of the many factors which affect reproduction, the most pivotal factor is probably *fertility*, whether or not one is able to reproduce at all. We rarely recognize the essential vulnerability of our reproductive organs, or the host of factors that can interfere with (or permanently destroy) our ability to conceive and bear children. But the ovaries and testes are among our bodies' most sensitive barometers—easily damaged by mutagens and teratogens and quick to malfunction when compromised by malnutrition or toxicity. While many adults of childbearing age choose to be sterile (either through temporary contraception or more permanent surgical measures), a surprising number of individuals *cannot* conceive or bear children, even when they want to.

Data from the National Center on Health Statistics shows that there are 28.2 million married couples in the United States in which the wife is of childbearing age (fifteen to forty-four years old).[1] Of these, 2.4 million (8.5 percent) are unable to conceive. One million of them are trying to conceive their first child.

Not all children are born to married couples, of course, so the data on couples is only part of the picture. Of the 54.1 million women in the United States who are of childbearing age, at least 4.5 million (more than 8 percent) are unable to either conceive or carry a pregnancy to term.

Some of these difficulties are age-related—the children of the postwar "baby boom" are waiting until later in life to have children of their own and are facing the natural problems of late childbearing. But there are other, more ominous and preventable causes for these fertility impairments as well.

It has been estimated that as much as half of all fertility problems are the result of cervical or tubal complications in the woman. The primary cause of such complications are sexually transmitted diseases, particularly pelvic inflammatory disease (PID). As of 1987, 14 percent of all women of childbearing age had been treated for PID. A previous history of pelvic inflammatory disease increases the likelihood of both miscarriage and inability to conceive. Black women, for example, have a much higher prevalence of PID (23 percent as compared to 13 percent in white women) and have a correspondingly greater incidence of infertility.

Pelvic inflammatory disease is only one of the sexually transmitted diseases that are known to impair fertility in both men and women. If current trends continue, it is estimated that 11 percent of the women born in the year 1955 will have been rendered involuntarily sterile by the year 2000.

Problems in the male account for up to 35 percent of fertility impairments. The most common are sperm difficulties, ranging from low sperm counts to poor motility, blocked tubes, or chromosomal aberrations in the sperm cells themselves.

Sperm cells (like ova in women) are exquisitely sensitive to changes in the bodily environment. Because they are, by their very nature, quick-replicating, they are among the first cells to respond when exposed to everything from radiation to marijuana. For example:

- Pesticides, chemicals, and hormonal food additives such as DES have been linked to both low sperm counts and impotence in men exposed to these agents, often for years after the initial exposures.
- Drugs used to fight cancer are equally toxic to sperm cells. Seminal fluid from patients treated with cyclophosphamide for four months or more showed no living sperm.
- Sexual dysfunctions have been reported in as many as 30 percent of patients treated with methyldopa (a high blood pressure medication).
- Even seasonal changes have an impact. Several studies have demonstrated that sperm motility, total sperm count, and sperm concentrations are lower during the summer months.

Drug addictions of any kind (and particularly of drugs that stimulate or inhibit the central nervous system) are damaging to sperm cells and can cause anything from temporary impotence to permanent hormonal changes and motility impairments. Infectious diseases (from syphilis to mumps) have a particularly devastating impact on sperm production and performance, and several "childhood" illnesses can render an adult male permanently sterile.

While delayed childbearing has brought the issue of infertility more into the public eye in recent years, it has not increased our awareness of the vulnerability of the reproductive process. Each year, millions of men and women discover that conception is not an easy, automatic by-product of ceasing contraception. Tragically, many of them also learn that their difficulties in conceiving are a result of preventable factors in their pasts—including sexually transmitted diseases, drug or alcohol use, and occupational exposures to chemicals or radiation. If more of us understood the delicate balance of conception—and the host of nutritional, environmental, behavioral, and infectious factors that threaten it—many of these fertility impairments could be avoided.

Lifestyle

We now know that the womb is not an impervious cocoon, protecting the fetus from all threats and providing it with all the necessary nutrients. The fetus is ***completely dependent*** on the condition of the mother, and every food, drug, or stress experienced by the mother has a corresponding effect on the fetus. Nowhere is this more clear than in the impact of lifestyle factors on birth outcomes—particularly in the infants of mothers who use or abuse drugs and alcohol. For these children, birth is an entry into the throes of withdrawal, and the rest of their lives will be marred by the neurological and physiological damages of drugs in the womb.

"Drugs" includes alcohol, caffeine, nicotine, and other legal substances, as well as illicit drugs like cocaine, heroin, marijuana, amphetamines, and hallucinogenics. Although women throughout the United States continue to believe that if it's legal and/or from a doctor it must be safe, prescription drugs and over-the-counter drugs can be incredibly hazardous to fetal development. It has been estimated that the average woman takes eleven different medications during pregnancy, all of which carry inherent risks.

- In 1983, the manufacturer of Accutane (an acne treatment) began issuing warnings against its use by pregnant (or soon-to-be pregnant) women because it can cause central nervous system defects in fetuses and newborns.

- Anesthesia during childbirth can cause severe fetal hypoxia and shock, depress fetal respiration, and slow fetal heartbeat to a dangerous degree.
- Labor-inducing drugs such as oxytocin restrict oxygen supply to the fetal brain and produce subtle brain impairments that are not easily detected at birth.

Data such as these have led the American Academy of Pediatrics to warn that *no drug* can be considered safe for an unborn child.[2] Similarly, the editors of the British medical journal the *Lancet* have denounced the misuse of labor-inducing drugs as a "pernicious practice which has no place in obstetric care."[3]

The very same women who recognize the risks of psychoactive medications or illegal drugs are still likely to underestimate the risks of America's "big three" drugs of abuse—cigarettes, caffeine, and alcohol. These ubiquitous drugs have extremely damaging effects on the developing fetus.

At least one third of all pregnant women smoke during the year prior to their pregnancy, and approximately 10 percent of pregnant women continue to smoke throughout. With each puff, these mothers deliver a corresponding dose of carbon monoxide, nicotine, and cyanide to the developing fetus, and deprive fetal tissue of much-needed oxygen. As a result, the infants of smokers are of significantly lower birthweights than those of nonsmokers. Further, children exposed to the effects of cigarette smoke in the womb are more prone to:

- Congenital heart disease.
- Respiratory illnesses, bronchitis, and pneumonia.
- Sudden Infant Death syndrome.
- Possible hyperactivity and lowered IQ.
- Postnatal nicotine withdrawal.

Although the FDA has yet to regulate caffeine, the evidence of caffeine's damaging effects has led the National Academy of Sciences to recommend that pregnant women either eliminate or drastically reduce caffeine intake.[4] The FDA itself has suggested that pregnant women avoid caffeine altogether.[5]

But the greatest of the legal risk factors is, by far, alcohol. In 1987, up to ten thousand infants were born with frank evidence of Fetal Alcohol Syndrome, which includes low birthweight, slightly deformed facial features, retarded growth, cardiac defects, central nervous system dysfunctions, and minor anomalies of the joints and limbs. Learning disabilities, hyperactivity, attentional deficits, and speech and language problems will continue to dog these children throughout their lives, often despite educational support.

The dangers of excessive alcohol use—during pregnancy and in general—are well documented but not well recognized. For example, in 1988 only 43 percent of high school seniors were aware that drinking five or more drinks on the weekends is dangerous to health. This is well below the government's 1990 goal of 80 percent awareness, and is particularly ominous since this same age group has a high percentage of unplanned pregnancies.

The fact that children of alcoholics are four times more likely to become alcoholics than the rest of the population is usually ascribed to an inherited genetic predisposition to the disorder. It is also possible that the fetus of a heavily drinking mother may develop a gestational predisposition to alcoholism: The fetus's nervous system develops in the presence of high levels of alcohol, which entail specific neurological impairments; during the trauma of birth the infant is abruptly withdrawn from it. When alcohol is encountered again—in high school or earlier—the relief is enormous and addicting. In fact, numerous studies over the last ten years have shown that children of alcoholics actually respond differently to alcohol than the children of nonalcoholics. Several studies by Dr. Mark Schuckit of the University of California have shown that sons of alcoholics experience *improved* performance and less feelings of drunkenness when they drink levels of alcohol that prompt deterioration in others.[6] These differences—whether prompted by genetic predisposition or in-utero programming—may be crucial to the development of excessive drinking and eventual physical addiction to alcohol.

Beyond legal drugs such as alcohol, an increasing number of infants are being born to women addicted to illicit drugs.

- In 1986, more than 24,000 children were born to substance abusers in New York State alone.
- Also in New York, an estimated 63 percent of women between the ages of eighteen and thirty-four regularly use "recreational" drugs.

- In a 1989 study of pregnant women in a region in Florida, Dr. Ira Chasnoff and colleagues found that an average of 14 percent tested positive for illegal drugs during their pregnancies. The prevalence was so consistent across all classes and economic groups that Chasnoff stated: "The use of illicit drugs is common among pregnant women regardless of their race or socioeconomic status."[7]

And research has shown that even an "innocuous" drug such as marijuana increases the risk of birth defects in animals if ingested during the first trimester of pregnancy, when fetal tissues and organs are differentiating.

This epidemic of drug use during pregnancy is taking a tremendous toll. These children face not only the pain of withdrawal but also the threat of maternally transmitted AIDS. In the course of five years (1983 to 1988), the incidence of AIDS in children under one year old has risen by 916 percent, and the numbers are increasing. In fact, heterosexual women and their children are the fastest growing group of AIDS patients, primarily because of the unsafe sexual practices that frequently accompany drug addiction.

Teen Pregnancy

Of the many factors that are correlated with "high-risk" pregnancies—defined as those having an increased likelihood of miscarriage, abortion, prematurity, low birthweight, and handicapping conditions—the most prevalent and severe is early childbearing (or teen pregnancy). America's children are becoming sexually active at progressively younger ages, and they are not physically, emotionally, or socially prepared for the experience. Sexually active teenagers are the prime candidates for unplanned, unwanted, and unsuccessful pregnancies.

The teenage fertility and childbearing rates of the United States far exceed those of most other developed nations, and they are on the rise. Between 1986 and 1987 the birth rate for fifteen-to-seventeen-year-old mothers increased by 4 percent, and in 1987 there were 10,300 births to "women" younger than fifteen years of age. (These rates do not take into account the 53 percent of teen pregnancies that ended in abortion or miscarriages.) Teenage mothers now account for almost 20 percent of all live births in the United States.

In addition to severe social, educational, and emotional consequences, adolescent pregnancies are fraught with medical problems. The mothers' physical immaturity, inadequate nutrition, poor health prior to conception, lifestyle risk factors (including drug use), and inadequate prenatal care result in alarmingly high obstetric risks.

The prospects for infants born to adolescent mothers are bleak. When compared to the children of more mature mothers, these children are:

- Twice as likely to weigh less than five and a half pounds at birth.
- Three times more likely to die before they are one month old.
- Two and a half times more likely to die of Sudden Infant Death syndrome.

Should they survive past infancy, these children are typically destined for a life of small size, substandard performance, and very often abuse and neglect. According to the Alan Guttmacher Institute, children of teenage mothers are also likely to suffer learning and emotional problems, have lower IQ and achievement scores, and quite often become teen parents themselves, completing the vicious cycle.

The impact on the young parents is frequently devastating as well. All too often, the immediate result is the end of formal education. Only half of teenage mothers will get their high school diplomas. In part because of this educational deficit, 75 percent of the households headed by women under the age of twenty-five are in poverty. Teenage fathers are equally at risk—adolescent fathers are more likely to experience academic, drug, and conduct problems than adolescent males in general.

Unfortunately, the cycle of teen pregnancy does not stop at the first child. Premature parenting actually leads to higher subsequent fertility. In a 1987 report from the National Center for Health Statistics it was noted that one white mother had her fourth child before she reached her fifteenth birthday.[8]

Low Birthweight

Low birthweight is the common denominator in the many conditions that compromise infant and child health—and is a leading cause of infant mortality in the United States. Nearly all social and racial differences in infant mortality can be reduced to differences in birthweight—teenagers, minority groups, substance abusers, and the poor are all more likely to give birth to dangerously underweight (and therefore underdeveloped) infants. As Dr. Myron Winick, professor of nutrition at Columbia University, explains:

> Pound for pound, the poor baby does as well as the rich baby; black babies do as well as white babies. The difference in mortality can be entirely explained by the fact that babies from disadvantaged groups weigh on average half a pound less at birth than middle-class babies.[9]

Low birthweight is defined as anything below five and a half pounds (2,500 grams), while very low birthweight is defined as anything less than three pounds, four ounces (1,500 grams). The lower an infant's birthweight, the greater its risk of:

- Infant mortality (LBW infants are forty times more likely to die within the first twenty-eight days of life than normal birthweight infants).
- Sudden Infant Death syndrome.
- Neuromotor impairments such as diminished muscle tone and unresponsiveness.
- Decreased mental capacity and ubiquitous brain damage.
- Respiratory and circulatory defects.
- Hypoglycemia and impaired nutrient absorption (which will further damage an already underdeveloped brain).
- Disorganized sleep cycles.
- Impaired physical growth.
- Death from infectious disease during the first months of life.
- Long-term immune deficiencies.

The incidence of both low and very low birthweight has been on the increase since the mid-1980s, after almost a decade of steady declines. In 1987, nearly fifty thousand very low birthweight infants were born in the United States, primarily to minority women in their teens. In fact, more than 12 percent of all black infants have low or very low birthweight, and the rate of low birthweights in black infants has consistently been more than twice that of white infants. Maternal age is also intricately linked with birthweight outcomes—the younger the mother, the greater the chance of a low birthweight infant.

The disabilities and intensive health care that are the inevitable concomitants of low birthweight place an enormous drain on our already overburdened economy. It has been estimated that LBW-related disabilities cost the nation up to $3.7 billion each year. The lifetime medical and societal cost of caring for a LBW infant can exceed $400,000—the cost of preventing LBW through prenatal care, on the other hand, can be as little as $400 per child. Statistics such as these have led some authorities to conclude that each averted incidence of low birthweight would save the U.S. health-care system up to $30,000.[10] If only half of the low birthweight incidence in 1987 had been averted (through prenatal care, effective contraception, or prepared pregnancy), the nation would have saved approximately $4.5 billion.

Beyond these economic considerations, the sheer human potential that is lost in each low birthweight infant is almost unfathomable. In 1969, researchers at the University of Edinburgh tracked the school performance of children of different birthweights born between 1953 and 1960.[11] They found that "the incidence of moderate or severe mental, neurological, or physical handicap increased steadily with decreasing birthweight." These problems persisted throughout the children's school careers. Well into secondary school, low birthweight children displayed lower IQs and were less likely to be selected for classes requiring high-level academic ability than their normal birthweight peers. Findings like these indicate that at least some of low birthweight's legacy is irreversible.

Infant Mortality

In 1984, the Public Health Service set a series of health promotion/disease prevention goals for the year 1990. Foremost among them was lowering the infant mortality rate to 9 infant deaths per 1,000 live-born infants. As of 1987, the news for white infants was good—an average infant mortality rate of only 8.6 deaths per 1,000 live births. For blacks, however, the news was dismal—17.9 deaths per 1,000—99 percent above the 1990 goal.

Throughout the world, infant mortality rates have been in decline for several decades. In the United States, however, the decline has progressively slowed, so that by 1987 our international standing had dropped to twenty-first place (in a tie with Italy). Twenty other nations had lower infant mortality rates than the United States—including Singapore, East Germany, and Taiwan. Not only that, twenty-six countries are showing better rates of improvement than the United States, including Cuba, Kuwait, Northern Ireland, and Trinidad and Tobago.

Individual American states and cities are faring even worse. In 1985, for example, an infant born in America's capital had less chance of survival than an infant in Trinidad and Tobago, Costa Rica, or Cuba. The 1987 rate for black infants in Mississippi was nearly 18 deaths per 1,000 births, for poverty-stricken Jamaica—16. Something other than poverty appears to be at work in America's infant deaths.

Birth defects are the leading cause of infant death, accounting for more than 23 percent of all infant mortality in 1986. The most common fatal birth defects are those that involve cardiovascular abnormalities, central nervous system defects (such as spina bifida), and respiratory abnormalities. After these the most common killers are: Sudden Infant Death syndrome, complications of low birthweight and/or prematurity (which can include most birth defects), respiratory distress, and maternal complications at birth.

Birth defects can be triggered by both hereditary gene variations and environmental conditions (such as malnutrition and toxicity) that cause conditions that mimic hereditary defects. Many environmentally and malnutrition-induced birth defects could easily be averted through effective prenatal care and maternal education. Concerning this last factor, Kathleen Newland of the Worldwatch Institute in Washington has noted that studies from throughout the world have conclusively demonstrated "the link between a mother's education and her children's chances of survival. . . . The impact was particularly strong on postneonatal mortality, suggesting that education enables a mother to meet the challenges of a hazardous environment more successfully."[12]

Once children have survived the perils of entry into the world and the first few years of life, death becomes rare. Mortality rates in school-age children (five to fourteen years old) are the lowest of all age groups.

Despite these drops, the *causes* of childhood death have shifted in a disturbing direction. In 1940, infectious diseases ranked first, followed by accidents, gastroenteritis, tuberculosis, and congenital malformations.

By the mid-1980s, infectious diseases had disappeared from the top five, replaced by accidents (particularly motor vehicle injuries), congenital malformations, cancer, and homicide.

It is understandable (albeit regrettable) that accidents should be a leading cause of death among school-age children. But that cancer, congenital malformations, and murder are among the top killers of our children is appalling. The fact stands in ghostly contrast to the affluent image of America.

Birth Defects

Even among the babies who survive gestation, birth, and early infancy, all is not necessarily well. At birth or during the neonatal period (the first twenty-eight days of life) many are found to have disorders that will impede their development and perhaps the entire course of their lives.

The March of Dimes once noted: "Every other minute a baby is born with a birth defect." This translates to more than a quarter million handicapped babies born in the United States each year.

Birth defects can be either structural ("congenital") malformations or functional disorders. About 7 percent of all infants are afflicted with significant structural or functional defects, such as spina bifida, abnormalities in the gastrointestinal tract, or congenital heart disease. Less than half of these disorders are diagnosed during the first twenty-eight days of life, despite the fact that early identification and intervention can prevent later difficulties. It has been estimated that congenital malformations account for up to 15 percent of the death rate in children under fifteen.

Functional disorders include inborn errors of metabolism in which defective enzyme formation leads to an inability to properly metabolize substances such as carbohydrates, amino acids, certain vitamins, minerals, pigments, and so forth. When left unchecked, these metabolic errors can cause severe central nervous system abnormalities, culminating in spasticity, seizures, and even mental retardation or death. The earliest possible diagnosis is of utmost importance.

Less obvious malformations and most metabolic anomalies may only become apparent in later months or years. Many reproduction-related disorders may not even manifest themselves until puberty or, like Huntington's chorea, late adulthood.

Learning and Behavior Disorders

Sometimes the impact of an inadequate intrauterine environment is clear—the deformed features of fetal alcohol syndrome, the stunted growth of a low birthweight infant, the disorganized movements of a child with cerebral palsy. But in many cases the effects of the deficient or drugged womb are not evident until well after birth—when the child begins to walk, talk, or learn to read.

Learning disabilities, and the behavioral disorders that accompany them, have become widespread in the past quarter century, and the number of school-age children exhibiting difficulties in learning and behavior continues to rise. At present, it is estimated that between 15 and 20 percent of all schoolchildren are affected; and the progressive decline of many of the most traditional performance measures of youth indicates the probable impact of these disorders.

- The U.S. Department of Education has estimated that 1 million functionally illiterate young people graduate from high school each year.
- Nationally, school drop-out rates now exceed 40 percent, with rates in some areas exceeding 50 percent over the four years of high school.
- Since the 1950s, the United States literacy rate has steadily declined in contrast to the rest of the world, and we are now in the bottom two thirds of the 158 UN members.
- Homicide is now the second leading cause of death for persons fifteen to twenty-four years old.
- Suicide rates among young men (fifteen to twenty-four years old) have tripled since 1950. And according to a 1986 report, the number of children under fifteen who kill themselves jumped from less than forty in 1950 to more than three hundred in 1985.[13]
- The proportion of violent crime being committed by young people has skyrocketed. In one fifteen-year period (1960 to 1975) the juvenile crime rate increased at nine times the adult crime rate. This trend has continued to such an extent that in 1990 the Senate Judiciary Committee attributed the current wave of violent crime and murder on a "baby boomerang"—as the children of the baby boomers enter their high-crime years.[14]

While it is difficult to quantify how much of this trend can be attributed to learning and behavior disorders, it is well documented that children who have been diagnosed and treated for hyperactivity are at markedly greater risk of social and legal difficulties later in life. And children who are maintained on Ritalin or other medications are at considerable risk of later drug problems.

Children with learning disabilities are of average or above-average intelligence, with one or more *specific dysfunctions in performance* in any of four basic areas: coordination, language, attention, and perception. These dysfunctions are subtle clinical phenomena, basically maladaptive styles of learning that may be representative of unusual factors in the fine tuning of the body or mind. Learning disabled children find themselves inexplicably blocked by tasks that other children pick up with ease—writing, understanding the rules of games, tying their shoes.

All children will, at one time or another, exhibit the "classic" symptoms of learning disability, such as reversing numbers, letters, or words; distractibility; or poor memory. But the learning-disabled child will be dogged with these difficulties year after year.

Many of these children are further hampered by "hyperactivity"—an adjective, not a disease, that is used to label thousands of children. The child who prefers playing tag to reading a book or who enjoys climbing trees and running after the dog when his mother would like him to sit down and be quiet is not necessarily hyperactive. The child who literally cannot sit down for more than a few moments at a time, who cannot remain at the dinner table long enough to finish more than a few bites, who is up and roaming the house in the middle of the night, who is incessantly touching (and breaking) things probably is. But the reasons for this hyperactivity can be many and varied. "Hyperactive" is, of itself, no more illuminating a diagnosis than "nervous." It is a description that tells us nothing of the etiology of the problem. Such is the essential problem with all the learning disorders.

Over the years, there have been almost as many theories about the causes of learning disabilities as there have been names for them. Most theories have been based on a medical model, and looked for evidence of brain damage but failed to discern evidence of gross abnormalities. As technology has become more sophisticated, however, subtle differences are being discovered.

Recent research has revealed some anomalies in the brains of learning-disabled (particularly dyslexic) individuals. For example, a significant proportion of learning-disabled persons are also left-handed or ambidextrous. Existing knowledge of the lateralization of the brain and language functions, combined with a growing body of evidence on the connections between the immune and neurological systems, seems to point to a functional, physiological abnormality in learning-disabled brains.

Of course, knowing what's different about these brains does not explain *how* they got that way. Or how we should deal with the concrete problems that arise from these abnormalities. The learning and behavior disorders defy the search for a specific cause-and-effect relationship. The brain, like every organ in the human body, is subject to biological individuality, and a wide range of variables can impair its functions.

Several researchers have theorized that children with learning and behavior disorders have unusually high requirements for specific nutrients or unusual sensitivities to certain additives or sugar. These children appear to be a subgroup of the learning/behavior-disabled population.

Beyond the complexities of their individual biochemistry, learning-disabled children are often further wounded by labeling and a long history of academic and social failure. These children need help from parents, schools, special education programs, school psychologists, and other support groups to deal with their psycho-social problems as well as special attention to their biochemical needs.

It has long been recognized that the human brain is at its most vulnerable when it is developing in utero and during the early part of postnatal life—a time when severe-to-subtle structural damage can occur. Prenatal and paranatal insults to the developing brain can come from a variety of sources. The fact that learning disabilities seem to "run" in families (it has been estimated that nearly 90 percent of dyslexics have parents and/or siblings with similar difficulties) has led some researchers to theorize that there is a genetic component at work as well.

Keeping in mind that the learning/behavior disorders are a problem with no clear definition, no definitive taxonomy, no obviously effective therapies, and very little integrated research, an overview of the work done thus far indicates that there clearly is a nutritional, indeed a much broader biological, basis to these disorders, and it has been widely ignored.

- In a study of experimentally induced protein-calorie malnutrition in rhesus monkeys, it was found that there were "widespread abnormalities in social behaviors shown by those monkeys with induced protein malnutrition." Positive social behaviors were depressed, and negative behaviors—such as fear and aggression—were enhanced.[15]
- In 1963, a study showed that a group of undernourished children in South Africa (who had been malnourished throughout their first year of life) suffered lasting effects. "Both brain growth . . . and the IQ of the undernourished groups were significantly lower than in the control groups; and there was no improvement during the period of up to seven years during which they were followed."[16]

In cases of chronic undernutrition and toxicity—so prevalent in lower-income groups—one is faced with the dilemma of nature versus nurture. Are the problems of these children due to their poor nutritional status and toxic load, or the deprived environment (both physical and intellectual) in which they live? Is the problem biological or social? The question, while intellectually interesting, is beside the point. An entire complex of factors—ranging from the mother's diet and drug use to the composition of the paint in the home—can impede and damage a child's intellectual development. Given the enormous number of nutritional, environmental, and lifestyle threats currently facing the developing child, it is little wonder that the number of children with learning and behavioral disorders is growing.

WE HAVE already chronicled the biological transformation of our environment, diet, and lifestyles in recent decades. The developing fetus is not immune to these changes. In fact, it is now evident that our offspring are extremely vulnerable to them and that the nervous system—their neurological development—is most vulnerable of all. During the crucial growth spurt of brain development (from the third trimester of pregnancy until about eighteen months of age), our children need all the nourishment and biological protection they can get. Until American society recognizes the profound impact of these changes and makes broad progress in turning them around, our children's health—as well as their social and scholastic performance—will continue to suffer.

But if these measures are to be taken, young men and women entering their reproductive years must be shown what is involved in having healthy babies with bright futures. At present, this understanding exists but is not widely shared. Even physicians are often unaware of the factors involved in successful reproduction. There is no stronger indication of this problem than the simple facts of pregnancy and its outcome in the nation today.

9

The Limits of Modern Medicine

SHORTLY BEFORE noon on May 30, 1985, a thirty-five-ton crane collapsed into the excavation of a New York City construction site, trapping a woman passerby on the edge of the pit beneath its precariously balanced weight. Her legs crushed and partially severed below the knee, the woman remained under the crane for six agonizing hours as rescue workers tried to devise a way to lift the crane without causing it to topple completely into the pit, crushing her to death.

Just minutes after the collapse, a team of paramedics arrived and administered emergency treatment. They ascertained the extent of her injuries, inserted intravenous lines, and administered painkillers, a blood transfusion, and liquids. Emergency personnel talked with the trapped woman continuously for the six hours, explaining what was being done to free her. Once she was extricated an ambulance rushed her through mid-Manhattan streets that had been cleared of traffic to giant Bellevue Hospital. There, a team of eight surgeons—specializing in microsurgery, plastic surgery, orthopedic surgery, vascular surgery, and trauma—worked to reattach and restore her legs. Miraculously, they were successful and the woman began the long process of recovery.

This true story is but one example of the feats modern American medicine can accomplish. Whether in crisis intervention after an accident, delicate repair surgery, curing an infection, or halting the spread of contagion, modern medicine has become, routinely, the miracle worker. If ever in history a person had to be hit by a vehicle, develop a serious infection, be wounded in battle, have an inflamed appendix removed—or be trapped by a giant crane—today in America is the time and place.

Unfortunately, modern medicine's heroic and specialized techniques are not nearly as effective at addressing the increasingly complex etiology of today's chronic diseases. This chapter reviews the tremendous strengths of modern medicine and some of its presevering weaknesses.

THE MODERN APPROACH to illness and health developed over centuries of battles against a host of diseases. During most of those years, medicine was not particularly effective. Plagues and contagions wiped out entire populations as medical practitioners labored in vain to find a cure.

These centuries of medical failure made the relatively recent century of medical success all the more impressive. The discovery and destruction of the germs responsible for disease led doctors (and their patients) to place their faith in the scientific model that had so miraculously saved humanity from its most ancient enemies. In the process, medicine has abandoned (or forgotten) some its most ancient and worthwhile traditions.

From the earliest days of medical science there have been two distinct but complementary approaches to health—the pursuit of well-being (the naturalistic school) and the cure of disease (the allopathic school). Hippocrates combined both approaches in his practice and medical teachings—stressing that the physician must be skilled in Nature and understand the patient in relation to his or her food, drink, and occupation, as well as the effect each of these factors has on the others. Health was an equilibrium between the mind and body and the external world, disease a disruption of this natural harmony. Treatment involved creating the conditions in which the body could maintain and cure itself through its internal healing mechanisms. When disease did manifest itself, specific interventions would be applied, but natural cures such as dietary changes were preferred over drugs.

The naturalistic and allopathic approaches existed in harmony for centuries. Over time, however, a growing body of information on the human body and how it could be manipulated increased the popularity of the interventionist approach and caused a gap between the naturalistic and disease-oriented schools. Allopathic medicine developed new methods for intervening with sick patients, taking an increasingly aggressive stance toward disease. Purgatives, emetics, various bleeding techniques, and a host of pills, tonics, and powders entered the medical armamentarium. Some had genuine therapeutic value, but the vast majority were at best worthless and at worst deadly.

During these years, many physicians believed that the human body was controlled by the stars and planets, and based their actions (or inactions) on vague ideas of cosmic determinism. When, in 1637, Descartes proposed that the body was actually a machine—composed of replaceable parts that could be understood and fixed "mechanically"—medical thought was profoundly and permanently altered.

Embracing the Cartesian view, medical theorists and physicians embarked on a search for the scientific and mathematical laws that would simplify medical practice, moving further and further away from the bedside, the individual patient, and the naturalist viewpoint. The critical break came more than two hundred years after Descartes, with Robert Koch's discovery of germs as the cause of infectious disease.

It has been said that "in the nineteenth century men lost their fear of God and acquired a fear of microbes." Koch's work was crucial to establishing that fear. In studying anthrax and other infectious conditions, Koch established the ground rules for proving that a microorganism is pathogenic (capable of causing disease). These rules (known today as Koch's postulates) when combined with Koch's ground-breaking work in the isolation and growth of bacteria, laid the foundation for the field of microbiology. By 1878, Koch had not only proven that microorganisms *can* cause disease, he had given science the tools to isolate and identify the culprits.

Many of the most fearsome microbes were identified and named during the last two decades of the 1800s. Koch himself isolated the organisms responsible for cholera, amebic dysentery, two types of conjunctivitis, and tuberculosis. Other scientists soon identified the organisms responsible for diptheria, tetanus, syphilis, tularemia, typhoid, and typhus. In an astonishingly short time, science "broke the code" of some of the most deadly scourges of mankind.

During this same period, Louis Pasteur used Koch's methods to refine the ancient practice of vaccination, which had been introduced to England in 1720. In 1796 Edward Jenner made history by using a related but less serious disease (cowpox) to vaccinate patients against smallpox. Pasteur improved on these early methods, using weakened or killed bacteria and viruses to inoculate animals (and people) against anthrax, cholera, and eventually rabies. But although Pasteur's work showed medicine how to prevent microorganisms from causing disease, it still could not *stop* these deadly microorganisms once disease had developed.

That barrier was broken in 1890, when Paul Ehrlich and Emil von Behring developed an antitoxin against diphtheria. From there, Ehrlich went on to try to develop chemical "magic bullets" that would selectively kill parasites or other infectious agents without simultaneously killing the host. He achieved spectacular success in 1911, with the arsenic compound Salvarsan, which was effective in killing the syphilis spirochete and apparently harmless to the patient.

By the 1930s the German laboratories of Bayer and I. G. Farben were making great strides in pharmaceutical research, including the development of the miraculous sulfa drugs. And, in 1928, came the greatest advance of all—Alexander Fleming's accidental discovery of penicillin. The antibiotic and drug revolution was definitely under way.

Successes such as these guaranteed the ascendancy of the allopathic approach to medicine. The rapid identification of the causal agents of so many deadly diseases seemed to point to a time when the causes of *all* illnesses would be known. And once the microorganism had been identified, it was only a matter of time before medicine would find the way to neutralize or kill it. For the first time, physicians were not battling in the dark against enemies that struck at random. Now they could actually *see* their opponents, and, using Koch's methods, *prove* that they were causing disease. The microbe hunters were the new heroes in the battle against disease, and medicine was quick to embrace this new, effective, and scientific approach to illness.

Indeed, as early as 1911, the historic Flexner Report proposed new standards for American medical education that were based on this scientific model of medicine. Flexner advised much more rigorous scientific training for physicians, with more hard sciences such as physics and chemistry. Actual involvement with patients was pushed to the final phase of medical education. Instead, doctors were to be trained in the basic "laws" that governed the body and the specifics of microbiology and bacteriology that determined disease. It seemed that the human body, like the universe, was governed by immutable laws and operated just like a machine, just as Descartes had theorized.

The result of all these breakthroughs has been a tremendous overall improvement in health and mortality. Contagious diseases and infections have gradually ceased to be a major threat to human welfare in all developed countries. The germ theory brought asepsis and antiseptics to fruition in germ-free childbirth and surgery, and germ control in hospitals, food preparation, and personal hygiene. Moreover, the cause-effect focus on agents and events proved powerfully fruitful against not only infections by bacteria, parasites, fungi, and certain viruses, but also injuries (from accidents or violence) and shock or trauma (from surgery, toxins, or injuries)—as well as in diagnostic advances in lab work and X rays, and in surgical operations.

Many battles in this struggle remain to be won. Wholly new infectious diseases continue to emerge and baffle medical science, at least for a time: Lyme disease, for instance, or (in 1976) Legionnaire's disease. Viruses, since they are not living cells, are impervious to antibiotics and remain a continuing problem. We successfully vaccinate against a few—measles and polio, for example—and are now developing toxic agents effective against some strains of viruses. And of course, the most imposing challenge to contemporary medicine, AIDS, is both a newly emergent disease and viral in origin. Yet, even with AIDS, the swift and decisive progress made already in identifying the nature of the disorder and its causative agent gives hope that the brilliance of modern medical science will find a way to intervene against such a deadly enemy.

So successful was medical research's adoption of classical scientific methodology that modern medicine wholeheartedly accepted specific etiology/specific treatment as its model. The complex systemic interactions of nutrition were neglected even as they were being discovered. And there has been even less interest in the interactive effects of environmental agents or of long-term behavioral patterns.

Yet as the infectious diseases became less and less prevalent, and the chronic diseases advanced to the forefront of illness, cracks have begun to appear in the fortress of allopathic medicine. The methods that had produced the successes of Jenner, Pasteur, Koch, Fleming, and Salk no longer seemed to be working. Further, flaws in, and abuses of, modern medical techniques have become all too apparent. The unqualified successes of earlier decades have come up against the failures of modern medicine.

THE EPIDEMIC of chronic illness in the United States, particularly arterial disease and cancer, is the stellar embarrassment of medicine and its high-technology weapons. These degenerative disorders—far from being bull's-eye illnesses—are complex dysfunctions of bodily systems that must be approached systematically. With them, the model of specific cause/specific intervention simply isn't working.

What is worse, many interventions, from prescription drugs to expensive surgery, cause more harm than good when they are overused or abused by doctors and patients.

Ironically, the wonder drugs of the last century may *never* have worked as well as we thought. Medical historians report that the dramatic improvements in morbidity and mortality rates in the past hundred years were not exclusively, nor even mainly, due to doctors' interventions. The death rate from many of the most virulent infectious diseases had begun to drop well before wonder drugs came on the scene. With the exception of the smallpox vaccine and the diphtheria antitoxin, most of medicine's disease-specific weapons were not even developed until the 1930s—well into infectious disease's decline.

But if doctors' interventions—mainly vaccinations and drugs—were not the chief eradicators of infectious disease, what was?

The great wave of progress that led to vaccines and penicillin and the rest led much more broadly, and earlier, to major society-wide improvements in the basic biological systems that underwrite human health. Even as the microbe hunters were unlocking the secrets of the anthrax and cholera bacilli, social reformers were waging their own war against poverty, squalor, and disease. As René Dubos notes, these reformers:

> . . . naively but firmly believed that, since disease always accompanied the want, dirt, pollution, and ugliness so common in the industrial world, health could be restored simply by bringing back to the multitudes pure air, pure water, pure food, and pleasant surroundings, the qualities of life in direct contact with nature.[1]

The Industrial Revolution had been accompanied by a host of social and environmental ills that contributed to the spread of infectious disease. Urban overcrowding resulted in wretched slums with inadequate sanitation and contaminated water supplies. The burgeoning factories belched clouds of soot and filth into the air, making some sections of London as dark as night at high noon. Unemployment and crime were rampant in the cities, and orphaned or abandoned children were common. In 1858, Charles Dickens (who eloquently depicted the plight of London's orphans in many of his novels) described the slums of Edinburgh thus in a speech on behalf of the Hospital for Sick Children: "In the closes and wynds of that picturesque place—I am sorry to remind you what fast friends picturesqueness and typhus often are—one saw more poverty and sickness in an hour than many people would believe in a life."

Scenes such as these prompted widespread social reforms, including the establishment of workhouses and orphanages, which—while far from luxurious and often downright harsh—at least provided orphans and indigent and homeless individuals with food, a clean and sanitary living place, and medical care.

While the reasoning of the social reformers might not have been scientific, their impact on public health was significant. Improved sanitation systems, coupled with a clean water supply, were of critical importance in reducing the incidence of water-borne infectious diseases such as cholera and typhus. In their efforts to provide the masses with pure water and a cleaner environment, the social reformers of the nineteenth century also eliminated a major vector of disease transmission.

During the same period in which reformers were cleaning up the water supply and improving urban sanitation, the science of agriculture was going through improvements of its own. Between 1702 and 1851 food production in England and Wales increased by at least 300 percent. This abundance of food, coupled with improved methods of transport, made for a better nourished population, with a concomitant increase in disease resistance.

At the same time, improved sanitation and agricultural methods were drastically reducing the number of pathogens that were actually contaminating the food supply. For example, the introduction of pasteurization contributed significantly to the drop in nonrespiratory tuberculosis, gastroenteritis, and infant mortality after 1900.

The great health improvements of the nineteenth century were not, then, the result of medical interventions per se, but of basic improvements in nutritional and living conditions that coincided with (and often preceded) these interventions.

Such observations are far from new. More than a decade ago, Thomas McKeown, Professor of Social Medicine Emeritus at the University of Birmingham in England, extensively evaluated medicine's impact on infectious disease in his book *The Role of Medicine: Dream, Mirage, or Nemesis?* As he succinctly points out, we owe the improvement in health

> not to what happens when we are ill, but to the fact that we do not so often become ill; and we remain well, not because of specific measures such as vaccination and immunization, but because we enjoy a higher standard of nutrition and live in a healthier environment.[2]

The continued importance of these factors—and the problems medical interventions face when they do not take them into account—was graphically illustrated in the outcome of the Navajo-Cornell project of 1955 through 1960. The failure of this Field Health Research project shed a new and discouraging light on some of modern medicine's techniques and showed that the nineteenth-century reformers might have been more wise in their naive beliefs than many of our modern medical technologists.

The project was designed to bring the full array of medicine's skills and technology to the aid of the Navajo people, whose disease rates (particularly for tuberculosis) and infant mortality rates were appallingly high. It provided access to sophisticated diagnostic technology, tuberculosis-screening techniques, and modern illness care.

At the end of the five-year project the mortality rate from tuberculosis had dropped somewhat, but the Navajo's overall health picture remained distressingly bleak. The incidence of other infectious diseases remained high, and the total death rate had changed remarkably little. Most discouraging, however, was the infant mortality rate—which was still three times the national average. What had gone wrong?

Then, as now, the living conditions of Native Americans on "reservations" were far from ideal and often positively squalid. Prior to their relocation to the arid lands of the reserve territories, the Navajo lived in agricultural communities, herding sheep, goats, and cattle and growing their own food in fertile regions such as Canyon de Chelly in Arizona.

The shift to nonarable reservations destroyed this lifestyle, making the Navajo dependent on commercially produced foods and forcing many to make their livings as transient workers. Reservation living brought with it social disenfranchisement, nutritional deficiencies, and a devastatingly high rate of alcohol and substance abuse.

The project provided screening and care for disease, it was true, but it treated these diseases as if they were completely independent of these social, nutritional, environmental, and behavioral factors. The importance of proper nutrition to disease resistance and effective reproduction was completely disregarded. The effect of a contaminated environment was not even considered. And the extremely high incidence of alcoholism and other forms of addiction was virtually ignored. Given these striking oversights, it is not surprising that the project made barely a dent in the Navajo's health status.

The Navajo people have experienced serious disturbances in the basic systems that underlie health. These disturbances can make themselves known in a variety of ways—from dying babies to alcoholic adults—but their resolution requires much more than the antibiotics and tests offered by the project. Such measures, while worthwhile, will not resolve the fundamental disorders.

In this respect, the Navajo community involved in the project is a microcosm of the modern world. As we have seen, the years since the dawn of the Industrial Revolution have been accompanied by dietary changes, environmental contaminations, subtle disenfranchisements, and less subtle lifestyle and cultural shifts that have affected every member of our society. And, as Eric J. Cassell pointed out when discussing the Navajo-Cornell project in *The Healer's Art: A New Approach to the Doctor-Patient Relationship:*

> Just as medical care played a minor role in reducing death rates in the past, so we should not expect that it alone will relieve us of our present burdens. . . . Medical care did not get us out of our past troubles, it will not get us out of our present ones.[3]

The medical community is still learning this fundamental lesson. By dealing proficiently with—and truly believing in—a world of events and agents, direct causes and effects, medical people are largely unprepared to do justice to the broader biological parameters of disease. They do not regard them as specifically "medical."

Drugs

Modern medicine's most common intervention is a drug. When we go to the doctor we expect, and usually get, a prescription that we assume—or at least hope—will "cure" what ails us. Unfortunately, the assumption is often groundless.

Paul Ehrlich, the founder of the pharmaceutical industry, realized the inherent difficulties of the concept of a "magic bullet" to cure disease. Toxic drugs administered systemically are not selective, and the complexity of the human organism makes it difficult if not impossible to predict exactly what a substance will do when taken into the body. Unfortunately, drug companies tend to a more simplistic view, and gear their research, advertising, and treatment efforts accordingly.

"Among modern drugs, some may be considered more magic, or be better aimed, than others," wrote Arabella Melville and Colin Johnson in *Cured to Death: The Effects of Prescription Drugs*. "But the concept of the carefully aimed bullet can easily degenerate into the casual lobbing of a speculative hand grenade."[4]

These "hand grenades" have done considerable damage over the course of pharmaceutical history. The best-known example was the tragedy of thalidomide, the tranquilizer that resulted in thousands of deformed children in Europe and Great Britain. Yet the pharmaceutical industry continues to produce and market drugs that have the potential to cause a comparable tragedy.

Witness the case of DES (diethylstilbestrol), a synthetic female hormone that was enthusiastically given to pregnant mothers from the late 1940s to the early 1950s. Few adverse effects surfaced at the time. But twenty years later the *daughters* of these women evidenced an extraordinarily elevated rate of cervical and vaginal cancer, and their sons a high rate of genital malformations. The most alarming aspect of the DES tragedy is that as early as 1940 experimenters had noted that prenatal exposure to DES caused damage in rats. How is it that follow-up tests were not done? That DES was approved for and was used on humans? That the uproar over its damaging effects did not come until the 1970s?

The drug industry is a business. In a regrettable Catch-22, the main sources of information for the regulation of the pharmaceutical industry are the companies themselves. The "watchdog" of the industry, the Food and Drug Administration, sets testing standards and then evaluates the test results submitted by the companies. In determining whether a drug is "safe," the FDA does not perform clinical trials of new drugs and only rarely runs toxicity tests. As a result, the FDA must make its decisions based on information provided by the very company that wants to market the drug. If the information provided is fraudulent, the FDA (and the public) is unlikely to find out about it until a significant problem occurs.

A recent example of misleading reporting is the case of Selacryn, a blood pressure drug marketed from May 1979 to January 1980 by the SmithKline Beckman Corporation. This drug, which has been linked to at least thirty-six deaths and five hundred cases of liver and kidney damage, was sold with a statement that there was no known relationship between Selacryn and liver damage, in spite of the fact that SmithKline had received reports (from the laboratory that developed Selacryn) that the drug had damaged patients' livers. The data, which were received a month before the drug was approved and on the market, never made it to the FDA. According to the lawyer for a former SmithKline official, the information dropped through the cracks as a result of human error. In the end, SmithKline Beckman pleaded guilty to failing to report to the FDA the lethal effects of Selacryn.

One of physicians' most important responsibilities today is the correct prescribing of drugs, yet so out of date is the structure of medical education that they are still given only a few hours of pharmacology training. One result of this shortfall is that most doctors are not prepared to make informed critical judgments of the flood of advertising and "testimonials" routinely provided by drug companies. And since the companies are also the principal sources of funding for drug research reports and symposiums, it is always a question how unbiased these ostensibly objective exercises are. The physician who receives glowing testimonials about a new drug (and there were many such testimonials for thalidomide) has no way of knowing whether the reports are accurate. In a recent study of faculty and residents at seven hospitals, 90 percent of physicians indicated that they felt they had not been properly prepared to deal with sales representatives from pharmaceutical companies.[5]

The extreme competitiveness of the drug industry exacerbates the situation. By nature, profit-based drug manufacturers need to develop new markets continually, whether or not a medical need for them exists. If the disease isn't already out there, it sometimes takes a little inventing ("diagnosing").

Despite the conflict of interest inherent in such situations, drug companies continue to be the major funders of research on most common diseases and their potential treatment. And it is no surprise that the research focuses on finding new chemical methods of managing disease—or at least symptoms. Indeed, could one expect A. H. Robins or SmithKline or Ciba-Geigy to fund research on therapies (such as nutrition) that cannot be patented and will not significantly increase their market share? Drug companies are in business for the same reason as oil companies or amusement parks: to make money for management, shareholders, and employees.

However drugs are produced and distributed, a separate and equally important issue is how doctors prescribe them. As noted, physicians prescribe largely on the basis of information from the drug houses. If the packaging and copy are effective and persistent enough, the physician will probably prescribe the product.

Even if a drug has been well tested, with accurate information available, physicians and patients often fail to read the fine print. The disregard of contraindications for the use of drugs causes thousands of unnecessary illnesses every year.

Mixing medications creates an equally deadly situation and is often disregarded by physician and patient alike. Patients frequently fail to inform their physicians of drugs they are already taking, and physicians too often fail to inquire. But *any* drug, from aspirin to over-the-counter laxatives to a daily oral contraceptive, will alter the body's chemistry and the effects of other drugs.

The fact that many Americans routinely ingest recreational drugs—cigarettes, coffee, alcoholic beverages, street drugs—is usually ignored by both patient and doctor. And each year thousands of people die as a result of mixing medications and alcohol, for example, completely inadvertently. And the effect of caffeine or nicotine on a drug treatment is almost never considered when drugs are being prescribed.

Further, the patient's biochemical individuality is often lost sight of in the magic-bullet use of drugs. Patients who respond "inappropriately" are often treated as if they had another illness, not an adverse reaction to the original medication. And the usual treatment for the "new illness" is often yet another drug.

The "when in doubt, write a prescription" mentality has become so pervasive that patients feel they have not really been treated if they don't leave the doctor's office with prescription in hand. As many doctors admit privately, this patient expectation has led to rampant overprescribing of drugs (including addictive and deadly drugs such as Valium and Darvon) that can mask important symptoms. It has led to the overuse of antibiotics, resulting in resistant strains of pathogens. And it has led to a host of drugs that are little more than placebos but are propagated as highly effective and priced accordingly. In the end, it is the patient who pays—physically, mentally, and economically.

Unhealthy Hospitals

In cases such as the woman trapped by the falling crane, described earlier, hospitals serve their classic function superbly well. But in other ways the hospital can actually be detrimental to the health of its patients.

THE UNPALATABILITY of hospital food has long been a source of grim amusement. But the problem goes beyond the taste buds. Numerous studies have found that ***malnutrition*** is widespread among patients hospitalized for two weeks or more, and that this malnutrition has a deleterious effect on the healing process. One such study found that "protein-calorie malnutrition affects 44 percent of general medical patients and as many as 50 percent of surgical patient populations."[6] The result is that many of these patients—just when they most need to be well nourished—are worse off nutritionally at discharge than they were on admission.

This state of affairs is due to a combination of factors, only one of which is the quality of hospital food.

> Illness, regardless of its cause, often results in a reduced desire to eat and enjoy food. In addition, if the gullet, stomach or intestines are involved, there may be a mechanical impediment to eating and absorbing food as well. In any case, the net result is starvation because of reduced intake of food.[7]

And unfortunately hospital diets do little to increase the patient's appetite. The situation is further aggravated by physicians who are unaware of their patients' poor nutritional status and rely on the usual magic-bullet treatments to the exclusion of basic nutritional principles, including: excessive reliance on antibiotics (which can damage intestinal linings and affect nutrient absorption), prolonged use of mechanical life support, and performing surgery on nutritionally compromised patients (who are likely to have more difficulty in healing and be more prone to complications).

Hospital malnutrition renders patients much more susceptible to postoperative complications, lengthens the time they must spend in the hospital, and increases the likelihood of their succumbing to ***nosocomial infections or disease*** (any infection or disease that originates in a hospital). Since hospitals are allegedly safe, sterile environments, the idea of infections *originating* there may seem contradictory. The truth is that hospitals are often far from sterile, that hospital personnel often bring germs to the bedside, and that many of the most common cleansing procedures provide breeding grounds for bacteria. Since hospital patients are already vulnerable physiologically, normally nonthreatening bacteria can cause devastating, or fatal, illness.

As for normally innocuous bacteria, strangely enough, the sterile procedures designed to protect patients sometimes serve to promote the growth of many of these bacteria, which are quite resistant. By killing off not only threatening pathogens but the body's natural bacteria that control normally nonthreatening pathogens, the drug therapy leaves an open field for these latter to multiply into serious infections. The dubious credit for the virulence of these usually harmless bacteria (such as *Pseudomonas* and *E. coli*) and for much of the high prevalence of nosocomial infections must go to the widespread use of antibiotic drugs.

Failed Technologies

Illnesses caused by physicians or their procedures are called "iatrogenic" (*iatros* means "doctor" in classical Greek). In the delicate phraseology of *Stedman's Medical Dictionary*, iatrogenic illness is "an unfavorable response to therapy, induced by the therapeutic effort itself."[8]

In 1981, Steel and co-workers evaluated the incidence of iatrogeniic illness at a university hospital, defining it as "any illness that resulted from a diagnostic procedure or from any form of therapy. In addition, we included harmful occurrences . . . that were not natural consequences of the patient's disease."[9] At least one third of the patients suffered some ill effect during the course of their stay, and 9 percent had "a major untoward event." Overall, they concluded that the risk "has almost certainly not diminished in comparison with the situation 15 to 20 years ago, and the risk of a serious problem may well have increased."

The riskiness of physicians' procedures can be attributed to a number of factors: hospital-induced malnutrition (which lowers the patient's natural defense systems and which most doctors are not alert to); exposure to drugs (which correlates with increased severity of complications); and continuous monitoring techniques (which often involve additional therapeutic procedures or drugs that carry high risks). In sum, doctors' efforts are becoming riskier in proportion to the increasingly sophisticated procedures they submit patients to. The acutely difficult question—for physician and patient—is, "Is the possible benefit worth the risk?"

Often—as in the case of diagnostic X rays—the answer should be no, but the procedure is carried out anyway. For example, Blue Cross/Blue Shield has estimated that up to $140 million is spent each year on unnecessary use of X rays and similar diagnostic procedures. While the instinct of most insurers (and patients) is to blame such phenomena on physicians' greed or irresponsibility, the reality is more complex.

The American medical system—as it stands now—places the bulk of the reponsibility for health maintenance in doctors' hands even as it prevents physicians from taking the steps necessary to actually provide such health maintenance. Physicians who try to address the complex problems that underlie most chronic disease—such as subclinical malnutrition, toxicity, addictions, or destructive behavior patterns—are penalized by third-party insurers who view such care as unnecesssary. Government insurance plans (such as Medicaid and Medicare) not only refuse to pay for such care, they pay so little in general that basic operating costs are not covered, and physicians must often wait months for reimbursement.

With so little support for comprehensive care and disease prevention, physicians are also facing the ever-present threat of malpractice suits. Patients, believing that the doctor not only should but *must* know best (and reinforced in this belief by all too many lawyers), tend to view any treatment failure as the fault of the physician. This prevailing attitude has led to a rash of malpractice suits, rising malpractice insurance, and corresponding increases in the cost of care. Even the most competent physician—practicing at the highest state of his or her art—often has to pay up to $100,000 in malpractice insurance a year.

Given these conditions, it is not surprising that physicians—concerned with malpractice suits and wishing not to miss anything in the diagnosis of a patient—tend to carry out extensive diagnostic testing. They are, in effect, being forced to practice "defensive medicine"—doing everything they can to both help their patients and protect their own careers.

Ironically, even in cases where the risk-benefit ratio favors potentially risky testing and treatment, technology often fails to have a significant impact on the incidence and outcome of the condition being addressed.

Each year, more than 1.7 million years of potential life (before age sixty-five) are lost to heart disease, stroke, and other vascular disorders. Although much has been made of the decline in mortality from cardiovascular disease (age-adjusted mortality dropped 40 percent over the last thirty years), it has not been accompanied by a decline in incidence. Although fewer Americans are *dying* from cardiovascular disorders, many are still *developing* them.

Recently a group of researchers evaluated three groups of men who were involved in the long-term Framingham Heart Study.[10] One group consisted of men who had been fifty to fifty-nine years old in 1950, the others consisted of men who were in that age range in 1960 and 1970. Each group was evaluated to determine cardiovascular disease incidence and mortality.

While it was true that the members of the 1970 cohort had a much lower mortality risk from cardiovascular disease than their 1950 counterparts, they also displayed a higher prevalence of these disorders—despite having a better overall health profile.

Data such as these give the lie to our seemingly "improved" mortality rates and show that while it is true that heroic medical procedures and diagnostic technologies are improving survival from these diseases (although the quality of that survival can be questioned), they are clearly not preventing their occurrence.

Similarly, despite the billions of dollars we have spent on the "war on cancer," we have yet to put a significant dent in the incidence of these terrifying disorders. Detection methods have become more sensitive and treatments more refined, but these are all "after the fact" measures—

instituted after the cancer cells have begun their activity. While many cancer therapies are tremendously effective (breast cancer, for instance, is eminently treatable if caught early), others are of dubious efficacy.

The conventional medical approach to cancer attempts to destroy existing cancer cells. Progress is measured by the degree of selectivity a treatment exhibits—how well it kills off malignant cells without annihilating healthy cells as well. Nearly two thirds of all cancer patients will eventually die of their diagnosed cancer, either before or after the arbitrary five-year limit. In 1955, the late Dr. Hardin Jones, professor of medical physics at the University of California, after studying cancer statistics for the previous thirty-three years, concluded that untreated cancer victims lived up to four times longer than treated individuals. Dr. Jones pointed out that the cure rates most often cited were (and continue to be) based only on the conventional treatment of the most favorable cases.[11] If the less "curable" cases were figured in, therapies would emerge as having little, no, or even aggravating impact on cancer patients overall.

The dubious efficacy of medical technology is not limited to cancer and heart disease. In evaluating the recent increase in asthma mortality (up 31 percent since 1980), an editorial in the *Journal of the American Medical Association* recently raised the possibility that asthma "treatment may be harmful or that patients and physicians fail to appreciate the seriousness of an individual episode of asthma, the severity of the chronic disease, or a steady deterioration in function."[12] Since the current approach to asthma treatment is to alleviate symptoms (either with inhaled corticosteroids or bronchodilators) rather than identify and treat causes, it is not unlikely that the treatment methods themselves are suspect.

The remarkable advances from the mid-nineteenth to the mid-twentieth century led to a false sense of confidence in technological innovation. As a result, major funding is poured into the development of artificial hearts or kidneys for some tenuous gain for a few patients, while the basic values of nutrition and preventive medicine continue to be ignored by most medical school and funding sources.

Health Care as an Industry

The industrialization of medicine, from ultrasound to learn the fetus's sex to painkillers as death approaches, is now a major American business;

and as such it is all the more resistant to change. Hospitals have bills to pay, drug companies have each other to fear, medical manufacturers have profit margins to improve. In medicine, the need to supply often dictates demand.

The more time Americans spend at hospitals and doctors' offices, the more money they spend; and Americans *are* spending more time at hospitals and doctors' office. In a little over two decades (between 1960 and 1982), hospital admissions increased more than 57 percent, and outpatient visits skyrocketed by almost 76 percent.

In 1988, the medical care component of the Consumer Price Index rose by 6.5 percent—compared with an overall inflation rate of 4.1 percent. The bulk of this rise was the result of steady, significant increases in the cost of health services and supplies—from physicians' services to medications.[13] For example:

- The cost of an average inpatient stay rose 477 percent between 1971 and 1987—from $667 to $3,849.
- The cost of physicians' services rose 15 percent between 1989 and 1990.
- The overall yearly cost of personal health care rose 507 percent between 1966 and 1982.

Although many hospitals are closing their doors, nursing homes continue to thrive. Approximately 1.4 million people were living in such homes as of 1985, an 82 percent increase since 1963. Nursing home care accounts for approximately 8 percent of our total national health-care bill—$48 billion each year. And just as hospital and physician costs have been rising, nursing home care costs progressively more each year.

- The monthly charges for nursing home care rose 683 percent between 1964 and 1985. Interestingly, the cost of "nonprofit" and government facilities increased by a much greater percentage (1,020 percent) than that of private, proprietary institutions (573 percent).

Mental health facilities, like nursing homes, are also booming. Between 1982 and 1986 the number of inpatient and residential treatment beds for mental illness increased by 8 percent—still insufficient for the growing numbers of mentally troubled individuals in our society. Mental illness, like the other chronic diseases, is consuming more and more of our gross national product. Between 1969 and 1986 total mental health expenditures rose by 461 percent—so that in 1986 our mental health bill was nearly $18.5 billion.

Costs such as these have reduced many politicians, policy makers, and insurers to a state of apoplexy. Faced with the prospect of spending more than a trillion dollars on health care by the end of the century (if the current trend continues)—these individuals and organizations are screaming that something has to change. They are calling for an end to unnecessary and expensive testing, the closing of underutilized hospitals, and limitations on the amount and type of care covered by insurance. The overwhelming message, from insurers and legislators alike, is that we cannot afford any more of this.

They're right, of course; we can't afford any more of this—the sicker we become the more it costs us, in every sense of the word. But rationing health services and limiting the procedures a physician can use in evaluating a patient are not panaceas for the current health-care crisis. As Dr. Arnold Relman noted in a recent *New England Journal of Medicine* editorial: "We are already restricting services through our failure to provide health insurance to many who cannot afford it."[14] And since the real nature of a patient's problem is not always apparent from the presenting complaint, limiting diagnostic options is bound to also limit diagnostic accuracy. To again quote Dr. Relman: "With each procedure, the cost-benefit assessment depends so heavily on individual circumstances that it is almost impossible to devise medically sound rules applicable to all patients."

If we are ever to bring the nation's medical bill back into line we must first develop a better understanding of the diseases that are presently afflicting so many Americans. This will not be accomplished by limiting access to care or diagnostic procedures. Nor will it be accomplished by an increased proliferation of the after-the-fact technologies that are currently straining the medical budget.

Instead of the symptom/disease-oriented approach that currently characterizes medicine (which is largely a matter of closing the barn door after the horse has left), the medical establishment—and the patients it serves—needs to return to a more broad-based approach to *health,* as opposed to illness.

The scientific method, from Koch's postulates to statistical significance, is as valid as it ever was, but in biology and medicine it is so only in the larger context of living and life-giving systems. When investigating the phenomena of chronic disease in the immeasurably complex human organism, simplistic applications of the methodology fail to take this diversity into account. Searching for discrete, consistent cause-and-effect relationships often does not yield much useful information. Not putting together what *is* learned in different fields is self-defeating. And looking for "proof"—as defined in the mathematical and physical sciences—can be even less productive. As the late Dr. Michael Halberstam wrote:

> Very little in medicine *is* proven. Diagnosis and treatment move haltingly, ahead a few steps here, back a few there, into blind alleys often enough. Breakthroughs are rare, increments are common. The practicing physician learns to live with this frustration, though not to enjoy it.[15]

10

A New Paradigm for Medical Care

IN GENEVA in 1980, the World Health Organization declared the world free of smallpox. The last remaining case had been cured. Modern medicine had eliminated the virus from the face of the earth—the only extant specimens are sealed in guarded laboratories.

The conquest of smallpox is the ultimate triumph of modern medicine, and as such it illuminates modern medicine's difficulties with chronic disease. For the bald biological fact is that cancer, as an intrinsic systemic disorder, will never be eliminated from the face of the earth. The laboratory will never exist that ardently guards the last surviving specimen of malignant tissue. Nor will a glass vessel ever contain, floating like Einstein's brain, the world's last diseased heart. These and the other chronic conditions are aberrations of life itself, and the two—biological life and its systemic disorders—are inseparable. It is conceivable that, except for patients with weakened resistance, mankind could for all practical purposes wipe out infectious disease. But it is not conceivable that we will someday wipe out all chronic conditions. They arise in the surpassing complexity of biological life, beyond medicine's powers of specific intervention. Instead of specific causes, these conditions have an entire range of contributing factors that lead to their development—factors that vary from individual to individual and situation to situation.

The chronic diseases, in their intransigence, point all too clearly to just how much medicine still has to learn.

Today there remain large areas of biochemistry, molecular genetics, cellular biology, enzymology, neuroendocrinology, immunology, nutrition—the emerging *basics* of medical science—of which we know little or nothing at all. As Dr. Lewis Thomas writes:

> We do not know enough about ourselves. We are ignorant about how we work, about how we fit in, and most of all about the enormous, imponderable system of life in which we are imbedded as working parts. We do not really understand nature, at all. We have come a long way, indeed, but just enough to become conscious of our own ignorance. . . . It is a new experience for all of us. Only two centuries ago we could explain everything about everything, out of pure reason, and now that most elaborate and harmonious structure has come apart before our eye. We are *dumb.*[1]

Dr. Thomas is far from the first to note the limits of what medicine knows and understands of the human organism in its relation to health, illness, and the surrounding world. Indeed, even as the bulk of medical science was embracing the cause-effect mind-set of Descartes, Newton, and the germ theory, several noted medical scientists were calling for a return to a broader, more systemic view.

Foremost among these was the French physiologist Claude Bernard, known today as the founder of experimental medicine. Bernard's work on the body's internal environment, or *milieu intérieur,* is of crucial significance to the problems of modern medicine.

Bernard held that the body functions as an organic whole that instinctively "knows" what is best for itself and continually adjusts to maintain this state—the *milieu intérieur.* He maintained that the body—far from passively accepting and/or reacting to changes around it—actively creates and maintains its own internal living environment in the midst of widely varying external conditions. Hence, the body's response to an external threat, such as a bacteria, may be more important in the eventual development of disease than the threat itself.

It would take Pasteur more than thirty years to admit, on his deathbed: "Bernard was right. The pathogen is nothing. The terrain is everything." Bernard was not alone in his focus on the "terrain" as the crucial component in disease and its prevention. At the turn of the twentieth century, a group of doctors—including a Russian pathologist named Elie Metchnikoff (who later discovered the white blood cells of the immune system)—proved Bernard's point by purposely consuming cultures containing millions of cholera bacilli. Although some of the experimenters experienced mild diarrhea, and all had cholera bacilli in their feces, none came down with cholera. But this dramatic demonstration of the importance of the host in the development of disease was lost in the excited uproar over germs.

Ironically, even as medicine was embracing the classical, specific cause/specific effect view of the universe, a new revolution was occurring in the field of physics that would fundamentally change that view. By 1920, some of the most entrenched assumptions of "classical" science had been challenged and revised by a variety of brilliant scientists.

First, Max Planck's theory of quantum energy upset a fundamental aspect of Newtonian physics. In asserting that energy did not increase in a steady flow, but instead held at one level and then "leapt" to the next, Planck showed that it could no longer be assumed that for *every* action there is an equal and opposite reaction.

Then Albert Einstein, with his theory of general relativity, put an end to the concept of absolute time and space, and effectively destroyed the possibility of discovering the absolute and inviolate "laws" that govern the universe.

Finally, in the 1920s, Werner Heisenberg and others developed a theory called "quantum mechanics," which incorporated the inevitable element of random chance into a powerful predictive model. Instead of anticipating a single, definitive result, quantum mechanics predicts several outcomes and their relative likelihoods—possibilities instead of certainties.

These advances caused a major shift in the scientific view of the universe and matter (including living beings). Instead of the solid, rational universe of classical science, this contemporary scientific view finds a strangely provisional cosmos in which "reality" is a blurred image cast by countless random events, and "knowing" is merely weighing different probabilities.

- Where classical science sees the universe as a permanent physical geometry composed of a variety of bodies in mathematical relationship to each other, contemporary science views the universe as an *event*—a slow-motion explosion that includes living beings in complex ecological relationships.

- To classical scientists, all bodies—inert and living—are uniformly governed by the laws of physics and chemistry. The contemporary scientist, on the other hand, recognizes the essential uniqueness of all living beings and the potentially vast implications of that uniqueness in individual responses.
- Similarly, in classical science "bodies" are considered unitary or—at their most complex—aggregates of replaceable parts. In contemporary science, these entities are organic wholes—developing from within and self-governing. This is true not only for individual living bodies but for entire systems of life—from the most simple collection of algae to the most complex human society. In each of these systems the various components are interdependent and interconnected, and that which affects one necessarily affects every other component of the system.
- Classical science, believing that every effect has a cause, defines scientific understanding as knowing the cause of every effect. Contemporary science—recognizing that much of the natural world is governed by apparently random (though organically coherent) forces—seeks *patterns* of activity, association, and relation, rather than individual causes.
- Further, classical science assumes a continuity between cause and effect—the higher the heat, the quicker the water boils, the stronger the medication, the greater the effect, and so on. Contemporary science, following Planck's discovery of the quantum effect, has discovered the limits of "to every action there is an equal and opposite reaction."
- Finally, classical science assumes that bodies and the relations between them are objective and understandable as dependent realities. Its belief is that the universe is an absolute that can be analyzed, quantified, and understood. Contemporary science has come to appreciate the limits of such a view—and the true complexity of the old notion of objectivity. Far from seeking absolute truth, contemporary scientists develop provisional models of experience, to be improved in time or eventually replaced with a better approach.

Medical science, enjoying the heady success of the germ and drug revolution, paid scant attention to the upheaval in the world of physics. At the time Descartes's theories revamped medical thought, doctors were still waging a losing war against plague and contagions. When general relativity theory supplanted Descartes and much of Newton, that war seemed well on its way to being won. Already equipped with a seemingly invincible paradigm, most medical researchers and practitioners saw no reason to consider a new approach. Today—as cancer, heart disease, diabetes, and other chronic diseases defy the modern medical paradigm—the time for a new approach is at hand.

METHODOLOGY IS a stuffy and abstract word. But what your doctor does—or doesn't do—about the pain in your side is neither stuffy nor abstract. Methodology, in clinical medicine, is doctors' whole way of going about doctoring—their mind-set regarding what disease is, what their proper role should be, how to carry out diagnosis, and what is the goal of treatment. And flowing from that, it includes their detail work—how thoroughly they conduct the physical, whether they're interested in the medical history, how many and what kind of lab tests they order, how readily they recommend surgery and prescribe drugs.

Because methodology is largely implicit, its limitations lie beyond the horizons of most physicians' awareness. And because doctors of a given time or place are trained in the same schools and practice within a common medical culture, they share a general methodology characterized by their current knowledge and traditions of medical understanding. Similarly, medical researchers share in the same methodology, tailored to their work in the laboratory or clinic. And what unifies all these disparate elements, inspiring in them a coherent outlook and pattern of procedures, is the paradigm of that medical tradition—the inherent model and shared examples of good medical research and practice.

Much of modern medicine's methodology is nothing short of miraculous—encompassing knowledge and technologies that were not even dreamed of in Pasteur's day and that are capable of both prolonging and improving life. Other aspects, as we have seen, are spectacularly unsuccessful. While we must not "throw the baby out with the bath water," we *must* reintegrate the lost lessons of the naturalistic approach. In treating illness of all kinds, the physician's strongest ally is the patient's natural defense system. In the words of Rhazes—the twelfth-century Muslim theologian and medical theorist:

> When the disease is stronger than the patient, the physician will not be able to help him at all, and if the strength of the patient is greater than the strength of the disease, he does not need a physician at all. But when both are equal, the one needs a physician who will support the patient's strength and help him against the disease.

Although the knowledge and methods exist to test for nutritional deficiency, toxicity, allergy, immune status, and many other aspects of metabolic functioning, they are rarely investigated during the diagnostic process. This is because most physicians are poorly trained in monitoring biochemical parameters beyond the most commonly used laboratory tests.

The current structure and focus of medical research, education, and practice make it extremely difficult for physicians to gain this important information, and even more difficult for them to implement it with their patients. As Thomas McKeown pointed out in the preface to *The Role of Medicine*: "There are no grounds for criticism in the fact that medical education, research, and practice are based on quite different premises. In their assumptions about the determinants of health, doctors have been under the same misapprehensions as everyone else."[2]

Medical Training

Future doctors must be educated more broadly—to help them become better physicians than today's cool and busy technocrat and to prepare them to deal more effectively with patients' needs. A broader education should lead to greater understanding of science and the scientific method, the proper roles of technology and drugs in treating patients, and the meaning of scientific advances as they emerge during the physician's practicing years. In other words, a more intelligent and scientific practice of the art of medicine. As the Commission on Medical Education (Association of American Medical Colleges) noted in 1932:

> The medical course cannot produce a physician. It can only provide the opportunities for a student to secure an elementary knowledge of the medical

> sciences and their application to health problems, a training in the methods and spirit of scientific inquiry. . . . Medicine must be learned by the student, for only a fraction of it can be taught by the faculty. The latter makes the essential contributions of guidance, inspiration, and leadership in learning.[3]

Medical school should emphasize interactions between students and professors, with students held responsible for their own education, developing problem-solving skills, and becoming self-directed lifelong learners. As Dr. Artemis Simopoulos of the National Institutes of Health has said: "We need physicians who look at the whole individual and work with his health problems in the context of his nutrition, the home and work environment, and his lifestyle."[4]

Accordingly, doctors of the future will need more and better science training—not less. Medicine is going to improve most of all through scientific breakthroughs. Doctors' practice and basic knowledge will be significantly different in the 2000s. Their training must ensure they achieve fundamental scientific insights and a firm grasp of methodology so they can continue to educate themselves as the breakthroughs occur. The keys are insight and understanding, not a large body of factual information infected with creeping obsolescence.

The basic medical school curriculum must incorporate sophisticated training in nutrition, environmental effects, toxicology, addictions, biological individuality, and the myriad other factors that we now know to be involved in human health and illness. This training must explore the role of these factors in diagnosis *and* treatment, as well as how to counsel and prescribe nutrition, exercise, and lifestyle changes for healthy patients in order to prevent the development of degenerative disease.

In 1985, the Committee on Nutrition in Medical Education made the following recommendations in reference to nutrition education in medical school:[5]

- Nutrition should be taught as an independent, required course at the same time as the other preclinical courses.
- Nutritional precepts should be reinforced during clinical training, and their application in patient care should be emphasized.
- Nutrition programs should be established and led by persons with "strong backgrounds in nutrition science, research, and applications to clinical medicine."

- In order to keep programs up-to-date, a monitoring system should be established to oversee "periodic changes in the status of nutrition education in medical schools."

The thrust of these recommendations is equally applicable to other neglected subjects in medical training, from genetics to behavior.

In a separate set of recommendations, the American Association of Medical College's Professional Education Panel advised that medical school faculties and students be encouraged to form mentor relationships, possibly by increasing the number of faculty members. Such mentor relationships should aid in the development of each student and provide a more coherent and relevant education than the current approach. To facilitate this, the panel also recommended that medical schools set up programs "to assist members of the faculty to expand their teaching capabilities beyond their specialized fields to encompass as much of the full range of the general professional education of the students as is possible."[6] The medical student will profit from such a personal, interdisciplinary model that provides a useful framework for acquiring new information and organizing and using that information in medical practice.

Such a framework will be particularly useful in dealing with the complexities of *medical pharmacology*—a field in which few physicians have sufficient training. As recently as 1988 the American College of Physicians acknowledged that training in the area of pharmacotherapeutics is inadequate. In the absence of such training, practicing physicians must rely on the dubious and potentially biased information supplied to them by pharmaceutical companies. More effective training in pharmacotherapy will give physicians a more wary attitude toward medications—one that seeks to *avoid* prescribing drugs wherever possible. It will also prompt doctors to keep up-to-date on new developments and watch for and educate patients about possible complications or side effects.

This training should be combined with intensive education about addiction. Alcoholism and other substance abuses are virtually ignored by doctors in their histories, physicals, or courses of treatment. Nearly 71 percent of physicians surveyed in a 1982 AMA poll indicated that they felt incompetent or ambivalent about treating alcoholism. Addiction training must therefore include:

- The genetics and biochemistry of alcoholism and other addictions.
- Recognition and diagnosis of the alcoholic or addicted patient.
- Familiarity with laboratory tests that can identify at-risk patients before the problem ever arises.
- The nature of nicotine addiction.
- The broad field of prescription addiction and how to avoid it.
- And most important, how to manage and successfully treat alcoholics, smokers, and other addicted patients.

Dartmouth, the University of Washington (where Fetal Alcohol Syndrome was first identified), Brown, Morehouse in Atlanta, New York University, and Johns Hopkins medical schools are pioneering in integrating addiction studies into medical training. It is urgent that all health-training institutions be required to follow suit.

From the rigidly structured, passive world of lecture halls, young doctors proceed to the chaotic, demanding world of the hospital—where the *practice* of medicine is learned. Unfortunately, these crucial years are also the most grueling and dehumanizing portion of medical training.

Despite the recognized dangers of working young doctors for days on end with little to no sleep, in September 1990 the American Board of Medical Specialties vetoed universal work hour reforms that would have limited overnight calls to no more than once every third night and required that residents have one day off a week. In New York State, reforms have limited residents to a work week of a mere *80 hours,* and even this limit is frequently ignored. No labor union in the nation would permit its members to work under these conditions, yet thousands of young doctors in training are expected to make complex diagnostic decisions when they are critically exhausted. It is more than absurd—it is dangerous.

The American Association of Medical College's Professional Education Panel's recommendation included a series of measures to reduce the recognized stresses and limitations of clinical training. Among their suggestions:[7]

- Students should be given clearly stated goals.
- They should be given "consistent supervision and guidance by experienced faculty members and residents who are fully aware of the specific knowledge, skills, values, and attitudes that their partic-

ular discipline is to contribute to the . . . education of medical students."

- Faculty members and residents should "have adequate preparation and the necessary time to guide and supervise" the students they are teaching.
- "Medical faculties should provide support and guidance to enhance the personal development of each medical student . . . [and] each medical school should develop a system for effective support and counseling of medical students."

Medical students need to be trained to deal with the unique characteristics and problems of each patient. They need the intellectual and technical tools to evaluate illness based on broad biological principles. As an essential of their profession, they need to become "lifelong learners"—keeping up with science's advancing understanding of the human organism and its place in the biosphere, because once they get out into the real world of sickness and health, they will discover the truth in Dean Burwell's 1984 statement to the medical students of Harvard: "Half of what we have taught you is wrong. Unfortunately, we do not know which half."

Medical Practice

No physician can treat illness intelligently without knowing what it is. If the patient's sore throat is caused by a virus it will not respond to antibiotics; if it's the result of a bacterial infection, it will. Both conditions manifest the same symptoms—it is the task of the physician to differentiate between the symptoms and the actual illness. Such diagnosis is part art and part science. If the physician misses a key sign of the disease or makes a wrong inference, the treatment will almost certainly be wide of the mark and perhaps harmful. For this reason, diagnosis is widely recognized as the central event of medical practice. Legend has it that Sir William Osler used to tell his medical students that there are three principles of good medicine—diagnosis, diagnosis, and diagnosis. From these, all else follows.

The importance of diagnosis in effective medical practice has long been acknowledged by members of the profession, and doctors adept at diagnosis always have been esteemed by their colleagues. In *The Youngest Science,* Dr. Lewis Thomas cites Dr. Robert F. Loeb as an example:

> Loeb was a master diagnostician . . . he could walk on a ward and recognize, by some kind of instinct, each of the patients in whom something deeply serious was going on. He was also a master at the art of raising interesting questions, unanswerable but nevertheless interesting, about the possible mechanisms that underlay the disease with which we were confronted. What did we think was going on, *really* going on?[8]

At the time Loeb was practicing neurology, such skill was particularly awe-inspiring since many of the diagnostic techniques in use at the time were crude at best, relying on the observation of reflexes elicited by a rubber hammer, a pin, and a feather.

Over the last three decades, of course, much of that lack of rigor has been corrected. The pin, feather, and hammer have been augmented by noninvasive CAT scans, Brain Electrical Activity Mapping (BEAM), the injection of radioactive dye into cerebral blood vessels to locate embolisms, the radiation-free Nuclear Magnetic Resonance (NMR) technology, and so on. We are, in fact, in a golden age of diagnostic technology. Hundreds of new instruments, techniques, and tests appear, are evaluated, and are put into use yearly. If medical methodology is to improve and become more effective in treating disease states, physicians must learn to use these technologies to perform truly thorough diagnoses of their patients—evaluating them in the full context of their nutritional, behavioral, and environmental status.

In this process, an essential tool is the patient's *history,* establishing details of past and present illnesses, nutritional habits, behavioral patterns, and potential environmental exposures at home, in personal products and foods, on the job, and outdoors. This work provides a profile of the patient's biological and medical background that can be used by the physician to explore issues during the personal interview.

It is *after* these evaluations that the careful *physical examination* and array of *laboratory tests* needed to clarify the patient's state of health are performed. If the combined result of these investigations indicates that the patient is decompensated by reason of malnutrition and toxicity, the physician pursues more detailed biochemical and metabolic questions using the sophisticated diagnostic tools now available. For example:

- How severe is the malnutrition, and does it have specific features or reveal a pattern? Are there indications of a distinctive deficiency in any one enzyme, vitamin, mineral, or trace element?
- How extensive is the patient's chemical reactivity or toxicity? Are there signs of a unique pattern? For example, is a particular environmental agent, such as aluminum or carbon monoxide, implicated? Are there indications of possible allergies or food reactions?
- What evidence is there of a genetic disease or propensity to a disease? Of a metabolic anomaly?
- What is the functional profile of key organs and bodily systems—the liver, thyroid, pancreas, pituitary, adrenals and kidneys, circulatory and nervous systems, and so forth?
- What is the status of the patient's immune system?
- How does he metabolize fats? Protein? Carbohydrates? Other nutrients?

When these examinations indicate that the patient is suffering from malnutrition, toxicity, or both, the diagnostician's task should be to detoxify and nutritionally restore him or her. Until the deck of symptoms is cleared in this way, the doctor cannot tell if the patient's chronic complaint is a function of a decompensated state or a specific disorder.

In today's conditions, most adult patients have to be detoxified and nutritionally restored before a specific diagnosis can be formulated. Otherwise, the interaction of biological factors may very well obscure what really is going on. The underlying pathologies can manifest in dozens of deceptive ways, including the vague symptoms of "chronic fatigue syndrome"—lethargy, irritability, fatigue, recurring headaches, muscle weakness, depression, anxiety, fear, hostility. The routine workup performed by most physicians doesn't provide enough detailed information to get past this smoke screen of nonspecific symptoms. On the other hand, once these biological realities are brought under control and clarified, the doctor can begin to make a specific diagnosis with a reasonable measure of confidence.

At a recent professional meeting involving several Canadian Ministry of Health officials as well as many prestigious psychology professionals, a case was presented of a young woman suffering from severe depression. After several months of unsuccessful treatment with antidepressant drugs, it was discovered that there was a severe natural gas leak underneath her bedroom. In the medical workup that followed it was also discovered that the patient was a chronic smoker and alcohol abuser suffering from several severe nutrient deficiencies. The ensuing treatment—which entailed a range of medical and psychological interventions—succeeded in "curing" her depression (as measured by several objective scales) within two months.

In discussing the case, several of the medical officials at the meeting repeatedly tried to determine "the cause" of the seemingly remarkable cure. Like the blind men and the elephant, these men and women—many of whom are at the top of their profession—failed to see the most central point of the case. No one factor had helped the young woman—all of them had, in a dynamic, interrelated fashion.

In many ways, the process of detoxifying and renourishing the patient is the most difficult part of the diagnostic process. As we saw in earlier chapters, many of the things that are giving patients health problems are also what they're most fiercely attached to. Hence, the physician usually has to take a firm, even aggressive stand on the dangers of continuing with the destructive pattern and ways to reshape it along healthier lines.

In 1981, then Surgeon General Dr. C. Everett Koop delineated the measures that physicians should take to help their patients give up smoking. They included:

- Information on the risks associated with smoking.
- Clarification of the benefits of giving up smoking.
- Encouragement of abstinence through advice and direct service.
- Referral to smoking cessation programs.
- Specific strategies for cessation and maintenance.

Dr. Koop's recommendations are equally relevant to the other risk factors that can malnourish and toxify a patient. There is no defensible reason why personal physicians should not take an active role in leading their patients to develop better nutritional habits, avoid reactive chemicals, and pursue a healthier lifestyle.

Medical Research

Research today is engaged in an attempt to fit nature into the rigid (and remarkably limited) conceptual boxes supplied by professional education. Unfortunately, these boxes are defined by the specific etiology/

intervention approach, which is at a distinct disadvantage in dealing with the degenerative diseases. Current research techniques and criteria cannot address the complex systems involved in chronic disease.

In order to effectively research these disorders, and therefore come up with useful information for clinician and patient alike, medical researchers must remember that:

- Each human organism is governed by a unique DNA/RNA code of immense complexity. The variation between individuals can be enormous, with substantial differences in the biochemical and physiological makeup of human beings. This biological individuality means widely differing susceptibilities to environmental and nutritional conditions, which makes replication an unreliable standard for validating research findings. In dealing with human subjects, it is naive to expect that investigators will be able to produce identical results. If consistent replication were the sole criterion, we would not be using digitalis for congestive heart failure—since we do not know exactly how it works, and toxic levels vary from patient to patient. Fortunately, the value of digitalis was discovered long before the prospective, replicated double-blind study, so that it is prescribed on a highly individualized basis, within certain general guidelines.
- When studying nutrition, every link in the chain of life is important. The attempt to investigate the impact of a single nutrient without regard for the complexity of human processes will frequently reach distorted conclusions.
- Susceptibility to specific factors or agents will vary even in the same individual at different times. Someone who was not allergic or reactive to wheat products or bee stings or gasoline fumes while growing up may well become allergic to them in middle age. The human organism is in a constant state of flux and evolution. This is particularly evident in women, whose susceptibility to a number of disorders (such as atherosclerosis) changes after menopause.
- Research must also deal with the macroeconomic social and commercial considerations that directly affect the well-being of populations. A research methodology that ignores the impact of socioeconomic factors runs the risk of missing crucial variables with important treatment implications.

- Finally, a broader, better integrated research methodology needs to be developed that takes information from related fields into account, that is not bound by the straitjacket of the "project mentality," and that examines problems of human health in terms of the actual situations of individuals. In medical treatment the patient should serve as his or her own control whenever possible. We should not confine our concept of proof to double-blind studies.

Hyperspecialization and competition are the norm in modern medical research. There is very little crossover between fields, and paranoia over being the first to publish new data can prompt almost pathological secretiveness. Continued funding is so inextricably linked to "results" that many research groups find themselves working more in the interests of their funders than the interests of science. If Robert Koch and Louis Pasteur were alive today they would probably be unable to get funding—their goals were too vague.

Medical research needs to be freed from the constraints of this mindset. Methodology should not be allowed to inhibit scientific intuition. The human mind is capable of far more than can be achieved merely through scientific method and statistical analysis. Most of the great scientific breakthroughs have been made through individual observations and human intuition rather than rigid methodological procedures. Proven intuitive genius, as well as strict scientific and statistical research, should be generously supported, not discouraged. To cite only the most illustrious recent cases, it is a national embarrassment that Nobel laureates such as Linus Pauling (the only living soul to have won the Nobel Prize in two different fields) and Albert Szent-Gyorgyi have been denied research funding by the "peer" review system of the National Institutes of Health.

If medicine's goal is the "integrated application" of science, medical research must take definite steps to correct the current, tunnel-vision approach to health and illness.

1. Medical researchers need to be more aware of the momentous advances happening in other scientific disciplines, and think in terms of their relevance to human health issues.

2. Research funders must give researchers the freedom to investigate these issues, with less emphasis on narrow, simplistic research goals.
3. The gap between lab research and clinical trials must be narrowed, so that the human applications of new techniques and treatments can be understood more quickly.
4. Finally, the critical information gulf that currently separates medical research from medical practice must be bridged. Information on new advances should be rapidly disseminated to practicing physicians for use in the "real world."

A lot of the most important research—into nutrition, human behavior, and the environment, to cite the subjects of this book—has little commercial potential, little glamour, and dismally little funding each year. Now that U.S. corporations have passed the federal government in total spending on research and development, the odds against noncommercial research are even slimmer. Industrial priorities—which are by their very nature profit-dominated—distort research enterprises and deplete talent and money from areas such as health, nutrition, and the environment. These areas may not have commercial value (you cannot, after all, patent a vitamin), but they are the best hope of understanding and limiting chronic disease processes. All the more reason for the government and the research-support community to ensure that these vital subjects are pursued.

Food science research, for example, is now conducted almost exclusively by the giant food processors for motives that are largely antinutrient in impact. No wonder we get so few nutrition breakthroughs on our grocery shelves.

We also need much more intensive study of human nutrient requirements. As long ago as 1975, the Working Conference on Research to Meet U.S. and World Food Needs, sponsored by the USDA, rated as our highest priority the need for further studies on human nutrient requirements. Distorted research priorities have left a nation of experts stumbling in the dark when it comes to food. As Dr. Jean Mayer, president of Tufts University, has noted: "For too long has nutrition been denied its proper role in American medicine. Billions of dollars are spent on the treatment of disease each year, but very little is spent in research on nutrition, which is often the key to the prevention of disease."[9]

What is true of nutrition is equally true of the environment and other noncommercial subjects of central importance to the health of Americans.

It is time to alter the criteria of biological research from the interpretation of single-factor results, to the design of multifactorial and interdisciplinary studies, to declaring a treatment valid. As biology and medicine move toward this goal, they must always keep in mind that we still know very little about the workings of the human body. The brain alone conceals innumerable mysteries that science has only begun unraveling. How can we understand disease processes if we do not understand the host that succumbs to the disease? Understanding the host's *milieu intérieur* and relationship to the rest of the world is integral to progress against chronic disease. And we can only arrive at such an understanding by more and better research, which recognizes its limitations and draws on the knowledge of a variety of sciences.

IMPROVING MEDICINE is not a panacea for the ills of the modern world. But it can have a significant effect on the health of individuals and the public policies that arise from the medical model. And despite the depth of modern medicine's paralysis, there is no question that a revolution is ahead—too much is at stake for everyone.

Specific intervention is an essential and often primary tool of medicine, but its utility is always limited to the confines of man's specific knowledge of disease. When treating conditions of unknown etiology (and there are still hundreds of them) and particularly the complex life-process disorders that give rise to chronic disease, much broader *systemic* measures take primacy. To that end, medicine must move toward an integration of all that is good in "the miracle of modern medicine" with the complementary strengths of systemic care. It is essential that environmental, nutritional, and lifestyle factors be incorporated into medical practice, and that medical science—at all levels—develop a much broader understanding of illness and a comprehensive approach to diagnosis and treatment.

11

What We Can Do

WITH CHRONIC DISEASE afflicting every family in America, it's natural to wonder what, if anything, can be done. We can't afford to wait for the medical establishment to embrace a new paradigm of medical care while industries continue to pollute the environment, the food-production system adds chemicals to our food, and pharmaceutical companies peddle dangerous drugs without adequate testing or full disclosure.

But we are not powerless. As individuals, we can choose to avoid many of the pitfalls that surround us. We can eat whole foods, avoid drugs, and clean up our home environment. We can exercise more, drink less alcohol, avoid radiation, and so on. Just as there are limits on what others can do to undermine our health, there are limits on what others can do to restore our health. In the words of the late Dr. John Knowles, who headed both the Massachusetts General Hospital and the Rockefeller Foundation: "The people have been led to believe that national health insurance, more doctors, and greater use of high-cost, hospital-based technologies will improve health. Unfortunately, none of them will."[1]

Despite this truth, most of us persist in focusing our dissatisfactions and expectations outside ourselves in an ever-hopeful belief that agents and agencies such as physicians, public-health officials, and clinics are the ones to protect our health.

The truth is just the opposite: *Self-care is the only effective way to ensure good health and longer, fuller life.* The many—and well-meaning—individuals and policy makers who believe that socialized medicine or a government-run health-care system (on the order of the already disastrous systems of Medicaid and Medicare) is the solution to our health-care problems are missing the central point of the current crisis. While it is true that far too many individuals do not have sufficient access to care, it is more true that the care itself is based on an outdated and ineffective model—based on end-stage results of the broad, systemic problems that arise from malnutrition, toxicity, and unhealthy lifestyles. If we are to restore the health of the American people (and truly cut the cost of health care) we must correct these fundamental, underlying problems—through a comprehensive approach to the diagnosis and treatment of disease that includes doctor *and* patient. Achieving this goal will require all the brilliance, creativity, and intellectual flexibility that we can muster—all of which are discouraged and often destroyed by government bureaucracy.

Self-care is not, then, a way of making the doctor obsolete. Its aim is to reduce the likelihood of disease, disability, and early death from illnesses where controllable lifestyle factors have been shown to be important in disease development. A person educated in self-care is also better equipped to make judicious choices when selecting the right doctor and more capable of working *with* the physician in the treatment of illness.

Lifestyle and Self-Care

Most of us have become addicted, for all practical purposes, to our lifestyle habits. Whether they include smoking, drinking a little heavily, working at high stress, or avoiding exercise at all costs, changing them is like major surgery, without anesthesia. The tenacity of unhealthy behavior can be blamed partly on the addictive substances involved (caffeine, alcohol, nicotine, drugs), but equally powerful are our basic *attitudes* toward life, health, and illness. It is only by overhauling some of these attitudes that many of us can hope to break our most risky habits.

For a start, we would all be a lot better off if we would simply believe the Surgeon General's various warnings. In recent years we have witnessed a tremendous increase in the amount of health warnings on potentially deadly products—including alcohol and cigarettes—but most of us still haven't quite gotten the point. Just a few of the recognized lifestyle risks we should be avoiding are:

- Cigarette smoking.
- Heavy drinking (more than one and a half ounces of 86-proof alcohol a day).
- Driving without a seat belt.
- Overeating.
- Illicit drug use.
- Overuse of caffeine.
- Unsafe sexual practices.

For the millions of individuals who are already addicted to cigarettes, alcohol, or drugs, the simple formula of "Just say no" is about as effective as telling a depressive to "Have a nice day." If you are battling an addiction you should not do it alone. See a physician with expertise in the field of addiction medicine, and get involved in a support group. Start repairing your damaged body through improved nutrition and avoidance of other toxins. If you aren't sure where to go for help, contact one of the many nonprofit support groups (notably Alcoholics Anonymous and Narcotics Anonymous) that can assist you in getting help.

If someone you love is suffering from an addiction, these groups can help you to intervene and get the person into treatment. Most addictions, once they become entrenched, are no longer lifestyle *choices*, they are life *imperatives*—dictated by the body's radically disordered biochemistry. Addicted individuals need comprehensive treatment and care—not punitive measures—and the treatment needed to repair the biological damage caused by the addiction.

The tremendous power of addictive substances—particularly alcohol, nicotine, and caffeine—makes it imperative that children be taught to avoid their use and/or abuse. Children need useful knowledge, not scare tactics and morality fables, if they are going to avoid the pitfalls of addiction. And that means education on *all* addictive substances—not just the illegal "drug of the week." Alcoholism kills and disables more people than all the other drugs put together, but 70 percent of high school students have no understanding of how dangerous a drug it is.

Smoking killed 300,000 people last year—heroin approximately 5,000. Let your kids know the real risks of all the drugs of abuse—not just the ones you don't happen to use.

Sex is another lifestyle variable that is widely disregarded—a possibly fatal oversight in today's world of AIDS, syphilis, pelvic inflammatory disease, herpes, gonorrhea, venereal warts, chlamydia, and various other sexually transmitted diseases. Our children need to be versed in the realities of sex and contraception before they find out the hard way. No child should have to die of AIDS because his or her parents felt uncomfortable about discussing condoms. In the modern world, inadequate sex education could mean death.

We adults also need to be more realistic about our sexual behavior. The "risk-free" sex of the sexual revolution—a by-product of effective antibiotics and accessible contraception and abortion—is long gone. We are back to the historical reality of sex as a serious and sometimes dangerous proposition for both partners. It is shocking that only 12 to 20 percent of sexually active women report using condoms as their contraceptive method of choice. Everyone who is not involved in an exclusive, monogamous relationship in which both partners have tested HIV negative should either be using condoms or abstaining altogether. Individuals in high-risk groups—particularly intravenous drug users (or past users) and their partners—should be tested for HIV at least every six months. Early detection and optimization of overall health can help prevent the development of full-blown AIDS even in patients who are HIV positive, and new pharmacotherapies are still under development.

Beyond avoiding known risks, we can also increase behaviors that are known to be beneficial. Exercise, for example, can improve cardiovascular fitness, raise the metabolic set point, and increase the brain's production of important neurotransmitters. Cardiovascular fitness is also improved with "aerobic" exercise (sustained high burning of oxygen rather than isolated spurts of activity) for at least thirty minutes at a time at least three days a week. Such activity should elevate the pulse to about twice its resting rate. Brisk walking, bicycling, and swimming are good aerobic exercises that don't place undo stress on the joints and muscles. Whatever exercise you choose, make it something you actually like and remember not to overdo it.

Just as exercise can increase your energy level, decrease your weight, and even improve your overall outlook on life, relaxation and a balanced living pattern can protect you from a range of stress-related disorders, including hypertension, gastrointestinal disorders, and headaches. Regular sleep-wake schedules are crucial to a healthy lifestyle, and chronic disruptions of the sleep cycle (including those induced through dream-suppressing drugs or alcohol) take a serious physical and psychological toll.

Stress is largely a matter of how we perceive our experiences. Getting "worked up" over life's events only worsens the physical impact. Healthy interpersonal relationships, when coupled with various relaxation techniques, can restore a sense of perspective and "defuse" potentially negative stresses. Give yourself time to relax and wind down every day (without alcohol or other chemical "assistance"). If you find it impossible to relax, therapists specializing in biofeedback can help you learn techniques that will induce what stress researcher Herbert Benson has called "the relaxation response"—the physiological state that is almost exactly the reverse of the stress response. It has proved useful in treating a number of disorders including hypertension. And it is certainly less toxic and less expensive than drugs or a coronary bypass.

If You Do Get Sick

The ability to assess your own state of health and either care for yourself properly or recognize when it's time to get a doctor's help is integral to self-care.

Today, many of the tools that were once reserved for doctors are available to laypersons. Blood pressure cuffs; thermometers; instruments for examining the ears, nose, and throat; and even the classic stethoscope can be purchased and made a part of any medicine cabinet. We are strongly advised to do simple, quick, manual self-exams for breast and skin cancer, which are far more easily cured if caught early. The means to take responsibility for your own health have never been so readily available.

Some doctors resent it when a patient takes an informed or skeptical stance, particularly if they are used to spending a minimum of time explaining things to patients. Nonetheless, you have the right, and a duty, to know what is being done to you or your family member, and why.

Since drugs are often prescribed incorrectly, excessively, or without an adequate explanation of interactions and side effects, the active patient should have a copy of the *Physician's Desk Reference* (the PDR) at home. It is available at most large bookstores and libraries. *Drugs are not to be taken lightly.* One should know as much as possible about the risks as well as the benefits of any drug before ingesting it. There may be contraindications the doctor is not aware apply in your case or possible side effects you should know of while taking the drug.

The same healthy skepticism should be applied to all nonemergency procedures, particularly those that require exposure to or ingestion of radioactive materials. X rays, barium milk shakes or enemas, kidney scans, and so on, are common, risk-laden procedures that are sometimes performed even when they are not necessary. Try to avoid any invasive or risky diagnostic procedure unless you are convinced it is needed. "Second opinions" should be sought during diagnosis, as well as treatment, whenever you become uncertain about the risks involved.

Finally, since many of us do not have a single "family doctor" but go to several different physicians over the course of a lifetime, it is important to have a comprehensive understanding of our own medical histories. Dr. Lawrence Weed of the University of Vermont has suggested that individuals should learn to keep their own health records, perhaps by keeping copies of all physician's reports and records (which should be requested in writing).

The push for self-care programs needs to come from individuals as well as the health professions. Look for a self-care program in your community, or a good book on self-care at the library. Ask questions. Learn all you can about how your body works and what you can do to maintain it. It is, after all, *your* health and long life that is at stake—not your doctor's.

Ecology and Self-Care

While the environment is not our doing, it pervades us physically all our lives. And through the constant promotion of chemical-laden foods and products, it pervades us socially and psychologically as well. The modern technological society in which we live is also, invisibly, a swamp of chemicals. These substances are in the soil beneath us (and in which our children play) and throughout the air we breathe, the food we eat, the water we drink, the clothes we wear, the furniture we sit on, the toiletries and household products we use, the job we go to. In fact, this chemical contamination has become so ubiquitous that most assume it's not really a problem or it's beyond our control.

In truth, it *is* a problem, a major problem. Although many environmental threats are outside our immediate "sphere of influence," there are also many ways to reduce the chemical load of our daily lives. In the average American home, on any given day, there are many potentially reactive chemicals in use—the bleach to whiten clothes, the spray to kill insects, the foam to remove mildew from bathroom tiles, the "powerful new" oven cleaner, the formaldehyde "leather" on Dad's favorite chair. Since these substances are found in such commonly used items, few of us recognize their dangers so we can try to avoid them. Michael Colgan, then a visiting scholar at Rockefeller University, wrote of our ignorance about so many common potential carcinogens:

> It amazes me to see how people will protect their hands with gloves from many agricultural chemicals, while gagging on the smells. The same applies to household chemicals. Women especially go to great lengths to protect their hands from bleaches, oven cleaners, and insect sprays, while neglecting entirely the much more delicate tissues of the nose, throat, and lungs. Use a mask. Many cancers start from breathing in carcinogens. We have a strict rule around the laboratory. What it amounts to is: if you can't eat it, don't sniff it.[2]

If you must use a product that contains risky chemicals (manufacturers put fine-print warnings on some, though by no means all, of these items), you can reduce the risks by using gloves or a protective mask. But it is best to avoid such products so far as you can. Even if your deodorant bath soap doesn't give you a rash and your spray wall cleaner only makes you sneeze, and the pest spray just smells awful, many experts fear that the accumulation of all these minute chemical assaults poses long-term health risks. Despite industry disclaimers, even additives to food ("It's only coloring") continue to be found unsafe and should be avoided as much as possible.

There are several ways to prevent environmental risks on the home front. The first is to perform an environmental "diagnosis" of your home and its surroundings (if you are considering buying a house these factors should be investigated before you buy):

- Who are your neighbors? Are you downwind of a military base? A factory? A superhighway? If so, investigate their environmental consequences.
- Who lived there before you? Was the land once owned by the military? If so, it could well be contaminated with a number of toxins. Did the previous owners have a business that used toxic chemicals, such as mercury or formaldehyde? If so, you may need to have the house professionally decontaminated.
- When was the plumbing system installed? Newer homes (under three years) tend to have higher levels of lead in their water supplies. Have the water tested for possible contaminants. If possible, replace all lead pipes with copper pipes with mechanical fittings. (Pipes made of polyvinyl chloride can leach chemicals into the water supply) Failing that, install a filter between you and the pipes—at kitchen sinks, etc.
- How have the house and yard been treated for pests? Was the house fumigated for termites? Did the previous owners use chemical pesticides?
- Is the house new or recently remodeled? If so, chemical products used during construction may vaporize when the heat is turned on.
- Are there high-tension wires running over or near the house? Electricity emanating from these areas can interfere with the body's natural electromagnetic field.

Local environmental protection groups and state agencies can help you arrange to test your home for a range of contaminants—including radon. If necessary, they can also help you decontaminate your home. On a less drastic level, you should as a matter of course install a water filter at the main water source or at the tap. Most municipal water treatment programs simply are not effective enough at purifying the water supply.

Similarly, individuals living near high-traffic areas would be well advised to install air filters in one or more rooms—since ambient lead levels are significantly higher near roadways, and children are particularly sensitive to such exposure. Lead is such a serious concern in the modern world that it is important to "de-lead" your home as much as possible. In addition to the measures already mentioned, you can:

- Avoid canned foods, which can contain twice as much lead as fresh foods. When using canned foods, do not store food in the can. Transfer it to a glass or plastic container.
- Beware outdoor and indoor dust, which can be contaminated with lead from the deposition of aerosols, weathering or removal of lead-based paint, and leaded emissions from gasoline. Children playing in yards and houses near roadways are at particular risk for ingesting lead from yard dirt and house dust. Moving to a less contaminated neighborhood is the best solution—and worth the trouble if it can be managed. Otherwise, water frequently to keep play areas clean and the dust down and wash the children's hands and clothes as often as practical.
- Remove coats of potentially leaded paints. Older houses, particularly in urban areas, should be considered risk factors for young children, and old coats of paint should be removed and recovered with nonlead-based paints.

If you are now feeling inclined to simply throw up your hands and move to Antarctica (where you'll only need to worry about the hole in the ozone layer), take heart. Several excellent books have already been written on the topic of cleaning up the home environment, and they can help you decide what to use and what to avoid. One of the best is Debra Lynn Dadd's *Nontoxic & Natural: A Guide for Consumers. How to Avoid Dangerous Everyday Products & Buy or Make Safe Ones* (Los Angeles: J. P. Tarcher, 1984; distributed by Houghton Mifflin, Boston). Arranged alphabetically, this resource book covers everything from afghans to sanitary napkins to Worcestershire sauce. There are also several citizens' groups that can provide information on specific products and sources for nontoxic alternatives.

These simple measures can drastically decrease your exposure to toxic chemicals via your food, air, water, and immediate environment. In moving in this direction the strength of your dollar will move with you, and the market will get the point.

Nutrition and Self-Care

Nutrition is in many ways easier to improve than either one's lifestyle or environment. While it is conditioned by many of the same forces as the environment—the American food-production system—and subject to the same deep drives as lifestyle habits, the reality is that good food and good eating are more enjoyable than lousy food and eating in a rush. If people eat poorly, it's usually not because they prefer to but because they're in a hurry, or they're alone and "don't cook," or they're under pressure and haven't got the patience for good food, or they don't know any better. Fortunately, the number of Americans seeking better diets continues to rise year after year, so much so that many major producers now have lines of "improved" foods.

Still, most of us don't eat as well as we should. We like "quick-and-easy" meals, refined carbohydrates, junk foods, and lots of sugar. We don't get enough fiber—and often not enough of certain vitamins or essential fatty acids. Many don't get enough key minerals or trace elements. Some don't even get enough protein. All these deficiencies undermine our health.

Good nutrition is essential to self-care. The human body, when properly nourished, is a remarkably resilient organism, and good nutrition will help you fight off infection and toxic assaults.

Despite the potentially vast differences in nutritional needs between individuals, it is possible to optimize your diet without getting a doctorate in biochemistry or having expensive testing done (although in the best of all possible worlds you *would* have your individual needs evaluated). Just keep in mind that your body's design is somewhat unsuited to the modern world, and try to maintain a diet that is closer to that of our ancestors—who lived in a world devoid of chemical additives, processed foods, refined carbohydrates, and other modern conveniences. Start reading the ingredients of the foods you buy. If you need a Ph.D. in industrial chemistry to decipher a food's ingredient list—don't buy it. Avoid foods that are colors that do not occur in nature, such as incandescent orange cheese. Just because the FDA hasn't banned a food coloring doesn't make it safe. Some other general guidelines include:

1. *Use whole foods*—fresh vegetables, fruits, nuts, eggs, cheeses, fish, poultry, meats. Keep preparation moderate. For example, steam rather than boil vegetables.
2. *Choose whole grain breads*, cereals, pasta, and baked goods. (Whole grains include rye, cornmeal, and brown rice, along with whole wheat.) Avoid white flour bread and bakery products as much as you can.

3. *Include fiber* (in the form of fresh fruits, vegetables, salads, sprouts, nuts, seeds, bran, and whole grain cereals and bread) in your diet daily.
4. *Avoid refined sugar* (as opposed to the sugars that are natural constituents of fruit and milk, for example) and products that are high in refined sugar (including corn syrup), as much as possible.
5. *Include some protein* food in each meal. Dairy products are particularly important, for their calcium as well as protein.
6. *Eat moderate amounts of natural fats*—found in fish, olives, nuts, butter, milk, cheese, cold-processed oils, wheat germ, and meat.
7. *Avoid margarine and other hydrogenated oils.* Cut down on highly processed polyunsaturated oils. Where needed, use butter, olive oil, and a variety of cold-pressed oils. Keep these products covered and refrigerated when not in use.
8. *Eat several smaller meals a day*, instead of a couple of big ones. Snacks—of whole foods—are good for you. Avoid drastic or imbalanced diets (such as single-item programs or modified fasts)—they are potentially dangerous and they don't work. If you feel you need to diet, do so under the care of a physician who understands nutrition.
9. If you have food allergies or sensitivities, learn to eliminate or rotate these foods.
10. If you suffer from hay fever, asthma, chemical sensitivities, or chronic gastrointestinal problems have your immune system evaluated by a physician and have any allergies or adverse reactions identified and corrected as soon as possible.
11. *Take a comprehensive multinutrient supplement* (with food) every day. Make sure that it does not contain chemicals, dyes, cornstarch, or sugar, and try to purchase one that has most of the essential nutrients.
12. Since agricultural practices often result in chemical and pesticide contamination of even "fresh" foods, try to purchase products that have been organically grown (without pesticides or chemical fertilizers) or bred on "free-range" farms (as opposed to those bred "intensively" on a minimum of space and a maximum of antibiotics and hormones).

Self-care through good nutrition is easy. All it takes is a little effort and an ongoing process of self-education. By listening and reading, inform yourself—and your children—about good nutrition. But keep in mind that nutrition is a relatively young field, and many specific issues are subject to wide-ranging debate. For example, Adelle Davis, who pioneered in educating Americans about nutrition, at times discusses large doses of certain nutrients for specific ailments. Such an approach has been shown to help in certain conditions, but some nutrients can become toxic at higher doses. Individuals should not take large doses of specific nutrient supplements without the guidance of someone knowledgeable in nutrition science.

For more recent examples, the Center for Science in the Public Interest, Jane Brody, and other regular columnists—in need of news to report—track what we have called the "hyperspecialized" scientists rather closely. As a result they tend to report (and seem to advocate) the most recent "discoveries" as the latest, best wisdom in nutrition. Usually such findings are highly particular, partial, and not yet tested by the larger progress of science over years. Some of their recommendations of just a couple of years ago—polyunsaturated oils, for example—are now being reversed by newer findings. By following tunnel-vision science, such recommendations tend toward simplistic formulas that, on the basis of present evidence, aren't applicable to most people—for instance, very low-fat, low-salt, or low-protein diets for avoiding heart disease or high blood pressure or cancer. There is considerable debate about the issues involved in these narrow recommendations, and many reputable researchers dispute such approaches for the general public or question the wisdom of advising diverse persons on the basis of fragmentary and unfolding evidence. Individual human beings' biochemistry is far more complex than any of these quick formulas would suggest.

It is wise, therefore, to follow such sources with a little balance and common sense. For good nutrition, what Americans need most of all is an instinctive preference for whole foods and a healthy sense of suspicion about processed foods.

DESPITE THE superb achievements of medicine, our best hope for a healthy life is not medical care but self-care. Current medical evidence, which implicates violations in lifestyle, environment, and diet as the driving forces in chronic disease, shows that many of us are not conducting our lives in a healthy way. Health as subjective behavior is ignored in favor of health as an objective entity that the designated expert (the doctor) ensures and maintains.

This abdication of responsibility undermines the development of healthy attitudes and healthy behavior. Kidding ourselves that we are forever young, or that the doctor will take care of us if something goes wrong, keeps us from doing what we can, learning how to take care of ourselves. It jeopardizes our health—a little more each day.

The medical establishment has, for the most part, accepted our abdication of responsibility. The doctor has become an almost mythic figure in our era. When something goes wrong, we individuals become "patients"—receivers of the physician's knowledge and skill. Information about how our human body works, and how our sickness is being diagnosed and treated, is not readily or patiently shared with us.

The importance of diet and environment and lifestyle in avoiding degenerative illnesses is beginning to change this situation. Doctors and laypeople alike are becoming aware that spiraling health costs and stubbornly high levels of chronic illness will not change unless *people* change. As we have seen, our society has been violating the broad biological systems on which we depend for our life and health. During this century, these violations have started coming home to roost—in greatly increased rates of chronic, degenerative disease. Meanwhile the medical establishment has largely ignored these biological systems, despite their obvious importance. The result is that, while we are threatened broadside by chronic illness, our doctors, with their special expertise, can't help us very much.

Americans are in the unique position of being able to change this situation, both in their own lives and in the broader systems of social, medical, and governmental policy. Every dollar of the nation's $4.5 trillion gross national product ultimately reverts back to individual economic choices. Every time we buy a product—whether it is an apple or the services of a physician—we are sending a small, subtle message to manufacturers and the government agencies that regulate them. The consumer dollar is therefore the most effective and powerful tool we individuals have. The prospect of an organized consumer boycott (of the kind recently mounted against the tuna industry) is enough to make any corporate structure tremble. But most manufacturers count on consumer apathy to protect them from such an organized display of consumer power.

Similarly, every time we don't go to the voting booth we are tacitly telling elected officials that they have free rein and that the "average" American neither knows nor cares what goes on in the distant halls of government. But the government, like industry, depends on the goodwill (or ennui) of the people. These individuals are in office because we put them there, and if the bulk of the nation is dissatisfied with their leaders, it is because the bulk of the nation has abdicated their power of the vote. It is high time that we as individuals—the much maligned "just one" persons of the world—took back the reins of control, both in our own lives and in the life of the nation. Only then can we begin to truly take care of ourselves and our children—both in this generation and in generations to come.

APPENDIX

Options and Resources

No matter what your opinion of the ideas expressed in this book, it is likely that there are scores of individuals who agree with you, and somewhere in the nation (or the world) these people have banded together—either to make their ideas known or to establish a network for information and resources. The following is only a partial listing of the scores of agencies and groups that deal with the issues discussed in this book.

Government Agencies

General Federal Information
1-800-327-1997
The operators at this toll-free number can provide information on federal policies, programs, and actions regarding everything from toxic wastes to school lunch programs. If they don't have the information, they can generally refer you to the individual or agency who will.

United States House of Representatives (Congress)
Washington, DC 20515
202-224-3121

United States Senate
Washington, DC 20510
202-224-3121

The operators at the Capitol switchboard (which serves both the House and the Senate) can tell you who your representatives are and their specific phone numbers, as well as connect you with various committees, subcommittees, and congressional offices.

The Environmental Protection Agency
401 M Street SW
Washington, DC 20460
202-382-4355
Since the EPA does not have a public affairs office, it is not always easy to get a straight answer from its pressured staff. If you have a specific question or concern (such as current regulations on a particular pesticide), the main operator can connect you with the appropriate person or office. For more general information, you may be better off calling your state or local EPA office.

The Environment

THE HOME:
The Household Hazardous Waste Project
Box 87
901 South National Avenue
Springfield, MO 65804
417-836-5777

WATER:
Water Pollution Control Federation
601 Wythe Street
Alexandria, VA 22314-1994
703-684-2438

TOXIC WASTES:
Citizen's Clearinghouse for Hazardous Wastes/Center for Environmental Justice
P.O. Box 926
Arlington, VA 22216
703-276-7070

THE WORLD AT LARGE:
Center for Marine Conservation
1725 DeSales Street NW
Washington, DC 20036
202-429-5609

Environmental Defense Fund
1616 P Street NW (Suite 150)
Washington, DC 20036
Hot line: 1-800-CALL-EDF

Greenpeace
1436 U Street NW
Washington, DC 20009
1-800-333-7717 (automated line)
202-667-7814

Natural Resources Defense Council
40 West 20th Street
New York, NY 10011
212-727-2700

The Oceanic Society
218 D Street SE
Washington, DC 20003
202-328-0098

The Rainforest Action Network
301 Broadway (Suite A)
San Francisco, CA 94133
415-398-4404

World Wildlife Fund
1250 24th Street NW
Washington, DC 20037

Worldwatch Institute
1776 Massachusetts Avenue NW
Washington, DC 20036

Nutrition

The Center for Science in the Public Interest
1501 16th Street NW
Washington, DC 20036
212-332-9110

National Coalition Against the Misuse of Pesticides
530 7th Street SE
Washington, DC 20003
202-543-5450

Informed Consumerism

The Council on Economic Priorities
30 Irving Place
New York, NY 10003
212-529-0890
Perhaps the best source for general information on the nutritional, environmental, social, and political records of manufacturers and corporations. The council publishes an easy-to-use guide to responsible shopping and investing, which can give you the information you need to "shop your conscience."

Addictions

There are literally thousands of addiction help lines and support groups throughout the United States—for everything from alcoholism to eating disorders and compulsive gambling. Most are listed in local phone directories and many—particularly Alcoholics Anonymous and its affiliates—can help you find treatment programs and assist in interventions. The resources listed here are some of the national sources of information on drug and alcohol addiction.

National Institute of Drug Abuse Hot Line
1-800-662-HELP (4537)
(9 A.M. to 3 P.M. Eastern Standard Time)

Alanon/Alateen
P.O. Box 862
Midtown Station
New York, NY 10018-0862
212-302-7240
(9 A.M. to 5 P.M. Eastern Standard Time)

National Cocaine Hotline
P.O. Box 100
Summit, NJ 07901
1-800-COCAINE (1-800-262-2463)

National Council on Alcoholism
12 West 21st Street
New York, NY 10010
1-800-NCA-CALL (1-800-621-2155)
(9 A.M. to 5 P.M. Eastern Standard Time)

Notes

Chapter 1: The Genetic Foundation of Health

1. A. Garrod, "The incidence of alkaptonuria: A study in chemical individuality," *Lancet* 2 (1902): p. 1616.
2. W. Brown, L. Pearce and C. M. Van Allen, "Organ weights of normal rabbits," *Journal of Experimental Medicine* 43 (1926): pp. 734–38.
3. B. J. Anson, *Atlas of Human Anatomy* (Philadelphia: W. B. Saunders Co., 1951).
4. R. Dubos, *Man, Medicine and Environment* (London: Pall Mall Press, 1968), p. 19.
5. R. Lewontin, *Human Diversity* (New York: W. H. Freeman & Co., 1982), p. 26.
6. T. Dobzhansky, *Mankind Evolving* (New Haven: Yale University Press, 1962), p. 288.
7. W. Tucker, "Thrifty diabetes," *Science '83* 4(2) (1983); pp. 92–93.
8. Ibid.
9. Sir F. M. Burnet, "Human biology as the study of human differences," in *The Impact of Civilization on the Biology of Man*, ed. S. V. Boyden (Toronto: University of Toronto Press, 1970), p. xvi.

Chapter 2: The Web of Nutrition

1. F. Rudell, *Consumer Food Selection and Nutrition Information* (New York: Prager, 1979).
2. J. Pierce, "Nutrition beliefs: More fashion than fact," *FDA Consumer* June 1976: pp. 25–27.
3. Ibid.
4. Agricultural Research Service, *Homemakers' Food & Nutrition Knowledge, Practices, and Opinions* (Home Economics Research Report #39) (Washington: U.S. Department of Agriculture, 1975).
5. Pierce, loc. cit.
6. H. A. Schroeder, *The Trace Elements & Man* (Old Greenwich, Conn.: Devin-Adair Co., 1973), p. 68.
7. R. J. Williams and G. Deason, "Individuality in vitamin C needs," *Proceedings of the National Academy of Science, USA* 57 (1967): pp. 1638–41.
8. H. Baker and O. Frank, "Deployment of vitamins in health and metabolic imbalances," *Journal of the International Association of Preventive Medicine* 7(2) (1982): pp. 19–24.
9. H. H. Hussey, "Taste and smell deviations: Importance of zinc," *Journal of the American Medical Association* 228(13) (1974): pp. 1669–70.
10. H. Popper and F. Steigmann, "The clinical significance of the plasma vitamin A level," *Journal of the American Medical Association* 123(17) (1943): pp. 1108–14.
11. F.R. Steggerda and H. H. Mitchell, "Variability in the calcium metabolism and calcium requirements of adult human subjects," *Journal of Nutrition* 31 (1946): pp. 407–422.
12. B.L. Vallee and J. G. Gibson. "The zinc content of normal human whole blood, plasma, leucocytes, and erythrocytes," *Journal of Biological Chemistry* 176 (1948): pp. 445–57.
13. R.J. Williams et al., *Individual Metabolic Patterns and Human Disease* (University of Texas Publication #5109, 1951).
14. M. Colgan, *Your Personal Vitamin Profile* (New York: William Morrow, 1982).
15. E. McCollum, quoted in W. Darby, "Nutrition science: An overview of American genius," *Nutrition Reviews* 34(1) (1976): pp. 1–14 (quote on p. 8).
16. W. Shive, F. Pinkerton, J. Humphreys, M. M. Johnson, W. G. Hamilton, and K. Matthews. "Development of a chemically defined serum- and protein-free medium for growth of human peripheral lymphocytes," *Proceedings of the National Academy of Sciences, USA* 83 (1986): pp. 9–13.

17. W. Shive and K. Matthews, "Nutritional requirements for growth of human lymphocytes," *Annual Review of Nutrition* 8 (1988): pp. 81–97.
18. K. Matthews, F. Pettit, J. Boghossian, and W. Shive, "Chemically defined medium for the growth of lymphocytes," *Methods in Enzymology* 150 (1987): pp. 134–46.
19. W. Shive, "Development of lymphocyte culture methods for assessment of the nutritional and metabolic status of individuals," *Journal of the International Academy of Preventive Medicine* 8(4) (1984): pp. 5–16.
20. K. Matthews, F. Pettit, R. Matthews, and W. Shive, "Lymphocyte responses in the assessment of individual metabolic and nutritional status" (Paper presented at the Castel Ivano Symposium on Nutrition, Castel Ivano, Italy, September 22, 1989).
21. Shive, loc. cit.

Chapter 3: Deadly Diet: Nutrition and Disease

1. Centers for Disease Control, *Ten-State Nutrition Survey* DHEW pub. no. 72-8129, 8130, 8131, 8132, & 8133 (Atlanta, Department of Health, Education, and Welfare, 1973).
2. National Center for Health Statistics, *Caloric and Selected Nutrient Values for Persons 1–74 Years of Age: First Health and Nutrition Examination Survey, United States, 1971–1974*, Vital & Health Statistics ser. 11, no. 209, DHEW pub. no. (PHS) 79-1657 (Hyattsville, Md.: Public Health Service, 1982).
3. E. M. Pao, "Nutrient consumption patterns of individuals, 1977 and 1965," *Family Economics Review* Spring 1980: pp. 16–20.
4. Senate Select Committee on Nutrition and Human Needs, *Diet and Killer Diseases* (Washington, D.C.: Government Printing Office, 1977).
5. J. A. T. Pennington, B. E. Young, and D. B. Wilson, "Nutritional elements in U.S. diets: Results from the Total Diet Study, 1982 to 1986," *Journal of the American Dietetic Association* 89(5) (1989): pp. 659–64.
6. United States Department of Agriculture, Human Nutrition Information Services: National Food Consumption Survey, Continuing Survey of Food Intakes by Individuals, Report #85-4 (Women 19–50 Years and Their Children 1–5 Years, 4 Days, 1985) and #85-3 (Men 19–50 Years, 1 Day, 1985). (Washington, D.C.: Government Printing Office, 1987, 1986).
7. A. Bianchetti, R. Rozzini, C. Carabellese, O. Zanetti, and M. Trabucchi, "Nutritional intake, socioeconomic conditions, and health status in a large elderly population," *Journal of the American Geriatric Society* 38 (1990): pp. 521–26.

8. American Medical Association Council on Scientific Affairs, "Vitamin preparations as dietary supplements and as therapeutic agents," *Journal of the American Medical Association* 257(14) (1987): pp. 1929–36 (quote on p. 1931).
9. R. J. Williams, *The Advancement of Nutrition* (Austin: Clayton Foundation Biochemical Institute, University of Texas, 1982), p. 14.
10. National Academy of Sciences, *National Academy of Sciences Recommended Dietary Allowances,* 9th ed. (Washington, D.C.: National Academy Press, 1980), p. 10.
11. M. Behar, "A deadly combination," *World Health* Feb./March 1974: p. 757.
12. E. B. Drew, "Going hungry in America," in Scientists' Institute for Public Information, *Hunger* (New York: SIPI, 1970), pp. 5–7 (quote on p. 6).
13. M. Brin, "Example of behavior changes in marginal vitamin deficiency in the rat and man," in *Behavioral Effects of Energy and Protein Deficits: Proceedings of the International Nutrition Conference,* ed. J. Brozek, DHEW pub. no. NIH-79-1906 (Washington, D.C.: Department of Health, Education and Welfare, 1979), pp. 272–77 (quote on p. 272).
14. D. Lonsdale and R. J. Shamberger, "Red cell transketolase as an indicator of nutritional deficiency," *American Journal of Clinical Nutrition* 33 (1980): pp. 205–211 (quote on p. 208).
15. B. Winikoff, "Changing public diet," *Human Nature* 1 (1978): pp. 60–65 (quote on p. 60).
16. H. Acosta-Sison, "Relation between the state of nutrition of the mother and the birth weight of the fetus: A preliminary study," *Journal of the Philippine Islands Medical Association* 9(5) (1929): pp. 174–76.
17. B. Pasamanick, The life and death sciences: Uses and abuses of epidemiology (Rema Lapouse Gold Medal Lecture) (Washington, D.C.: American Public Health Association, November 2, 1977).
18. R. S. Beach, M. E. Gershwin, and L. S. Hurley, "Gestational zinc deprivation in mice: Persistence of immunodeficiency for three generations," *Science* 218(4571) (1982): pp. 469–71.
19. T. L. Cleave, "The neglected natural principles in current medical practice," *Journal of the Royal Naval Medical Service* 42 (1956): p. 55.
20. J. P. Bantle, D. C. Laine, G. W. Castle, J. W. Thomas, B. J. Hoogwerf, and F. C. Goetz, "Postprandial glucose and insulin responses to meals containing different carbohydrates in normal and diabetic subjects," *New England Journal of Medicine* 309(1) (1983): pp. 7–12.
21. D. Burkitt, "Dietary fiber," in *Medical Applications of Clinical Nutrition,* ed. J. Bland (New Canaan, Conn.: Keats Publishing, 1983), pp. 269–87.
22. J. Yudkin, *Sweet and Dangerous* (New York: Bantam Books, 1973).

23. W. C. Hueper, "Experimental studies in cardiovascular pathology XIV: Experimental atheromatosis in Macacus rhesus monkeys," *American Journal of Pathology* 22(6) (1946): pp. 1287–91.
24. A. B. Nichols, C. Ravenscroft, D. E. Lamphiear, and L. D. Ostrander, "Daily nutritional intake and serum lipid levels: The Tecumseh study," *American Journal of Clinical Nutrition* 29 (1976): pp. 1384–92.
25. National Heart Institute, "Diet and the regulation of serum cholesterol," *Framingham Heart Disease Epidemiology Study* (Washington, D.C.: Dept. of Health, Education, and Welfare, 1970), sect. 24, p. 2414.
26. G. V. Mann, A. Spoerry, M. Gray, and D. Jarashow, "Atherosclerosis in the Masai," *American Journal of Epidemiology* 95(10) (1972): pp. 26–37.
27. D. A. McCarron, C. D. Morris, H. J. Henry, and J. L. Stanton, "Blood pressure and nutrient intake in the United States," *Science* 224 (1984): pp. 1392–98.
28. J. H. Laragh, "Calcium antagonists as a new treatment modality in hypertension," *Angiology* (1988) 39: pp. 100–105.
29. D. Lonsdale and R. J. Shamberger, loc. cit.
30. J. Mayer, "Toward a national nutrition policy," *Science* 176(4032) (1972): pp. 237–41 (quote on p. 239).
31. J. L. Brown, quoted in R. Pear, "Three doctors tell House panel of new medical data on hunger," *New York Times,* October 21, 1983, I, p. 18.

Chapter 4: The Industrialization of Food

1. R. H. Hall, *Food for Nought: The Decline in Nutrition* (New York: Random House/Vintage Books, 1976), p. vii.
2. J. Mayer, "Toward a national nutrition policy," *Science* 176(4032) (1972): pp. 237–41 (quote on p. 238).
3. Office of Technology Assessment, *Impacts of Applied Genetics: Micro-Organisms, Plants and Animals* (Washington, D.C.: Congress of the United States, 1981), p. 170.
4. R. H. Hall, op. cit., p. 144.
5. American Medical Association Council on Foods and Nutrition, "Some nutritional aspects of sugar, candy, and sweetened carbonated beverages," *Journal of the American Medical Association* 120(10) (1942): pp. 763–65 (quotes on pp. 763, 765).
6. O. Fennema, "Effects of freeze-preservation on nutrients," in *Nutritional Evaluation of Food Processing,* eds. R. S. Harris and E. Karmas, 2d ed. (Westport, Conn.: AVI Publishing, 1975), pp. 244–88 (quote on p. 282).
7. A. H. Ensminger, M. E. Ensminger, J. F. Konlande, and J. R. K. Robson,

Food and Nutrition Encyclopedia (Clovis, Calif.: Pegus Press, 1983), p. 2203.

8. D. Katz and M. T. Goodwin. "The food system: From the field to the table," in A. L. Tobias and P. J. Thompson, *Issues in Nutrition for the 1980s* (Monterey, Calif.: Wadsworth Health Sciences Division, 1980), pp. 147–54 (quote on p. 153).
9. R. S. Harris quoted in E. Cheraskin, W. M. Ringsdorf, and E. Sisley, *The Vitamin C Connection* (New York: Harper & Row, 1983), p. 29.
10. Senate Select Committee on Nutrition and Human Needs, "Eating in the Dark: Report to the 23rd Congress," quoted in A. L. Tobias and P. J. Thompson, *Issues in Nutrition for the 1980s* (Monterey, Calif.: Wadsworth Health Sciences Division, 1980), pp. 106–113 (quote on p. 111).
11. L. Hopkins, Presentation to the American Association for the Advancement of Science annual meeting, 1971, quoted in M. F. Jacobson, *Nutrition Scoreboard: Your Guide to Better Eating,* rev. ed. (New York: Avon Books, 1975), p. 93.
12. D. Katz and M. T. Goodwin, loc. cit.
13. H. A. Schroeder, "Losses of vitamins and trace minerals resulting from processing and preservation of foods," *American Journal of Clinical Nutrition* 24 (1971): pp. 562–73.

Chapter 5: Our Toxic World

1. Special Commission on Internal Pollution, "The chemical age," *Journal of the American Pharmaceutical Association* 17(6) (1977): pp. 369–73 (quote on p. 369).
2. K. R. Mahaffey, J. L. Annest, J. Roberts, and R. S. Murphy. "National estimates of blood lead levels: United States, 1976–1980: Association with selected demographic and socioeconomic factors," *New England Journal of Medicine* 307 (1982): pp. 573–79.
3. C. Benbrook, quoted in P. Shabecoff, "Pesticides finally top the problem list at EPA," *New York Times* March 6, 1986, II, p. 12.
4. Shabecoff, op. cit.
5. Ibid.
6. O. Schell, "A kind of commons," *The New Yorker,* April 23, 1984, pp. 50–83 (quote on p. 62).
7. M. F. Jacobson, *The Complete Eater's Digest and Nutrition Scoreboard* (Garden City, N.Y.: Anchor Press/Doubleday, 1985), p. 165.
8. J. F. Crow, "Chemical risk to future generations," *Scientist and Citizen* 10 (1968): p. 113.
9. Jacobson, op. cit., pp. 361–62.

10. Surgeon General of the United States, *Healthy People: The Surgeon General's Report on Health Promotion and Disease Prevention,* DHEW pub. no. PHS-79-55071 (Washington, D.C.: Department of Health, Education, and Welfare, 1979), p. 102.
11. R. W. Miller, "Areawide chemical contamination," *Journal of the American Medical Association* 1981; 245(15):1548–1551 (quote on p. 1550).
12. S. Shulman, "Toxic travels: Inside the military's industrial nightmare," *Nuclear Times* 8(3) (1990): pp. 20–32.
13. M. Synar, quoted in P. Shabecoff, "U.S. effort grows to protect water," *New York Times,* July 26, 1983, I, p. 1.
14. E. Mann, "L.A.'s smogbusters," *The Nation,* September 17, 1990, pp. 254–74.
15. A. V. Zamm, *Why Your House May Endanger Your Health* (New York, Simon & Schuster, 1982), p. 49.
16. Public Health Service, *Promoting Health, Preventing Disease: Objectives for the Nation* (Washington, D.C.: Department of Health and Human Services, 1980).
17. R. Lavelle, quoted in P. Shabecoff, "Concern growing over unclear threat of dioxin," *New York Times,* February 15, 1983, I, p. 1.
18. A. Pasztor, "Pentagon's waste sites represent huge, neglected crisis, critics say," *Wall Street Journal,* July 22, 1983, p. 19.
19. H. Caldicott, "Radiation: Unsafe at any level," *The Progressive,* December 1978, pp. 39–44 (quote on p. 39).
20. K. L. Kahn, *Health Effects of Nuclear Power and Nuclear Weapons* (Watertown, Mass.: Physicians for Social Responsibility, 1980), p. 9.
21. C. J. Johnson, "Cancer incidence in an area of radioactive fallout downwind from the Nevada test site," *Journal of the American Medical Association* 251(2) (1984): pp. 230–36.
22. D. J. Beninson, quoted in "Radiation limits to plunge," *Science News* 138(26) (1990): p. 405.
23. J. O. Mason, quoted in Associated Press, "New Chief discusses Disease Center policy," *New York Times,* December 13, 1983, III, p. 7.

Chapter 6: Ecological Illness and the Individual

1. J. Cohen, T. C. Gierlowski, and A. B. Schneider, "A prospective study of hyperparathyroidism in individuals exposed to radiation in childhood," *Journal of the American Medical Association* 264(5) (1990): pp. 581–84.

2. California Department of Consumer Affairs, *Clean Your Room: A Compendium on Indoor Pollution* (Sacramento, Calif.: State of California, 1982), p. 354.
3. R. A. Schreiber and W. A. Walker, "Food allergy: Facts and fiction," *Proceedings of the Mayo Clinic* 64 (1989): pp. 1381–91 (quote on p. 1381).
4. I. R. Bell, *Clinical Ecology: A New Medical Approach to Environmental Illness* (Bolinas, Calif.: Common Knowledge Press, 1982), p. 19.
5. M. A. Khan, "Systemic pesticides for use on animals," *Annual Review of Entomology* 14 (1969): pp. 421–36.
6. R. D. Gabovich and P. N. Maistruk, "On the therapeutic and prophylactic diet in the fluorine manufacturing industry," *Vaprosy Pitanica* 22 (1963): pp. 32–38.
7. O. Zaffina, G. Gala, R. Centi, and A. Salicone, "A new therapeutic method for acute oxycarbonism (with the method of Gala-Zaffini) with intravenous infusion of high doses of ascorbic acid," *Minerva Anestesiol* 37 (1971): pp. 332–39.
8. A. A. Yuince and R. D. Lindeman, "Effect of ascorbic acid and zinc sulfate on ethanol toxicity and metabolism," *Proceedings of the Society for Experimental Biology and Medicine* 154 (1977): pp. 146–50.
9. J. J. Chisolm, "Amino aciduria as a manifestation of renal tubular injury in lead intoxication and a comparison with patterns of amino aciduria seen in other diseases," *Journal of Pediatrics* 60 (1962): p. 1.
10. E. Cheraskin, W. M. Ringsdorf, and E. Sisley, *The Vitamin C Connection* (New York: Harper & Row, 1983), p. 182.
11. M. Chrapil, S. L. Elias, J. N. Ryan, and C. F. Zukoski, "Considerations on the biological effects of zinc," in *International Review of Neurobiology,* ed. C. C. Pfeiffer (New York: Academic Press, 1973), pp. 115–73.
12. C. K. Chow, "Effect of dietary selenium and vitamin E on the biochemical responses in the lungs of ozone exposed rats," *Federal Proceedings,* Abstract no. 4347, 36 (1977): p. 1094.
13. P. Noszczynski and A. Starek, "Activity of lysosomal betaglucoronidase in leukocytes of rats exposed to benzene and sodium selenate," *Folia Haematologica Internationales Magazin für Klinische und Morphologische Blutfershung* 105 (1978): pp. 230–38.
14. B. Kidman, M. L. Tutt, and J. M. Vaughn, "The retention and excretion of radioactive strontium and ythrium in the healthy rabbit," *Journal of Pathology and Bacteriology* 42 (1952): pp. 209–27.

Chapter 7: We Are How We Live

1. M. Harris, *Cows, Pigs, Wars, and Witches: The Riddle of Culture* (New York: Vintage Books, 1974), p. 2.
2. J. Mayer, in Pan American Health Organization, *Metabolic Adaptation and Nutrition,* Proceedings of the Special Session, 9th Meeting of the PAHO Advisory Committee on Medical Research, Scientific Pub. no. 222 (Washington, D.C.: Pan American Sanitary Bureau, Regional Office of the World Health Organization, 1971), p. 83.
3. R. S. Paffenberger, Jr., A. L. Wing, and R. T. Hyde, "Physical activity as an index of heart attack risk in college alumni." *American Journal of Epidemiology* 108(3) (1978): pp. 161–75.
4. H. O. M. King and A. A. Bleaney, "The low prevalence of hypertension in Falkland Islands men," *Journal of the Royal College of General Practitioners* 34(259) (1984): pp. 95–96.
5. R. J. Campbell, *Psychiatric Dictionary,* 5th ed. (New York: Oxford University Press, 1981), p. 473.
6. I. R. Bell and D. S. King, "Psychological and physiological research relevant to clinical ecology: Overview of the current literature," *Clinical Ecology* I(1) (1982): pp. 15–25.
7. C. Holden, "Cancer and the mind: How are they connected?" *Science* 200(4348) (1978): pp. 1363–69.
8. L. LeShan, *You Can Fight for Your Life: Emotional Factors in the Causation of Cancer* (New York: M. Evans & Co., 1977).
9. J. R. Eagleston, K. Kirmil-Gray, C. E. Thoresen, S. A. Wiedenfeld, P. Bracke, L. Heft, and B. Arnow, "Physical health correlates of type A behavior in children and adolescents," *Journal of Behavioral Medicine* 9(4) (1986): pp. 342–62.
10. M. Stein et al., cited in J. L. Marx, "The immune system belongs in the body," *Science* 227(4691) (1985): pp. 1190–92.
11. J. A. Sours, *Starving to Death in a Sea of Objects: The Anorexia Nervosa Syndrome* (New York: Jason Aronson, 1980), p. 282.
12. H. Selye, *The Stress of Life* (New York: McGraw-Hill, 1978), p. 1.
13. M. E. Seligman, J. Weiss, M. Weinraub, and A. Schulman, "Coping behavior: Learned helplessness, physiological change and learned inactivity," *Behavioral Research Therapeutics* 18(5) (1980): pp. 459–512.
14. T. H. Holmes and R. H. Rahe, "The social readjustment rating scale," *Journal of Psychosomatic Research* 11(2) (1967): pp. 213–18.
15. C. Wallis, "Stress: Can we cope?" *Time,* June 6, 1983, pp. 48–54.
16. Selye, op. cit., p. 299.
17. S. M. Murphy, R. T. Owen, and P. J. Tyrer, "Withdrawal symptoms

after six weeks' treatment with diazepam," *Lancet* 2(8416) (1984): p. 1389.

18. National Center for Health Statistics, *Health, United States, 1989* (Hyattsville, MD.: Public Health Service, 1990), pp. 43–44.
19. M. F. Goldsmith, "Sex tied to drugs = STD spread," *Journal of the American Medical Association* 260(14) (1988): p. 2009.
20. L. A. Fingerhut and J. C. Kleinman, "International and interstate comparisons of homicide among young males," *Journal of the American Medical Association* 263(24) (1990): pp. 3292–95.
21. R. Gould, quoted in G. Collins, "U.S. social tolerance of drugs found on the rise," *New York Times,* March 21, 1983, I, p. 1.

Chapter 8: The Next Generation

1. W. D. Mosher, "Fertility and family planning in the United States: Insights from the national survey of family growth," *Family Planning Perspectives* 20(5) (1988): pp. 207–217.
2. American Academy of Pediatrics Committee on Drugs, "Stilbestrol and adenocarcinoma of the vagina," *Pediatrics* 51(2) (1973): pp. 292–99.
3. Editorial Board, "A time to be born," *Lancet* 7890(2) (1974): pp. 1183–84.
4. National Academy of Sciences, *Alternative Dietary Practices and Nutritional Abuses in Pregnancy* (Washington, D.C.: National Academy Press, 1982).
5. Food and Drug Administration, cited in J. E. Brody, "Food, drink and medication: Risks during pregnancy," *New York Times,* December 8, 1982, III, p. 12.
6. M. A. Schuckit and E. O. Gold, "A simultaneous evaluation of multiple markers of ethanol/placebo challenges in sons of alcoholics and controls," *Archives of General Psychiatry* 45 (1988): pp. 211–16.
7. I. J. Chasnoff, Address to the 38th Annual Meeting of the American College of Obstetricians and Gynecologists, quoted in A. Skolnick, "Cocaine use in pregnancy: Physicians urged to look for problem where they least expect it," *Journal of the American Medical Association* 264(3) (1990): p. 306.
8. National Center for Health Statistics, "Final natality statistics, 1987, advance report," *Monthly Vital Statistics Report* 38 (1989) (3 suppl.).
9. M. Winick, "Food and the fetus," *Natural History* 90(1) (1981): pp. 76–81 (quote on p. 80).
10. P. Rowe, "Preventing infant mortality: An investment in the nation's future," *Children Today* 18 (1989): pp. 16–20.

11. C. M. Drillien, "School disposal and performance for children of different birthweight born 1953–1960," *Archive of Diseases of Childhood* 44 (1969): pp. 562–70.
12. K. Newland, *Infant Mortality and the Health of Societies,* Worldwatch Paper no. 47 (Washington, D.C.: Worldwatch Institute, 1981), p. 27.
13. Metropolitan Life Insurance Company, "Suicide: An update," *Metropolitan Life Statistical Bulletin* 67(2) (1986): pp. 16–23.
14. Senate Judiciary Committee, quoted in E. Tieber, "Murders soar in 'bloodiest year in U.S. history,' " *New York Post,* August 1, 1990, p. 17.
15. R. R. Zimmerman, P. L. Steere, D. A. Strobel, et al., "Abnormal social development of protein malnourished rhesus monkeys," *Journal of Abnormal Psychology* 80(2) (1972): pp. 125–31 (quote on p. 130).
16. M. B. Stoch and P.M. Smythe, "Does undernutrition during infancy inhibit brain growth and subsequent intellectual development?" *Archives of Disease in Childhood* 38 (1963): pp. 546–52 (quote on p. 552).

Chapter 9: The Limits of Modern Medicine

1. R. Dubos, *The Mirage of Health* (New York: Harper & Row, 1979), p. 20.
2. T. McKeown, *The Role of Medicine: Dream, Mirage or Nemesis?* (Princeton, N.J.: Princeton University Press, 1979), p. 79.
3. E. J. Cassell, *The Healer's Art: A New Approach to the Doctor-Patient Relationship* (New York: Lippincott, 1976), p. 74.
4. A. Melville and C. Johnson, *Cured to Death: The Effects of Prescription Drugs* (Briarcliff Manor, N.Y.: Stein & Day, 1982), p. 10.
5. W. P., McKinney, D. L. Schiedermayer, N. Lurie, D. E. Simpson, J. L. Goodman, and E. C. Rich, "Attitudes of internal medicine faculty and residents toward professional interaction with pharmaceutical sales representatives," *Journal of the American Medical Association* 264(13) (1990): pp. 1693–97.
6. B. R. Bistrian, G. L. Blackburn, E. Hallowell, et al., "Protein status of general surgical patients," *Journal of the American Medical Association* 230 (1974): pp. 858–60.
7. K. N. Jeejeebhoy, "Nutritional support of the depleted patient, presented at Bristol-Myers Symposium on Nutritional Management of the Seriously Ill Patient, Washington, D.C., November 9, 1980.
8. J. V. Basmajian, M. D. Burke, G. W. Burnett, et al., eds, *Stedman's Medical Dictionary,* 24th ed. (Baltimore, Md.: Williams & Wilkins, 1982), p. 688.
9. K. Steel, P. M. Gertman, C. Crascenzi, and J. Anderson, "Iatrogenic illness

on a general medical service at a university hospital," *New England Journal of Medicine* 304(11) (1981): pp. 638–42 (quotes on pp. 638, 641).
10. P. A. Sytkowski, W. B. Kannel, and R. B. D'Agostino, "Changes in risk factors and the decline in mortality from cardiovascular disease: The Framingham heart study," *New England Journal of Medicine* 322(23) (1990): pp. 1635–41.
11. H. B. Jones, "Demographic considerations of the cancer problem," *Transactions of the New York Academy of Sciences II* (18) (1955), pp. 298–333.
12. A. S. Buist and W. M. Vollmer, "Reflections on the rise in asthma morbidity and mortality," *Journal of the American Medical Association* 264(13) (1990): pp. 1719–20 (quote on p. 1720).
13. National Center for Health Statistics, *Health, United States, 1989* (Hyattsville, Md.: Public Health Service, 1990), p. 4.
14. A. S. Relman, "Trouble with rationing," *The New England Journal of Medicine* 323(13) (1990): p. 911.
15. M. Halberstam, "The legion disease: So little still is known about the body," *New York Times,* September 5, 1976, V, p. 7.

Chapter 10: A New Paradigm for Medical Care

1. L. Thomas, *The Youngest Science: Notes of a Medicine Watcher* (New York: Bantam Books, 1984), p. 145.
2. T. McKeown, *The Role of Medicine: Dream, Mirage, or Nemesis?* (Princeton, N.J.: Princeton University Press, 1979), p. vii.
3. Commission on Medical Education of the Association of American Medical Colleges, *Final Report of the Report of the Commission on Medical Education* (New York: Association of American Medical Colleges, 1932), p. 1.
4. A. Simopoulos, personal communication (New York, 1985).
5. National Research Council, *Nutrition Education in U.S. Medical Schools* (Washington, D.C.: 1985), p. 4.
6. Panel on the General Professional Education of the Physician and College Preparation for Medicine, *Physicians for the Twenty-first Century* (Washington, D.C.: 1984), p. 22.
7. Ibid., pp. 16, 17, 23, 24.
8. Thomas, op. cit., p. 72.
9. J. Mayer, "A note about the Tufts University diet and nutrition letter" (Boston: Tufts University, 1986).

Chapter 11: What We Can Do

1. J. H. Knowles, "The responsibility of the individual," in *Doing Better and Feeling Worse, Health in the United States,* ed. J. H. Knowles (New York: W. W. Norton, 1987), pp. 57–80 (quote on p. 59).
2. M. Colgan, *Your Personal Vitamin Profile* (New York: William Morrow, 1982), p. 208.

Index

ABOUT THE AUTHOR

JOSEPH D. BEASLEY, M.D., a board-certified practicing physician, is the director of Comprehensive Medical Care, a clinic in Amityville, New York, which takes a comprehensive approach to the diagnosis, treatment, and prevention of disease. He is a Bard Fellow in Medicine and Science and director of the Bard College Center's Institute of Health Policy and Practice. He has in the past served as chairman of the Department of Demography and Human Ecology at Harvard University, as dean of the School of Public Health at Tulane University, and as a member of the National Commission on Population Growth and the American Future. He is the author of several books, including *How to Defeat Alcoholism.*